# MORE PRAISE FOR *JUST ENOUGH ANXIETY*

"One of today's key leadership challenges is deciding how much change an organization can absorb at any point in time. Bob Rosen does an excellent job helping leaders think through this delicate balancing act."

—DENNIS NALLY, senior partner, PricewaterhouseCoopers

"Many great books have been written about the age of turbulence, global dynamism or business disruption focused upon firm level concerns. No great book has focused upon what it means to lead in these times. Finally, that book has arrived."

—BLAIR SHEPHARD, dean, Fuqua School of Management

"The ultimate goal of any leader is to create a winning company. Great leaders do this by mastering the human side of execution. Inherently they know how to turn up or turn down the heat. *Just Enough Anxiety* shows you just how to do this. The book is honest, heartfelt, and focuses on what really matters in business."

—MICHEL TILMANT, chairman and CEO, ING Group

"*Just Enough Anxiety* is a rare, new resource for leaders everywhere, at every level, and provides a challenging view of business success."

—FRANCES HESSELBEIN, chairman and founding president,
Leader to Leader Institute

"Change in the philanthropic sector today is immense. In *Just Enough Anxiety*, Bob Rosen offers us a great personal guide for managing the complex road ahead."

—STEVE GUNDERSON, CEO, Council on Foundations

"Bob Rosen totally gets it! *Just Enough Anxiety* is a must-read for executives who realize that understanding themselves and others is critical to success. His clear and insightful writing makes the book a pleasure to read while providing tools, tips and tactics to achieve peak performance and a well-balanced life."

—SUSAN SARFATI, CEO, Center for Association Leadership

"Bob Rosen's message is both critical and timely. I highly recommend this book to anyone struggling with demands and pressures of today's challenges, whether inside or outside of business."

—FRANK GUZZETTA, CEO, Macy's North

"Bob Rosen is really on to something in this timely book. It is one thing to trumpet that rapid change is a fact of life in every business; it is something else entirely to address the anxiety that is released in an organization where the 'human factors' struggle to change as rapidly as the world around. The leader has to both master those anxiety issues within him/herself, and find a way to turn the organizational anxiety into positive, productive energy. That is what this book is all about."

—STEVE MORRIS, CEO, Arbitron

"You'll never think about anxiety in the workplace the same way again after reading this book. Rosen's advice for harnessing anxiety to stretch to great performance is highly relevant and inspiring to leaders today."

—DONNA J. STURGESS, head of innovation, GlaxoSmithKline

"Tough challenges bring out the best in people, but continuous crisis management can be destructive. Bob Rosen's concept of *Just Enough Anxiety* captures this dilemma in a framework that CEOs can use to maintain the optimum amount of pressure to keep our business moving forward."

—MIKE TURNER, CEO, BAE Systems

# JUST ENOUGH
# ANXIETY

Also by Robert H. Rosen

*The Healthy Company*

*Leading People*

# JUST ENOUGH
# ANXIETY

## THE HIDDEN DRIVER OF
## BUSINESS SUCCESS

### ROBERT H. ROSEN

PORTFOLIO

PORTFOLIO

Published by the Penguin Group
Penguin Group (USA) Inc., 375 Hudson Street,
New York, New York 10014, U.S.A.
Penguin Group (Canada), 90 Eglinton Avenue East, Suite 700,
Toronto, Ontario, Canada M4P 2Y3
(a division of Pearson Penguin Canada Inc.)
Penguin Books Ltd, 80 Strand, London WC2R 0RL, England
Penguin Ireland, 25 St. Stephen's Green, Dublin 2, Ireland
(a division of Penguin Books Ltd)
Penguin Books Australia Ltd, 250 Camberwell Road, Camberwell,
Victoria 3124, Australia
(a division of Pearson Australia Group Pty Ltd)
Penguin Books India Pvt Ltd, 11 Community Centre, Panchsheel Park,
New Delhi–110 017, India
Penguin Group (NZ), 67 Apollo Drive, Rosedale, North Shore 0632,
New Zealand (a division of Pearson New Zealand Ltd)
Penguin Books (South Africa) (Pty) Ltd, 24 Sturdee Avenue,
Rosebank, Johannesburg 2196, South Africa

Penguin Books Ltd, Registered Offices:
80 Strand, London WC2R 0RL, England

First published in 2008 by Portfolio,
a member of Penguin Group (USA) Inc.

1 3 5 7 9 10 8 6 4 2

Copyright © RHR Enterprises, 2008
All rights reserved

LIBRARY OF CONGRESS CATALOGING-IN-PUBLICATION DATA

Rosen, Robert H.
Just enough anxiety : the hidden driver of business success / Robert H. Rosen.
p  cm.
Includes bibliographical references and index.
ISBN 978–1–59184–197–5
1. Leadership.  2. Performance anxiety.  3. Success.  I. Title.
HD57.7.R658 2008
658.4'09—dc22     2007042509

Printed in the United Sates of America
Set in Berkeley Old Style
Designed by Helene Berinsky

*This book is dedicated to you*
*as you live and lead*
*with just enough anxiety.*

# CONTENTS

*It is not the strongest of the species that survives, nor the most intelligent. It is the one that is the most adaptable to change.*

—CHARLES DARWIN

# JUST ENOUGH
# ANXIETY

# 1

# IT'S TIME TO EVOLVE

*The brave man is not he who does not feel afraid, but he who conquers that fear.*

—NELSON MANDELA, former president of South Africa

Anxiety is a fact of life. How you use it makes all the difference. If you let it overwhelm you, it will turn to panic. If you deny or run from it, you will become complacent. But if you use anxiety in a positive way, you will turn it into a powerful force in your life. You will uncover the hidden driver of business success.

Just ask Alan Mulally. Today, Alan is the new CEO of Ford Motor Company. I met him in 1995, when he was running the Boeing 777 business in Everett, Washington. When he took over at Ford in 2006, the automobile giant was in deep trouble. Its market share had been tumbling for more than ten years, due to a bloated cost structure and weak product lines. Plant closings had cost more than 30,000 people their jobs. The company had lost $12.6 billion in 2006, about $24,000 a minute. And both Jaguar and Land Rover were up for sale. So what possessed Alan to leave his job as president of Boeing Commercial Aircraft to take over the helm?

"The three Detroit carmakers had been losing their leadership position over the years," he told me. "So I made a balance sheet. Here are the reasons to come, and here are the downsides. Here are the risks. Here are the opportunities. But the biggest thing I had to decide was whether I could add value. I can remember struggling with that. Could I use my skills and experiences to serve in this new job?

"I thought, 'I've designed airplanes. I haven't designed cars. I'm going to need a whole new skill set.' But then I decided that the things that had served me well before would serve me well in the new job. What was important was having a compelling vision, working together, having a plan, and making sure that everybody is included in the plan. I could always rely on these working principles. And, of course, I would grow and learn on the job."

Alan's realization that his core beliefs, combined with his willingness to learn and adapt, gave him the confidence he needed to tackle the job. "I took the job to help a great American icon reverse its slide and start growing again." Then he rolled up his sleeves and went to work.

"When you come into an environment like this, the most important thing you can do is define reality. 'Do we want to give up? Do we believe we can make a viable business? Or should we liquidate this place?' Certainly I came in with the goal of making this a viable business. That might have created anxiety. But it was also liberating.

"Everybody knew what the status was. There were no secrets. Dealing with it directly was refreshing. The other side, of course, is that people got anxious. They wondered, 'Am I going to be here?' 'Am I going to be part of the turnaround?' 'Am I going to have to work differently?'"

Change and uncertainty make people anxious even when change is what they need to keep their company viable. Good leaders like Alan understand this—for themselves and the people around them. And they also know that anxiety can be planned, modulated, and channeled into productive energy.

"I started a Thursday business-plan review. And that always creates anxiety. You're either ahead of the plan or behind it. So right away, boom. You've built a gap between where you are and where you want to be. You've built in anxiousness, excitement, motivation. And, 'Oh, by the way, I'm going to see you next week. We're going to get back together.' And, of course, nobody wants to stand up and be behind again, right? We wouldn't want to let each other down. The meetings create the motivational anxiety, the energy we need to make progress."

Sustaining the right level of anxiety is Alan's strategy for success at Ford. He uses it to challenge and motivate himself and to drive the behavior required to turn the company around.

"Half the time, at the end of the day, I don't know how we're going to get it done. You always give it your best shot, and you can never get down or immobilized. So anxiety is a good thing. It means you're thinking about your goals, your objectives and plans, and the risks and opportunities. It's very useful and very enabling. If you're free and open to deal with the uncertainty of it all, then you have to be able to say you're anxious.

"Now there's still a lot of anxiety here. But we have a plan to get back to profitability in 2009. We are aggressively restructuring the business to changing market and customer demands. We've accelerated the new products and services that people really value today. We're making great progress on accelerating the plan. We have the financing in place. And we're really working together on our leadership skills."

Alan may succeed in turning the company around. Only time will tell. Ford won five top-quality awards from J. D. Power and Associates in 2007—more than any other carmaker—and that's a good indicator of its ability to produce great products. The company, maker of the Mustang, Lincoln, and Taurus, is in good hands, given Alan's track record and his mind-set for success. And things appear to be moving in the right direction.

So what do you have in common with a guy running a $160 billion company with approximately 260,000 employees? Maybe more than you think. Your inner experience of anxiety is the same as Alan Mulally's. In today's fast-paced world, with its pressures and problems, opportunities and options, we're all in the same boat.

Think about the times you have had to make tough decisions. You've wondered: Should I change jobs or stay where I am? Is a new job what I really want? Do the benefits outweigh the risks? Do I have what it takes to succeed? Can I make a difference?

These are the kinds of questions we ask ourselves whenever we're faced with change, whether we're a CEO or a new hire in the mailroom. Questioning ourselves is how we manage our anxiety when we are stepping into a new role, tackling a new challenge, or doing something to improve ourselves or our organizations. We examine our fears and hopes. We assess our strengths and weaknesses. We weigh our options. It's part of being human.

Yes, Alan Mulally is a great leader today. But before he was a CEO, Alan was a student, management trainee, middle manager, and division head. His ability to create just enough anxiety to motivate himself and others has evolved over his lifetime, just like yours.

But why is it so difficult to deal with our anxiety in the first place? If anxiety is a fact of life, why do we try to hide from it? Or let ourselves get hijacked by it?

I believe the problem lies with our faulty thinking. It goes something like this: Change and uncertainty make me anxious. Anxiety is bad, a sign of weakness. Therefore, I have to avoid change and uncertainty. I have to do whatever I can to avoid anxiety.

Our faulty thinking comes from centuries of viewing change as dangerous, even life threatening. It comes from medical models that frame anxiety as a mental health problem. And it comes from years of outmoded leadership practices that ignore the human side of business.

Our limited logic leads us to reject change, uncertainty, and anxiety as inherent and acceptable parts of life. We associate anxiety with fear, stress, and instability. We are afraid we can't understand or manage our anxiety, so we avoid, deny, resist, run away from, or medicate it. And we refuse to see our anxiety as a major source of energy, in ourselves and our organizations.

It's time to change our perspective on anxiety. It's time to make better use of our brain power to manage the anxiety that accompanies change and uncertainty. It's time to evolve.

I'm basing this conclusion on five decades of life and my thirty-year career as a psychologist, entrepreneur, and CEO adviser. It is grounded in the face-to-face meetings I've had with more than 250 top business leaders. In fact, my research has led me to three fundamental insights about leadership and life:

- It's time to embrace change, uncertainty, and anxiety as facts of life.
- We can use our healthy anxiety as a positive force for growth.
- Just enough anxiety is the key to living and leading in our complex world.

Let's face it: The world is changing at an unprecedented pace. Nothing is static, certain, or predictable. Anxiety is rapidly becoming our constant companion. If we continue to struggle against this natural process, we will remain locked in a closed loop of our own making. We will stop growing, as individuals and organizations.

Wait a minute. Is it possible to evolve intentionally? Can we overcome our inherited fear-based response to change and uncertainty? Based on two decades of research and my personal experience, I believe the answer to both questions is an emphatic "Yes!"

This book describes how. It provides a proven road map for using just enough anxiety to live and lead in a world of uncertainty. It is geared toward helping leaders at all levels and in all types of organizations to manage themselves, mobilize people, maximize performance, and accelerate sustainable growth. Yet its message is just as relevant to individuals in all types of situations. If you want to use your anxiety as productive energy and thrive in the midst of constant change, then this book is for you.

Where do we start? Let's take a close look at how I came to believe that now is the right evolutionary moment for reframing anxiety.

## OUR CRAZY WORLD

*We have data overload, emotional overload, sensory overload, and responsibility overload.*

—JUDITH BARDWICK, *Seeking the Calm in the Storm*

Imagine hovering above the Earth at 30,000 feet. Below you are beautiful mountains and rivers, fields and forests, towns and cities. And a lot of people. Like colonies of ants, they're scurrying frantically from place to place. The scene reminds you of a kaleidoscope as the patterns change from moment to moment. Life on this planet seems to be happening at an unprecedented pace.

At ground level, you know it's true. Life today is about keeping up with a rapidly changing world. Environmental, economic, and sociopolitical changes are more complicated and more unpredictable than ever. Terrorism and dramatic weather events threaten to turn our world upside down. Our jobs, relationships, financial status, health, and even the place we call home often change in an instant. Everything we think of as real and stable is more impermanent than we care to admit. We struggle to keep up and stay sane.

Business today is a whirlwind of change. The pressure on leaders—in all kinds of companies around the world—to navigate through these changes is palpable. I've spoken with top leaders from Toyota, Singapore Airlines, and Canon in Asia; to UBS, Cadbury Schweppes, and Deutschebank in Europe; to Procter & Gamble, Motorola, Boeing, and Kodak in the United States; to Foster's Brewing in Australia. They all agree: The very nature of business is changing, almost on a daily basis.

But change is nothing new. Our species has had to adapt to a changing world for hundreds of thousands of years. It is how we've evolved. Over time, however, the tempo of change has increased dramatically. Like a boulder rolling downhill, change has picked up speed. And with more change comes more complexity.

The pace of change is particularly hard on businesses. Leaders across industries and sectors struggle to keep up with changing global markets, disruptive technologies, and demanding consumers. They face economic uncertainties on a global scale. They grapple with virtual teams and privacy concerns. Many find their organizational identities and products reshaped by mergers, acquisitions, or downsizing. In the midst of all this, leaders have to keep cynical shareholders satisfied, adhere to demanding board directives, engage entitled employees, and stay ahead of the competition.

Continuous improvement is no longer enough. Businesses need constant innovation to stay ahead of the game. After all, there's no such thing as a stationary position in life or in business. If we're not moving forward, we're sliding backward. With so little time for trial and error, we could all be just a few decisions away from disaster.

The uncertainty created by so much change makes a leader's task challenging at best. How can anyone plan for unpredictable threats and opportunities? How can leaders achieve top-line growth, manage for value, globalize their businesses, build trust and transparency, develop their people, and stay on top—all at the same time?

The good news is that complexity and change offer us unprecedented opportunities. They enable us to grow as individuals and in business. They make it possible to communicate 24/7 and to gain new customers and employ the best talent from around the world.

But constant change is also unsettling, unnerving, and intimidating.

We get upset when things are out of control. We feel vulnerable, anxious, and helpless. As leaders, we have little time to respond to one change before the next wave crashes upon us. This puts us in a permanent state of transformation.

The bottom line is that the rate of change is outpacing our ability to reinvent ourselves. There's a limit to the complexity and speed we can handle. We can no longer find instant solutions to our problems or quick fixes that give us competitive advantage. Everything seems urgent and important.

Once upon a time the present marched slowly toward a seemingly predictable future. Today, the present races into an uncertain future, where the rules, and even the game, keep changing. While our forefathers may have had the luxury of musing about the future, we barely have time to understand today. So instead of the straight line we long for—based on the Newtonian model of cause and effect—life and business have become tangled webs of possible pathways through an unfamiliar landscape.

We're facing a moment of truth in our evolution. We have to learn to live and work in the midst of change. To feel at home in uncharted territory. To make friends with ambiguity and anxiety. Albert Einstein said that it's impossible to solve problems with the same minds that created them. I say it's impossible to live and lead in the world today with the same mind-set that worked so well just a few decades ago. We must adapt or die. But are we ready?

## OUR UNPREPARED HUMAN PSYCHE

*Neither a wise man nor a brave man lies down on the tracks of history to wait for the train of the future to run over him.*

—DWIGHT D. EISENHOWER, thirty-fourth president of the
United States

It's not easy to change your mind. Each of us is shackled by the chains of old mental models and layer upon layer of outdated mental circuitry. We are held hostage by our unmet aspirations, unresolved problems, and unrealized potential. We drag our prior experiences, expectations, beliefs, and attitudes around with us like overstuffed baggage. And we rely on our habits to manage uncertainty.

There's more. Many scientists and change experts say we're engineered biologically, socially, and psychologically to seek homeostasis. We search for security. We prefer order. We long for predictability and stability in our lives. These conditions, we've come to believe, are the signs that we have "arrived." We equate comfort with success.

No wonder we have resisted change up until now. But does this mean we have to continue on the same path? Are we programmed *only* to protect ourselves against the storms of change and uncertainty in our lives? I say no. If this were true, we'd have died out long ago. I believe we're also programmed to learn and grow. We're engineered to adapt to our changing world, to survive.

Here's the problem: The world is changing faster than ever before. We can no longer wait for some unconscious level of evolution to select us out of or into a new human species. We need to find a new way of dealing with the pace, kind, and amount of change we're facing today. We have to initiate our own evolution. To help us move forward, let's look back at how we got to where we are now.

Evolution has a way of teaching us great lessons. It can help us understand what makes us human and what makes us unique. It can also point the way to what we can do to make the next evolutionary leap, consciously and willingly.

The human brain has been programmed to detect danger for many thousands of years. It holds hardwired memories of our survival dos and don'ts. And like all traits that help keep a species alive, this capability has survived as well. There have been improvements along the way—most notably in the part of the brain responsible for higher reasoning, commonly called the *executive brain*. Yet the part of the brain that alerts us to potential threats has been with us for a very, very long time. This part is deeply embedded in our human experience.

In 1952, Paul MacLean, an American physician and researcher, defined this older, ancestral part of the brain. He called it the limbic system. Later researchers referred to it as the *emotional brain*. Most of our emotional memories and triggers reside here. It is where our anxiety originates—how we respond to threats and changes in our environment, including our desire to fight or flee from danger.

All animals have neural systems designed to help them survive in the world. Animals with backbones and brains have similar neural systems.

But while we are like other animals to some extent, the size and composition of our brains make us distinctly human.

Over many thousands of years, the human brain has undergone a profound change. The executive brain has gotten bigger and more diversified. Today, this part of the brain is actually much larger than it should be, given our body size. The part of the executive brain that has increased the most in size is what scientists call the prefrontal cortex, the gateway to consciousness. This area of the brain is thought to be involved in complex cognitive behavior and in the expression of personality.

The arrival of the expanding executive brain signaled a paradigm shift in human evolution. It provided us with a dynamically faster central nervous system and an exponential surge in computational power. It gave us the capacity for language. Our bigger brain facilitated the rapid ascent of the qualities that make us human: our creativity, ambition, planning, intentional learning, and adaptive decision making. It enabled us to recognize and label our different feelings. With our new brain power, we evolved from psychologically primitive to psychologically elaborate beings.

But there's a downside. The fact that our emotional brain has been in residence so much longer than our executive brain means that our emotions tend to take precedence over our thoughts. It means that our emotional reactivity usually wins out over our reason and logic. While our thoughts can easily trigger our emotions, we are not very good at willfully turning off our emotions with our thoughts. And because our emotional responses are hardwired, we can get stuck in unproductive or dysfunctional habits of mind. It's the price we pay for the efficiencies of the brain's fear system.

There's no doubt about it: Fear has been with us since the beginning of time—the guardian of our survival. Fear kept our ancestors from becoming some predator's dinner. It alerted generation after generation to situations that threatened their survival. It keeps us from walking down dark alleys at night. Sometimes fear propels us forward; sometimes it freezes us in our tracks.

Your relationship with fear—and its cousin, anxiety—has a profound effect on your life. It shapes how you see yourself and others, and how others see you. It influences how you think about problems and make decisions. It affects how you view and manage change. It's a key factor in how you lead teams, manage performance, and interact with customers.

Fear and anxiety are what we experience when we go through life on autopilot. But we can no longer allow ourselves to operate this way. Most of the dangers faced by our ancestors are long gone. Unless we live in the wilderness, there are no wild beasts lurking in our bushes. Instead, we face threats our ancestors could never have imagined. We live in the shadow of weapons of mass destruction, terrorism, nuclear energy, global warming, and high-speed everything. The dangers we face are not fewer or less significant, they're just different. And we need a radically different approach to handling them.

As I see it, our paradigm for thinking about change, uncertainty, and anxiety has run its course. It is limiting our ability to live in our modern world. As long as we stay immersed in it, we will be blind to its limitations. We will be seduced by its promise of an anxiety-free life of comfort and stability. We will remain stuck in a closed loop of circular logic. We need to break the bonds of this outdated perspective.

Ironically, we have the capacity to give ourselves what we need. Research in fields as diverse as brain trauma, creativity, psychology, peak performance, and meditation has demonstrated the brain's capacity to rewire itself in new ways—to create new thinking patterns and neural networks. I believe these findings point the way toward changing our faulty thinking. The brain's ability to add an unlimited number of new connections means we can develop new ways of thinking and behaving.

We are not locked into running for our lives every time we're in a scary situation, whether it's the loss of a major client or negative feedback from someone we care about. We can use our brain power more effectively. We can unlock the potential of our executive brains and give them more control over our emotional brains. We can bypass outdated circuitry and restrictive thought patterns and develop new habits of thinking and acting. We can reframe what we think about entering the unknown and make new choices about how we handle change. As we do so, our brains will form new neural networks that reinforce our new perspective. This will make it progressively easier for us to manage and modulate the anxiety we feel from so much change and uncertainty.

Where do we start? What does it take to break free of our outdated response mechanism? It takes clearly defining what we want to achieve.

It takes commitment and courage to persevere in the face of difficulty. And it takes an unwavering belief in our ability to succeed. But above all, it takes our *willingness* to see change, uncertainty, and anxiety in a new way.

## LOOKING THROUGH A NEW LENS

*When you make a choice you mobilize vast human energies and resources that otherwise go untapped.*

—ROBERT FRITZ, *The Path of Least Resistance*

I've been fascinated with human nature as long as I can remember. What drives people? What keeps them up at night? Why do some succeed while others struggle? How do people manage change? Questions like these led me to get my Ph.D. in psychology. They also led to my keen interest in business, where so much of what makes people "tick" plays out in real time. With a grant from the MacArthur Foundation, I began researching the characteristics of successful leaders and winning organizations. I also founded a leadership-consulting business (Healthy Companies International) and learned the basics of business "on the street."

My travels to interview and advise CEOs around the world took me to more than thirty-five countries. As I met and worked with top executives, I came to understand the profound effect that leaders have on their organizations—both intentionally and unintentionally. I also became aware of how culture influences the way leaders, and their people, think about change, uncertainty, and anxiety.

While traveling through Asia, I was especially struck by the Buddhist notion of impermanence. The idea is that change is the natural state of things, everything in life grows and decays, and uncertainty and anxiety are an inherent part of being alive. After exploring the notion further, I started to shift my frame of reference. I began looking beyond the offices of the leaders I was meeting to see real men and women, with personal aspirations, vulnerabilities, and fears. I began to see how we all live with some degree of anxiety throughout much of our lives.

And then it hit me. The success of great leaders is all about creating the right level of anxiety for growth and performance. It is their uncommon ability to create just enough tension—within themselves and their organizations—that unleashes the human energy that drives powerful leadership, accelerated growth, and winning companies.

These leaders are not caught in the faulty thinking that imprisons so many of us. They have a different mind-set, a new perspective that enables them to embrace change and uncertainty. They know how to manage and use anxiety to propel their organizations forward, even in the midst of chaos.

It's time to shine a bright light on our habitual and outdated views of change. It's time to rethink our understanding of uncertainty, our relationship to it, and our ability to manage it in our lives. And it's time to reframe our perspective on anxiety. We need to see our world through a new lens.

When you change your lens, you change your life. You see things you never saw before. Other, more familiar sights come into sharper focus. You're able to see a bigger picture, and nothing looks quite like it did before.

The new lens I'm talking about is made up of three life-changing insights. Let's look closely at each one.

*It's time to embrace change, uncertainty, and anxiety as facts of life.* This involves letting go of your desire for stability. It means giving up any notion you have that you can protect yourself from pain. Or that you can predict the future based on the past. It requires taking an honest look at what you can and can't control, and accepting what you discover. Such acceptance takes nothing away from your ambitions and goals or your desire to improve yourself or your business. It just changes your relationship to uncertainty and change. And that's the point.

*We can use our healthy anxiety as a positive force for growth.* Anxiety travels with change and uncertainty, and this is actually good news. Because it accompanies change, you always have a ready supply of anxiety to use for handling whatever comes your way. That's right: Your anxiety is exactly what you need to deal with the ups and downs of life. It can prompt you to make healthy changes in your life. It can push you to take advantage of unforeseen opportunities, or it can help you confront your most difficult issues. It can keep you out of harm's way. Your anxiety can help you better understand yourself and stretch you into fulfilling your potential. You just need the right amount of it.

*Just enough anxiety is the key to living and leading in our complex world.*

What exactly is just enough anxiety? It is the right level of anxiety—at any given moment in time—that drives you forward without causing you to resist, give up, or try to control what happens. It unleashes your productive energy and makes you want to do better. Just enough anxiety produces the optimal state of arousal that enables you to stretch beyond your current reality into your desired future. It allows you to close the gaps in your life—gaps between who you are and who you wish to be; between the life you have and the life you want; and between where your organization is and where you want it to be.

---

### Tips for Living with Change, Uncertainty, and Anxiety

- Be fully present in each moment.
- Distinguish what you can and can't control.
- Be willing to embrace the unknown.
- Befriend your anxiety.
- Cultivate self-confidence.
- Learn to manage your emotions.
- Look for the positive in every experience.
- Focus on your personal goal.
- Keep the bigger picture in mind.
- Practice patience and persistence.

---

As Lars Ramqvist, chairman and CEO of Sweden's Ericsson, told me as we looked out over the city of Stockholm, just enough anxiety is "healthy anxiety with a destination." It grabs your attention, and, if you're willing and able to examine what you're feeling and why, it moves you toward optimal performance and the deeper truths in your life.

Just enough anxiety has been my personal teacher and motivator for many years. It pushed me to mend the broken parts of my life that came from growing up in a broken home. It propelled me to stretch myself to get my Ph.D. It enabled me to step outside my comfort zone and start my own business. Just enough anxiety prompted me to look beyond our Western view to see the world through a fresh perspective, a new lens. And it continues to help me build a new relationship with change and uncertainty.

The idea of just enough anxiety is the culmination of twenty years of research into how great leaders champion change and motivate top performance. It is where my work with top leaders intersects with ongoing consulting by Healthy Companies International (HCI) on the human side of change. It holds a great promise: As you develop and nurture your ability to create and live with just enough anxiety, you will be better able to learn, change, and navigate in a complicated world. You will achieve more of what your heart desires. You will live a happier, more fulfilled life. And you will be a better leader.

## YOUR LEADERSHIP CHALLENGE

*There are no signposts in the sea.*

—VITA SACKVILLE-WEST, English poet

Leadership used to be about creating certainty. Now it is about leading uncertainty. Most businesses today operate in environments where constant change is the name of the game. Leaders can't keep playing the same game when the rules keep changing. What worked yesterday won't work tomorrow. What succeeds in one industry won't succeed in another. Let's face it: Effective strategies seem to come and go faster than they can be replicated. To thrive in today's chaotic seas, organizations and their leaders must dramatically change how they navigate their positions in the marketplace.

If you're like most leaders, you are managing one burning platform after another. You may be pursuing new opportunities or coping with a crisis. You may be launching a new product or fending off a competitive challenge. Or you may be wrapped up in people problems.

There is hope. Successful leaders stay ahead of the game by either shaping their world to suit themselves or quickly adapting to the world around them. The shapers actually drive change. By introducing new technologies or developing new products or processes, they redefine their organizations in fundamental ways. The adapters work creatively within existing structures. Their flexibility and willingness to explore possibilities helps them avoid problems and take advantage of opportunities.

These are fresh approaches to leadership. Instead of fighting to remain afloat on a river of change, these leaders are using uncertainty and anxiety to stoke the engine and move full steam ahead. They see change and anxiety as opportunities to grow and learn. As a result, their companies are thriving. They are winning organizations—agile, innovative, profitable, and sustainable. Building a winning company is every leader's dream. And leading people through change is every leader's job. It's about taking people from where they are to where they need to be. And it's about having the courage and commitment to drive and sustain change.

Two decades of research at Healthy Companies International shows that the leaders who succeed in accomplishing these goals have something striking in common. Without exception, they excel in the five key leadership tasks that are priorities in every organization: Leadership, Strategy, Engagement, Growth, and Innovation.

But that's not all. Successful leaders look at change, uncertainty, and anxiety through a new lens. They see themselves, their leadership, and their businesses much differently than do their less successful counterparts. As a result, they execute all five of the key leadership tasks in fundamentally different ways. Let's see how.

LEADERSHIP: *Successful leaders willingly travel into the unknown.* They take uncertainty in stride. In fact, they enjoy the challenge that constant change provides. Their inquisitive nature and capacity for being uncomfortable enables them to be open to new experiences. Their deeply held values guide them as they chart paths through unfamiliar territory, unanticipated

**THE NEW LENS ON
THE FIVE LEADERSHIP TASKS**

Leadership · Strategy · Engagement · Growth · Innovation

problems, and unforeseen opportunities. These leaders have the mental flexibility to manage the unexpected in a way that appears almost effortless, as if they were just going with the flow. In a very real sense, they are. But they are also firmly grounded in reality, constantly attuned to their changing environment and to themselves. They are composed, confident, and courageous.

STRATEGY: *Successful leaders set an evolving course through ambiguity, complexity, and change.* They turn uncertainty and adversity into advantages. Their sound judgment leads to sound decisions, even with incomplete information. Yet they are willing to change their minds and their course of action when necessary, rapidly refining and redeploying resources. They steer and support others through change after change with a sense of urgency. Simultaneously optimistic and realistic, they risk failure in pursuit of success.

ENGAGEMENT: *Successful leaders inspire and challenge people to perform beyond their own expectations.* They are relationship builders. They align people around a shared vision with honest and open dialogue—and open hearts. Comfortable with conflict and disagreement, these leaders foster dynamic debate and constructive impatience. They get people involved by earning their confidence and trust. Their empathy and compassion for others allows them to stretch people into their discomfort zones, while igniting their passion to win. Their ability to motivate, coach, and develop leaders at all levels enables them to build a culture of accountability and execution.

GROWTH: *Successful leaders learn and relearn in real time by stretching themselves and the business.* They willingly reinvent themselves and their organizations to adapt to change. They see lifelong learning as a priority and themselves as teachers and learners. They see both success and failure as good teachers. Their resilience in the face of adversity enables them to continuously experiment and explore possibilities. It also allows them to face seemingly unending difficult and complex issues. Because they believe in people, these leaders build talent for a changing marketplace. With a sense of urgency and commitment to achieving results, they champion informed risk taking and sustainable growth.

INNOVATION: *Successful leaders imagine possibilities, discover opportunities, and release creative energies inside their organizations.* They refuse to accept the status quo. There's always a new goal to reach or a new opportunity to grab. These leaders are masterful at accessing and channeling energy, in themselves and others. They expect change, think nimbly, and question deeply. They push boundaries. They create excitement. Because they value differences, they invite diverse input and create big, bold ideas by building on smaller possibilities. Their deep understanding of changing customer needs and expectations—and their ability to unleash the creative capabilities within their organizations—enables them to stay ahead of their competition with new and better products and services.

## The Power of Just Enough Anxiety

One capability makes it possible for leaders to succeed at these key tasks. It is the capability to live with and create just enough anxiety within themselves and for others. More than any other leadership quality, this ability propels great leaders to the top. It enables them to embrace uncertainty and manage the ups and downs of a crazy world. It brings out their best performance, enables them to build great teams, and inspires and challenges their organizations. It is the hidden driver of business success.

Leaders without just enough anxiety put their companies at risk. If they have too little anxiety, they run away from uncertainty and change, eventually becoming complacent and losing out to the competition. Their lack of anxiety gives people a false sense of security and fails to inspire continuous innovation. If they have too much anxiety, they are unable to manage change and uncertainty and soon become frozen in fear. Their excessive anxiety breeds chaos and confusion, lowers productivity, and destroys morale.

Successful leaders—whom I call JEA (just enough anxiety) leaders—understand themselves and the dynamics of change. They are at ease sitting with and talking about the anxiety that change produces, both in themselves and in those around them. They use their self-awareness to assess where they are, where they want to go in the future, and how much anxiety is just enough to get there. They know that just enough anxiety lives in the gap between their current reality and their desired outcome—where leaders do their most important work.

Over the past twenty years, I have watched scores of JEA leaders create the right amount of anxiety to move people forward in positive and productive ways. I have coached executives as they have learned to understand and use their anxiety in personal and organization-wide transitions. And I have learned through my own experience growing a small entrepreneurial firm what it takes to create and live with just enough anxiety.

## JEA Leadership in Action

Jean-Pierre (J.P.) Garnier at GlaxoSmithKline (GSK) can tell us a lot about how to lead people through change and uncertainty. Stepping into the CEO role following the merger of SmithKline Beecham and Glaxo Wellcome in 2001, J.P. wasted no time in shaping a new future for the company. His first step: Create a bold vision.

"The core of our vision was to create the best R&D organization in the world. We realized that the industry hadn't been very successful in discovering breakthrough medicines, and had underinvested in R&D. It was a fundamental new direction."

Resistance was high. So instead of trying to build a winning company on shaky ground, J.P. started from scratch. He realigned systems and structures, redeployed resources, and got the right people in the right jobs. He was visible, walking the corridors and making speeches.

"We saw a big jump in productivity, almost from day one," he recalls. "We put in place some very simple measurements, like the percentage of new drugs we are getting to the market. And by doing that we've gone from being in the back of the pack in terms of R&D productivity to being among the best."

J.P. understood people's anxiety in the face of change. But he didn't coddle them. "Too many CEOs feel they have to project the positive, tell people that everything is fine. I don't buy that at all. You can't treat employees like children and tell them everything is always good and great. You can't spend too much time on the positive or too much time on the negative. You need to be realistic to succeed." At the same time, "people need to know and feel confident that their leaders have solutions that they haven't thought about and that they're going to make things happen." It's the only way they will venture into the unknown.

"Fear is very paralyzing to an organization, as well as to a human being. If your fear shows, you end up passing it on to people, and they don't think they can win. People won't try as hard if they don't believe they can make it. They'll think the boat is sinking and jump ship. So you need people to believe that you're going to win. People want to be associated with winning teams and winning organizations.

"I'm constantly trying to push the organization to the limit," J.P. told me when we met at GSK in Philadelphia. "Sometimes I'll hold back because, if I push too hard, it's not going to work. You have to know when to pull your punches. You can't get everybody excited all the time because there's a fatigue factor. You need to have a good sense of how far you can push the organization." And getting people to change—one by one—is the only way to change an organization. After all, every change is personal.

J.P. created just enough anxiety to reinvent GSK. Because he was looking at change, uncertainty, and anxiety through the new lens, he was able to tackle the five key leadership tasks in fundamentally different ways. He demonstrated strong leadership through his vision and willingness to tackle the unknown. He laid out a clear course through change that people could understand and follow. He engaged people by challenging them to perform beyond their own expectations—stretching them as far as they could stretch to help them move through their resistance. This released the collective energy of the organization and resulted in measurable growth.

GSK sales in 2006 totaled $45 billion. It now supplies one-quarter of the world's vaccines and has 149 projects in clinical development. On the people side, GSK recently finished first in employee engagement among its peers worldwide. "We've created positive energy by turning the company around," says J.P.

But like a true JEA leader, J.P. is not resting on the company's laurels. As he describes it, "We've operated very successfully over the past five years, but we need to keep up the pressure and the intensity. We can't relax or spend too much time congratulating ourselves for what we have accomplished so far. We have to understand that while we have moved forward, the environment we operate in has become more complex.

"Every employee must be really focused on the work to get done. We've got to have lots of passionate people all over the place. We will provide an environment that is supportive, but we're not going to tell you that life is going to be easy. We need to be resilient. We can't be distracted from execution."

Now, that's how you put just enough anxiety to work.

## Are You a JEA Leader?

*Instructions:* Rate yourself on the extent to which you demonstrate the following behaviors, beliefs, and attitudes.

1 = Rarely
2 = Sometimes
3 = A lot of the time
4 = Almost always

___I value and seek change.
___I am comfortable with uncertainty.
___I use anxiety as a positive force for growth.
___I engender hope and optimism in others.
___I take calculated risks in my life.
___I treat failure as a learning opportunity.
___I demonstrate adaptability and agility at work.
___I use conflict to find more effective solutions.
___I face tough issues with confidence.
___I trust myself and others to think flexibly.
___I am constantly scanning my environment.
___I am adept at managing my emotions.
___I understand the emotions of others.
___I am able to energize myself and others.
___I maintain a positive attitude in the midst of adversity.
___People describe me as honest and authentic.
___My passion inspires people to do their best.
___I readily help others handle change and uncertainty.
___I challenge people to outperform themselves.
___I pride myself in knowing my strengths and shortcomings.

*Results:* Add up your score and compare to the results below. Focus on your lowest scores to strengthen your JEA leadership skills.

- 62 or higher: You are a strong JEA leader.
- 51–61: You are moving in the right direction.
- 40–50: You need to step up your game.
- 39 or below: You have a lot of work to do.

## FORGING A NEW PATH

*It is uncertainty that creates the space for invention. We must let go, clear the space, leap into the void of not knowing, if we want to discover anything new.*

—MARGARET WHEATLEY, *Leadership and the New Science*

We're breaking new ground here. Taking a fresh look at uncertainty, change, and anxiety is evolutionary. Yet it's an idea whose time has come. If we are to live and lead successfully in today's world, we must forge a new path.

This journey begins with you. To change your organization, you must first change yourself. You must learn to create and live with just enough anxiety inside yourself. Then you can help others do the same. You can lead your organization through whatever comes your way.

This book will guide you on your journey. It gives you a proven road map drawn from two decades of research and my interviews with more than 300 top leaders. It tells you what to expect and what you can do to chart your course, avoid pitfalls, and clear the obstacles along the way. And it helps you stay focused on where you're headed by sharing the stories of real-life leaders who are getting it right.

### ROAD MAP FOR LIVING AND LEADING
### IN A WORLD OF UNCERTAINTY

CHANGE & UNCERTAINTY → LEADER'S WORK → JUST ENOUGH ANXIETY → THE THREE PARADOXES → WINNING PERFORMANCE

The book is organized as a road map. Each chapter examines a specific section of the map, which is highlighted on the road map at the beginning of the chapter. In this chapter, we looked closely at how our outdated view of change, uncertainty, and anxiety is holding us back, keeping us locked in our faulty thinking. We learned that we have the capacity to change how we see things. Looking through the new lens, we discovered the three points of view we need to live and lead in today's world. We explored the implications of our changing world on leaders, and how successful leaders are mastering the five key leadership tasks to build winning organizations.

Chapter 2 focuses on how anxiety affects your work as a leader. You'll learn how physiology and psychology come together to produce emotions, and how research in diverse fields is helping us understand our amazing human brain. I'll talk about how we can use this information to befriend our anxiety. We'll explore some new ways of thinking that can help us live more comfortably with uncertainty and change. We'll look at the distinctions between healthy and unhealthy anxiety. And I'll offer ways you can use healthy anxiety as a catalyst for positive growth, for yourself and your organization.

Chapter 3 continues our exploration of the inner world of the leader. We'll look at how change creates gaps—between where we are and where we want to be—for ourselves and our organizations. You'll learn to see the gap as part of a dynamic human energy system. I'll give you practical advice on how you can use the anxiety that comes from these gaps to generate productive energy. And I'll explain in detail the importance of having an open mind and an open heart for living and leading with just enough anxiety.

In Chapter 4, we will explore the three distinct faces of anxiety. We'll look at how we all constantly balance between too much and too little anxiety in our attempt to find just enough. You'll meet successful leaders who travel the middle (JEA) road, unleashing productive energy to build winning companies. You'll also meet leaders who are doing it wrong. For example, those who create too much anxiety produce chaotic energy, while those who create too little anxiety produce ineffective energy. Both too much and too little anxiety lead to decline.

In Chapters 5 through 7, I'll share inspiring stories of JEA leaders who have an astounding ability to live in paradox. You'll meet men and women who are adept at realistic optimism, constructive impatience, and confident humility. And you'll learn how your ability to develop these seemingly contradictory qualities defines who you are, how you think, and how you lead others. In each of these chapters, you'll have the opportunity to identify your tendencies and learn practical tips for living in paradox.

Chapter 8 pulls it all together to give you an in-depth view of what it takes to be a JEA leader, create a JEA team, and build a JEA organization. You will see just enough anxiety in action. We'll look closely at the practices of leaders who are traveling the JEA path. And I'll talk about how you can transform your company from too little or too much anxiety into a JEA organization.

In Chapter 9, I'll share what I've learned on my own journey about making it all work. And I'll talk about the four qualities that will help you along the way.

Throughout the book, I will introduce you to successful top executives from around the world. These leaders have little in common. They did not graduate from the same business school. In fact, some never even went to business school. They work in different countries and industries. And they are not united by any single approach to operations, marketing, or financial management.

What these exceptional leaders do share, beyond their consistent success, is their ability to live and lead with just enough anxiety. They effectively embrace human challenges most leaders consider too soft or too mysterious to manage. And they dedicate themselves to creating an environment in which their people will consistently excel.

You will notice that these JEA leaders are always wearing two hats. One hat is personal, psychological. It reflects their inner work. The other hat is professional. It reflects their external work as leaders. They wear these hats simultaneously because real life is a combination of what goes on inside and outside of us. Our inner experience as humans is inextricably tied to our outer experience as leaders, managers, factory workers, or office heads.

I've written the book so you can wear these two hats as you read. It speaks to both your inner and outer experience by weaving together the personal and the professional. It combines principles from both psychology and business. That's the real work of leaders.

We stand at a critical juncture in human evolution. As the world continues to increase in complexity, accompanied by stronger and stronger winds of change, we have two choices. We can try to stand still and be blown about at random, fearful and anxious at every gust. Or we can lean into the wind. We can learn to live and lead with just enough anxiety. Each of us must make our own decision. What are you going to do?

# 2

# A NEW UNDERSTANDING OF ANXIETY

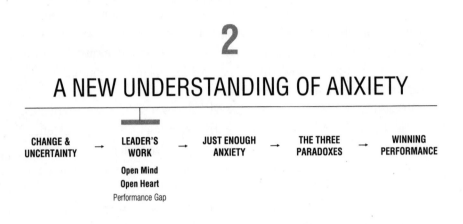

| CHANGE & UNCERTAINTY | → | LEADER'S WORK | → | JUST ENOUGH ANXIETY | → | THE THREE PARADOXES | → | WINNING PERFORMANCE |
|---|---|---|---|---|---|---|---|---|
| | | Open Mind | | | | | | |
| | | Open Heart | | | | | | |
| | | Performance Gap | | | | | | |

*Confusion is a word we have invented for an order which is not yet understood.*

—HENRY MILLER, American writer

Manuel (Manny) Pangilinan, managing director and CEO of First Pacific Company, understands anxiety. His picture was splashed all over the *South China Post* the day I interviewed him in Hong Kong. Manny's company, one of Asia's largest and most diversified—with interests in banking, telecommunications, real estate, trading, and packaging—was more than $900 million in debt as a result of the economic crisis in Asia. "Business is tough these days," he told me. "This crisis isn't limited geographically; it's endemic. It's not limited to currencies, but has an impact on liquidity and profit position. This is the first time I've seen this sort of crisis." It was a dilemma that would keep most leaders up at night.

But Manny is not just any leader. His Asian heritage has taught him to accept the way things are and to be comfortable with ambiguity. "In Asia," he says, "we generally accept nature's way of doing things. We're comfortable with both crisis and opportunity. We can hold different ideas in our heads at the same time." With this mind-set, and unlike many of his contemporaries who bailed out during the crisis, Manny was able to moderate his anxiety and find a constructive solution.

He faced the Asian crisis head-on, insisting that everyone rethink their assumptions about the business. But he was also deliberate about managing his employees' anxiety. He quickly articulated a new vision and plan for the company's future, and he communicated openly and honestly about the situation. "If the business feels the pain, the people feel the pain. And if the people feel the pain, so do I. CEO or not, I'm a human being." By both acknowledging the chaos and defining the future, and by both requiring quick action and giving people the understanding and support they needed, the Asian leader generated just enough anxiety to move the company forward.

Today, Manny continues to share his vision and invite people to join him in creating positive change. First Pacific has sharpened its focus, maintaining interests primarily in consumer food products and telecommunications. In 2005, First Pacific reported sales of $1.98 billion, with a net income of nearly $139 million.

We can learn a lot from Manny Pangilinan. If we want to navigate the change and uncertainty in our lives, we need to see anxiety as a positive and powerful force, as he did. We need to find a way to embrace anxiety as part of life and use it to move ourselves and our organizations forward. To accomplish these tasks, we must learn to let go of our long-held negative views of anxiety based on faulty thinking, old mental models, and an outdated fear response.

We can start by exploring how we ended up where we are. For example, how have cognitive, emotional, and physiological research and inquiry informed our understanding of ourselves and our anxiety? And what do we know about the brain that might help us create just enough anxiety to live and lead in a world of change and uncertainty?

## ONE HUNDRED YEARS OF BRAIN SCIENCE

Do we run because we're afraid of the bear? Or are we afraid of the bear because we run? These questions inspired the work of psychologist William James in 1884. In his view, action comes first. Our bodily response to danger precedes and shapes both our emotional experience and our cognitive understanding. James also believed that each of our emotions has its own set of physiological sensations.

In the 1920s, physiologist Walter Cannon refuted James's idea that different emotions correspond to different bodily sensations. According to Cannon, a single fight-or-flight response enables us to protect ourselves from threats by increasing our heart rate and blood pressure, pumping blood away from extremities into our large muscles, and enhancing our vision and hearing. Our feelings occur automatically, while our understanding of what is happening comes later.

Around the same time, Sigmund Freud theorized that fear and anxiety arise from deep-seated conflicts and desires linked to early childhood. These hidden impulses drive our thoughts and behaviors as we develop and mature. Uncovering the trigger events through psychoanalysis (talk therapy) can help people overcome their negative emotions. James, Cannon, and Freud set the foundation for linking anxiety to fear and seeing it as something beyond our control.

Around the 1930s, Anna Freud (Sigmund's daughter) and her followers turned their attention to how people cope with anxiety at the psychological level. They suggested that some anxiety is healthy and natural—it's not all negative. But our minds are always trying to protect us from anxiety. These mental processes—ego defense mechanisms—can be adaptive or maladaptive. With adaptive defenses such as humor or sublimation, we channel our anxiety into productive activities, like sports, music, or art. With maladaptive defense mechanisms, we stray from reality and toward pathology. If we use denial, for example, we close ourselves off to reality. If we use projection, we see our anxiety as being generated by something or someone outside ourselves.

### Ego Defense Mechanisms

| | | |
|---|---|---|
| • Compensation | • Intellectualization | • Repression |
| • Denial | • Introjection | • Somatization |
| • Displacement | • Inversion | • Splitting |
| • Dissociation | • Projection | • Sublimation |
| • Humor | • Rationalization | • Substitution |
| • Idealization | • Reaction formation | • Suppression |
| • Identification | • Regression | • Undoing |

The identification of ego defenses helped to legitimize our avoidance of anxiety. But the suggestion that anxiety could be healthy garnered little attention. Perhaps psychiatrists, whose focus at the time was solely on patients hospitalized with severe mental illness, were blind to the possibility of healthy individuals with "normal" anxiety.

But this was about to change. Psychiatrists who served in World War II noticed that the stress of combat contributed to mild "mental maladjustment" among healthy soldiers. They also found that early treatment in noninstitutional settings produced favorable outcomes. These observations had profound impacts, broadening our view of mental illness from a purely biological disease to one that could be precipitated by environmental factors. They expanded the range of mental disorders, from severe to mild. And they led to the first plausible classification system for diagnosing mental disorders.

Published in 1952 by the American Psychiatric Association, the *Diagnostic and Statistical Manual of Mental Disorders (DSM-I)* divided mental disorders into categories. It listed anxiety as a psychoneurotic disorder, along with phobic, obsessive-compulsive, and depressive disorders, and a variety of personality disorders. The *DSM-I* placed anxiety firmly in the realm of illness, something to be avoided, denied, or treated professionally. Today, the latest revision of the *DSM*, published in 1994, lists seven types of anxiety disorders:

- Acute Stress Disorder
- Agoraphobia (with or without a history of Panic Disorder)
- Generalized Anxiety Disorder
- Obsessive-Compulsive Disorder
- Panic Disorder (with or without Agoraphobia)
- Phobias
- Post-traumatic Stress Disorder

Meanwhile, back in the laboratory, science was digging deeper into the physiology of emotions. In 1952, based on his research at Yale Medical School and the National Institute of Mental Health, physician Paul MacLean postulated that our emotions are related to a group of structures in the center of the brain called the limbic system. The main components are the amygdala, hypothalamus, and hippocampus. Together, said MacLean, they initiate both our physiological response and our emotional experience. The limbic system became known as the seat of our fear response, and, as I mentioned in Chapter 1, was later dubbed the emotional brain.

Enter the concept of stress. In the 1950s, Canadian endocrinologist Hans Selye took MacLean's work and the experience of World War II psychiatrists a step further. He popularized what he called the general adaptation syndrome—the idea of a system-wide response to external stressors. According to Selye, stressful situations trigger not only the limbic system, but also our adrenal and pituitary glands, to release chemicals throughout the body. As the stress subsides, our bodily functions return to normal. Chronic stress, however, sends the body into constant hypervigilance, making us susceptible to severe fatigue and illness.

Selye's theory spoke to people's internal experience and their postwar desires to lead calm, controlled lives. They accepted that stress, like anxiety, was bad. One or both could destroy our health and happiness. And they were mostly out of our control. Once again, stress and anxiety remained on the top of the list of things to avoid.

The rise of psychopharmacology compounded the idea that anxiety could—and should—be suppressed or controlled. Among the first prescription drugs to hit the market, in 1954, was the antianxiety drug Doriden. In 1960, the FDA approved the use of Librium to treat anxiety. It approved Valium in 1963. Since then nearly two dozen drugs have been developed to treat anxiety disorders. While these provide legitimate relief for anxiety-related disorders, their use also bolsters the belief that anxiety is abnormal.

### Medications Now Used to Treat Anxiety Disorders

| | | |
|---|---|---|
| • Atarax | • Inderal | • Tranxene |
| • Ativan | • Klonopin | • Valium |
| • Benadryl | • Librium | • Visken |
| • Benzodiazepine | • Lopressor | • Vistaril |
| • Buspar | • Paxipam | • Xanax |
| • Corgard | • Serax | |
| • Diphenhydramine | • Tenormin | |

Experiments in the 1960s and beyond added a new piece to the puzzle. They confirmed the idea that our experience of emotions is not entirely biological. It results from our mental interpretation of bodily sensations. Although our original sensations might be genetically programmed, our assessment of what we're feeling is conscious. We can escalate or diminish what we're feeling with our thoughts.

Cognitive behavioral therapy (CBT) erupted on the scene in the 1980s. Its founders were Aaron Beck, a psychiatrist at the University of Pennsylvania, and Albert Ellis, a New York therapist. Focusing on the link between our negative thoughts and emotions, they developed a way of helping people overcome the self-defeating thoughts that perpetuate negative emotions. The effectiveness of CBT in treating a wide array of mental maladies—from anxiety and depression to Post-traumatic Stress Disorder—reinforces the notion that we can control our emotions with our thoughts.

Fast-forward to today. We now understand a lot more than ever before about the emotional brain, thanks to Joseph LeDoux, professor of neuroscience and psychology at New York University and director of the Center for the Neuroscience of Fear and Anxiety. In *The Emotional Brain,* LeDoux focuses on the power of the limbic system, particularly the amygdala, over the higher-functioning cortex to drive human behavior. This supports the view that our emotions tend to take charge of our thoughts, and that, while possible, it's hard to gain conscious control.

We also know more about the importance of emotions in general, and the interplay between our emotions and our intellect. In *Emotional Intelligence,* psychologist Daniel Goleman distinguishes between emotional and cognitive intelligence while arguing the importance of expressing and managing our emotions for personal and business success. And in his book *The Executive Brain,* Elkhonon Goldberg, clinical professor of neurology at the New York University School of Medicine, deepens our understanding of the seat of consciousness: our prefrontal cortex. His work offers considerable promise for our ability to moderate our anxiety by giving more control to our executive brain.

Science has illuminated our understanding of our thoughts and emotions. Its discoveries have improved health care and people's everyday lives. Yet it has also colored our perception of anxiety. It has led us to believe that anxiety is unhealthy, unconscious, and mostly uncontrollable. Science has made us feel vulnerable, afraid of our healthy anxiety. Millions of us seek treatment for anxiety on a regular basis. Fear and anxiety are a multibillion-dollar business.

### Anxiety in the United States Today

- Anxiety disorders are the most common mental illness in the United States, affecting 19.1 million (13.3 percent) of the adult population (ages eighteen to fifty-four).
- Anxiety disorders cost more than $42 billion a year, almost one-third of the $148 billion total U.S. mental health bill.
- More than $22.84 billion of costs are associated with the repeated use of health care services, as people seek relief for symptoms that mimic physical illnesses.
- People with an anxiety disorder are three to five times more likely to go to the doctor and six times more likely to be hospitalized for psychiatric disorders than nonsufferers.
- Twice as many people treat anxiety and depression with drugs than use talk therapy.

So why am I talking about brain science in a book about leadership? It's because these evolving scientific and societal views of anxiety have infiltrated the minds of leaders around the world. Business is about people. People naturally experience anxiety. And leadership is about modulating and harnessing the anxiety of others.

This is where your two hats come in. If you wear only your professional hat, while denying your personal feelings, you come to your job as a leader both blind and disconnected from your emotions. If you wear only your personal hat, while ignoring your professional role, you become preoccupied with your emotions and misjudge the emotions of others.

In my travels I've noticed that many leaders talk openly about the stresses of the job—feeling tense, concerned, worried, upset, uncomfortable, or apprehensive. Often they see stress as a badge of courage. Yet they are strangely reluctant to use the word *anxiety,* which they see as a sign of weakness. I believe their resistance to the word, and perhaps to the emotion itself, has stifled and suffocated many leaders' ability to lead the human side of change. They are simply running away from a natural condition of leadership and life.

Fortunately, a new group of leaders is starting to see anxiety for what it is, as well as the effect it has on them. Rand Construction Corporation founder Linda Rabbitt sees it clearly: "I try to embrace my anxiety every day. I get up in the morning and think about the most important thing I have to do, and it's usually something uncomfortable for me. My rule is to get it done by ten o'clock in the morning."

Todd Stitzer, CEO of Cadbury Schweppes in London, admits, "It's a constant challenge to modulate and manage your anxiety. To not let your anxiety overwhelm you or get transmitted to others in a negative way. That's why I exercise four or five times a week and have a wife as my partner whom I confide in and who supports me no matter how insane I get."

"Anxiety is intriguing" to Anne Bryant, executive director of the National School Boards Association (NSBA). "It can be positive or negative. It can make you reach or shut you down."

Ron Carlee, county manager of Arlington, Virginia, puts it this way: "In business, positive anxiety is good. We want to be pushing for the positive and the constructive and avoiding the negative and destructive."

In Amsterdam, ING CEO Michel Tilmant agrees: "When it comes to anxiety, you have to turn it off or turn up the heat. That means recognizing success and pointing out problems. You need to have these two approaches at all times to ensure the right level of anxiety throughout the organization."

Dennis Nally, senior partner of PricewaterhouseCoopers (PwC) in the United States, sums it up nicely: "What I get anxious about is knowing how much change our organization realistically can absorb at any one time. Knowing how much is too much, too little, or just enough, and constantly recalibrating. My job is to keep my finger on the pulse at all times."

Today, more than one hundred years after William James began the elusive quest to understand emotions, the debate continues. Researchers and scientists are working hard to clarify the interplay between thoughts and emotions, between physiology and psychology, and between our emotional and executive brains. But as I see it, these three areas of distinction are essentially one and the same. They are merely different ways of looking at the dynamic interaction inside our minds that produces our experience of anxiety. A closer look at this interaction will help us see how we can create just enough anxiety to live more comfortably with uncertainty and change.

Ask yourself . . .

- How do I think about anxiety?
- When and how have I avoided feeling anxious?
- When and how have I gotten hijacked by my anxiety?
- How does my view of anxiety affect my experience?

## HOW ANXIETY WORKS IN THE BRAIN

The brain has been described as a biological organ, a computational machine, and the furnace of our emotions. It is composed of 100 billion cells. Most are neurons that act as on-off switches for sending and receiving impulses via electrochemical signals. The signals speed along the longest part of a neuron (axon) and then travel across the space at the end (synapse) to reach the next neuron. The chemicals that enable this to occur are called transmitters, with names like serotonin, epinephrine, and dopamine. Neurons also have branchlike projections (dendrites) that allow

### ANATOMY OF A NEURON

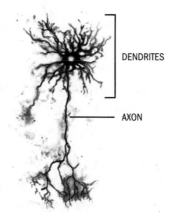

DENDRITES

AXON

## ANATOMY OF THE BRAIN

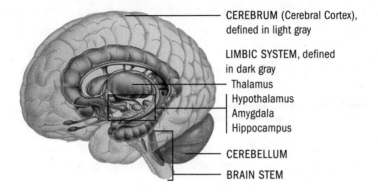

CEREBRUM (Cerebral Cortex),
defined in light gray

LIMBIC SYSTEM, defined
in dark gray
Thalamus
Hypothalamus
Amygdala
Hippocampus

CEREBELLUM

BRAIN STEM

them to "talk" with other cells and monitor the brain's internal environment.

There are three major parts to your brain. The *brain stem* controls your reflexes and automatic functions (heart rate, blood pressure), limb movements, and visceral functions (digestion, urination). The *cerebellum* integrates information about your body's position and movement and uses this information to coordinate your limb movements. The *cerebrum* (also known as the cerebral cortex) is divided into left and right hemispheres; it controls such functions as speech, memory, and intelligence, and integrates information from all of the sense organs.

The amygdala, hippocampus, hypothalamus, and thalamus are buried deep within your cortex. Together, they are known as the emotional brain. The amygdala is the source of your emotions, the hippocampus houses your memories, the hypothalamus regulates essential bodily functions, and the thalamus is the critical relay station that links your cerebral hemispheres to all other parts of your nervous system. The newest kids on the block are the prefrontal lobes of your cortex, commonly called the executive brain. These two brains within your brain are constantly competing with each other to gain the upper hand. Your older, emotional brain fights to let your emotions reign supreme, as they have for eons. Your newer, more evolved executive brain fights to exert control over those pesky, primitive emotions.

Here's how it works. Let's say you enter the conference room for an important, but routine, meeting. Before you are consciously aware of it, your internal sensors pick up the worried looks on people's faces. Your amygdala processes the emotional significance of the stimuli. If it recognizes a potential threat, based on stored memories (e.g., previous worried looks that signaled disaster), it alerts your hypothalamus, which activates your autonomic nervous system (ANS). Your ANS tells your adrenal glands to release stress hormones. These hormones, cortisone and adrenaline, prepare you for defensive action by raising your blood pressure, increasing blood flow to your muscles, and decreasing your blood supply to other body functions. They also shut down your thought process, making you less able to think creatively or figure out what's going on. The process occurs beyond your conscious awareness. Your heart begins to race. Without yet knowing why, you feel nervous, uncomfortable, and confused.

This all takes place in the blink of an eye. A few milliseconds later, your slower thalamus-cortex connection enables you to determine whether or not the incoming sensory data is a viable threat. This is where your higher-order thinking skills, reason, and speech reside. It's where you think about what you're feeling, analyze potential causes, and decide what to do. Without this capability, you might end up responding to threats that don't exist or ignoring threats that do.

Back in the conference room, you suddenly become aware of the looks on people's faces. You notice a feeling of tension in the room. Some people seem angry; others are sad or disengaged. In your mind, you sort through possible scenarios: Do they know something you don't? Did you lose that big account? Is there a problem with you? Maybe they're going to reject your budget proposal. Or maybe someone else is in trouble. Maybe something has happened that has nothing to do with you.

Hopefully, in a matter of seconds, you begin to calm yourself down. You tell yourself that you can handle whatever it is. You've done it before. So you override the urge to leave and take your seat at the table. Then you calmly ask, "Are we ready to begin?"

Our internal alarm system goes off every time our brains detect danger. It can be triggered by our memory of a past threat, our involvement in a current situation, or our dread of something that might happen in the future. We feel anxious over both real and imagined events. We tend to worry about things that haven't happened yet. We fear short-term dangers more than long-term risks. We're also more fearful of catastrophic events, like terrorist attacks, than we are of gradual threats, like global warming. We are less afraid of the devil we know than the devil we don't know.

Whatever triggers your anxiety reflects the dynamic interplay of your emotional and executive brains. Their constant chemical conversation gives rise to how you feel and what you think. As in the conference room example, your thoughts monitor, modulate, and interpret your feelings. Your feelings color, energize, and personalize your thoughts. This complex interweaving of physiology and psychology draws on your genetic makeup, development, memory, temperament, and life experience to produce your unique experience of anxiety.

Once your anxiety has been triggered, you have a choice: You can respond productively or unproductively.

Let's take another look at the conference room example. If you had denied your anxiety—not let yourself become aware of it—you would have been oblivious to the undercurrents in the room. You would have missed social cues, personalized the tension, or acted ineptly. On the other hand, if you had been hijacked by your anxiety, you would have gotten defensive or argumentative and blurted out something inappropriate. You would have lost your focus and ability to interact in the meeting. Or you would have left the room. These responses are all unproductive.

Each time you feel anxious, you have the same options. You can become defensive and try to deny, suppress, or ignore what you're feeling. You can exaggerate your anxiety or be overtaken by it. Or you can manage and use your anxiety in productive ways. Your body is talking to you, expressing excitement or concern. By paying attention, you can learn to lean into and through your anxiety.

What you do has a profound impact on your organization. If you try to dampen your anxiety, it takes every ounce of your energy to keep it from bursting forth. You become preoccupied with protecting yourself from your feelings, as well as suppressing anxiety in others. You get distracted

**TRIGGER** → **ANXIETY**

People's
worried
looks

Increased
heart rate,
etc.

**PRODUCTIVE RESPONSE**
Positive self-talk, deep breathing

**UNPRODUCTIVE RESPONSE**
Getting defensive or leaving

from making important decisions or necessary changes. Your ineffectiveness generates too little energy in your organization.

If you overreact to your anxiety, you create negative energy. You run around doing a lot and accomplishing little. Your diffuse focus causes you to misinterpret events and misunderstand others. Chances are you jump into action and make changes unnecessarily. The people around you sense danger, which raises their level of anxiety.

But if you take conscious control of your anxiety, through your understanding of its causes, you are able to use it in productive ways. You have the focus, concentration, and sense of direction you need to make important decisions and respond positively to change. You help others manage their anxiety, while inspiring their top performance. People are energized and results-oriented. Your organization has the productive energy it needs to face uncertainty and change.

Ask yourself . . .

- How satisfied am I with the results of how I manage my anxiety?
- How do I behave when I respond productively? Unproductively?
- What effect does my behavior have on my organization?

## WHAT MAKES YOU ANXIOUS?

*Your living is determined not so much by what life brings to you as by the attitude you bring to life; not so much by what happens to you as by the way your mind looks at what happens.*

—KAHLIL GIBRAN, Lebanese American writer

Life is like a poker game. In poker, you're dealt certain cards and then you have a choice: You can hold on to what you've got or trade in your less desirable cards for new ones. Each option has potential risks and rewards. Sometimes you win; sometimes you lose. In life, you're born with certain genes and into a particular family. As you get older, you have choices: You can hold on to the person you are or trade in your less desirable attributes (thoughts, behaviors, and negative emotions) for new ones. You can choose your life experiences. Sometimes you succeed; sometimes you fail.

You are playing the game of life with four major "cards" in your hand: your genetic makeup, personal development, life experiences, and beliefs

## SOURCES OF OUR ANXIETY

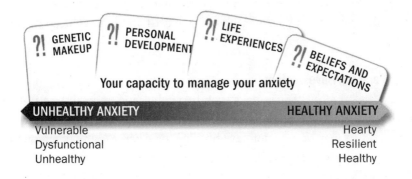

and expectations. Each one enhances or detracts from your ability to win with the hand you've got. Together, they determine your overall capacity to manage your anxiety. Let's look at each card more closely.

### Your Genetic Makeup

Your genes give you the raw materials from which your emotional experiences are built. They define how your nervous system operates, including your emotional and executive brains. They regulate the level of neurotransmitters responsible for carrying messages between your amygdala and prefrontal cortex, as well as those that allow or inhibit adventurous behavior. They establish your "set point" for anxiety and stress—whether you naturally tend to be highly sensitive and vulnerable or hearty and resilient.

How do we know this? Although genetic research in this area is relatively new, some findings are shedding light on the subject. Researchers have identified several specific genes that affect our sensitivity to life's stressors. These genes—and the chemicals they produce—make some of us high stress responders and some of us low stress responders. One gene in particular seems to play a major role in how anxiety prone we are. People with the short form of the gene are prone to twice the level of amygdala activation as people with the long form. They are easily overstimulated emotionally and vulnerable to feeling too much anxiety.

Additional evidence of the role of genetics in anxiety comes from research on twins. Studies suggest that identical twins—even those reared in separate homes—are far more similar in fearfulness than are fraternal twins. They are also more likely to have the same anxiety, phobic, and obsessive-compulsive disorders.

Your gene "card" defines your natural tendency for experiencing and managing anxiety in your life. It's the one card you have to keep in your hand.

## Your Personal Development

Whatever gene card you're dealt, you inevitably find yourself face-to-face with a family. You're in a relationship with your parents or other caregivers, and you may or may not have brothers or sisters. Your extended family may be large or small, functional or dysfunctional. Whatever your situation, your experiences in early childhood have a profound effect on how you experience anxiety and handle uncertainty and change.

Psychologists talk about this in terms of *attachment*. An attachment is a bond of affection that one person forms with another, usually a parent. As children, we develop our capacity for healthy relationships based on our early interactions with our primary caregivers. If those caregivers are overbearing or overprotective, we grow up anxious and overly dependent. If they are detached or avoid connecting with us, we grow up either as anxious and needy or detached and hyper-independent. If we have parents or caregivers who create healthy attachment—by loving us while fostering our independence—we grow up to be secure, independent, and loving adults. This allows us to hold healthy anxiety within ourselves, without withdrawing or overreacting. It enables us to handle change and uncertainty with confidence.

Your early attachments and childhood experiences formed the foundation on which you built your image of yourself and the world around you. You learned the extent of your personal power, and the power of uncertainty over you. You also developed your need for protection and your need to learn and grow. These unconscious lessons became embedded in your personality. They became the attitudes and behaviors that have guided you through life's twists and turns.

But don't worry. As someone once told me, the term *dysfunctional family* is a redundancy. We all have some level of dysfunction to overcome. It comes with being human. Whatever family you were born into, your personal development card is one you can choose to replace, as well as the next two.

## Your Life Experiences

Life is an unpredictable journey. You set out on a path, thinking you know where you're going. Along the way, you face obstacles, take detours, and even change direction from time to time. Sometimes you trudge up steep hills or get stopped cold by something unexpected. At other times you coast or gather momentum. One thing's for certain: You never know what's around the next twist in the road.

You can find yourself anxious about any aspect of your life at any time. You might experience anxiety around the physical, mental, emotional, or spiritual health of yourself or someone you love. You might feel anxious about a relationship—with a partner, parent, child, friend, or colleague. You might get anxious over personal finances, social or political issues, or the environment. Or you might experience anxiety concerning your performance at work, your career, your capability as a leader, or your ability to create work-life balance for yourself.

These are just snapshots in time. Some worries you can control; some you can't. Some are hardships that seem impossible to get through. Others bring love, hope, or joy. Wherever your life's journey takes you, remember: None of us gets out of here alive.

## Your Beliefs and Expectations

Early in my career I attended a meeting with many successful business-people. Eager to make connections, I walked up to a well-known CEO, hoping to introduce myself while wondering if he would talk with me. When he totally ignored me, I felt like a fork on the table in front of us. His behavior reinforced my insecurity and my belief that I wasn't important enough to warrant his attention. For some time after that, I felt trepidation every time I approached a top leader. As my confidence grew, however, things changed dramatically. I began to enjoy meeting leaders, and I have built my career on interviewing and advising them. After hundreds of CEO interviews, I now feel at home talking with any leader about any topic. In hindsight, it's easy to see how my beliefs and expectations about myself shaped my experience.

The same concept applies to anxiety. Your deep-seated beliefs and expectations—about yourself and the world around you—become self-fulfilling prophecies. They determine what makes you anxious. They affect the amount of anxiety you feel. And they influence how you interpret and label your experience.

## Top Twelve Self-Defeating Beliefs

Most of us sabotage our ability to manage change with one or more of the following deep-seated beliefs. We expect:

- to be right
- to do it all
- to avoid conflict
- predictable results
- love and admiration
- perpetual happiness

- things to go our way
- acceptance or approval
- things to stay the same
- never to make a mistake
- the past to predict the future
- never to feel anxiety

What you believe and expect can help or hinder you. If it's positive or self-affirming, it can push you to do your best. If it's negative or self-defeating, it can hold you back. Either way, beliefs and expectations can be tough to uncover. Stored deep within your memory banks—in the amygdala, hypothalamus, and cortex—they are a lot more accessible to your emotional brain than they are to your conscious mind. Because of this, they will continue to influence your experience of anxiety, for better or worse. If you want to change them, you'll need to devote time, attention, and patience to the task of digging them out. But it can be done.

Why bother? Because negative beliefs and expectations affect your performance. Studies show that performers who are moderately confident of success, and have positive expectations, see their anxiety as a positive influence. They perform well in both cognitive and motor-skills tasks. Performers who are less confident, and have negative expectations, see their anxiety as inhibiting their performance. They perform poorly.

The bottom line is that what you think is what you get. If you see yourself as highly sensitive, you will be. If you expect to feel anxious every time you are faced with change, you will. But if you consider yourself hearty and resilient, someone who thrives in the midst of uncertainty, your experiences will reinforce these beliefs and expectations as well.

All four of your life's cards—genetics, development, experiences, and beliefs and expectations—make up the hand you are currently holding. Each one contributes to your experience. Together, they point you toward healthy or unhealthy anxiety.

---

### How's Your Anxiety?

1. What is your set point for anxiety? Does it take a lot or a little to make you anxious?
2. How did growing up in your family contribute to the way you experience anxiety?
3. What childhood events still color your experience of anxiety—either positively or negatively?
4. Think of three life experiences that caused you considerable anxiety. How did you handle them?
5. What qualities do you have that help you manage your anxiety?
6. What qualities do you have that get in the way?
7. What self-affirming beliefs and expectations do you have?
8. What self-defeating beliefs and expectations do you have?
9. How would you rate your anxiety on a scale of 1–10, from unhealthy to healthy?
10. If you could change your relationship to anxiety, what would you change?

---

## Healthy Versus Unhealthy Anxiety

Anxiety is a fact of life. It keeps us safe and helps us grow. Scholars of the Kabbalah (an ancient Jewish text) assert that anxiety is "a requirement for learning and understanding the inner dimension of the Torah," the central and most important document of Judaism. It prompts us to seek answers to life's perplexing questions, such as: Why me? What does this mean? What is my purpose? Without a desire to resolve the incongruities of life, we would never develop, individually or spiritually. Our anxiety reflects our sensitivity. It shows that we care, that we're engaged in life.

These scholars are talking about healthy anxiety. It's the anxiety everyone deals with on a day-to-day basis. This kind of anxiety "can be a very positive motivator and driver," notes Jeffrey Akman, chairman of psychiatry and behavioral sciences at the George Washington University School of Medicine. "We can get to a healthier place if we learn how to manage and use this anxiety. We can gain pleasure in growing, in changing, or in searching for new experiences, just for their own sake."

Healthy anxiety is *just enough anxiety*. It is the exact amount you need to respond to danger, tackle a tough problem, or take a leap of faith. It is the right amount for you, given the person you are and what motivates you. Healthy anxiety is the right level of arousal, combined with the right attitude, that enables you to optimize your performance.

We've all experienced it. The athlete whose extra effort pushes her to her personal best. The scientist or artist who works late into the night. The leader whose perseverance enables the company to beat out the competition. These are examples of people using anxiety to push themselves beyond their own limits, to delve deep into themselves and discover their true potential.

Not all healthy anxiety leads to dramatic results, however. Sometimes it just helps you get through the day. It allows you to get to the meeting you would rather skip. It prompts you to tackle that niggling little problem that nobody else will. It propels you to stop at the gym on your way home, eat healthier, or work harder at keeping your relationships healthy and fulfilling.

Healthy anxiety has positive consequences. It boosts your confidence and ability to concentrate. It enhances your ability to learn. Healthy anxiety strengthens your commitment and increases your energy. It enables you to perform at your best. In the words of Jeffrey Akman: "You can develop a great sense of gratification and reward by mastering your anxiety. It has great positive, psychological outcomes."

But not all anxiety is healthy. Anxiety becomes unhealthy when it interferes with normal functioning or good judgment. Instead of spurring you on to action, it shuts you down. Or it sends you off frantically in all directions. Left unattended, unhealthy anxiety can lead to serious physical or psychological illnesses.

We often generate unhealthy anxiety within ourselves through faulty thinking. Our executive brains deceive us into making matters worse than they are. Common forms of such mental misperception include the following:

- *Overgeneralizing*—interpreting one negative event or failure as a regular pattern
- *Obsessive thinking*—selecting a single detail and amplifying it out of proportion
- *Disqualifying the positive*—insisting good experiences are isolated or irrelevant
- *Jumping to conclusions*—forming negative interpretations with only a few facts
- *Personalizing*—assuming inappropriate blame for situations or events
- *Magnifying or minimizing events*—exaggerating or belittling the significance of problems or mistakes

A long, uninterrupted period of unhealthy anxiety can have serious physical consequences. It can lead to stiff muscles, dizziness, sleep and stomach disorders, fatigue, and elevated blood pressure. It can also cause irritability, anger, self-criticism, and depression. High, long-term levels of unhealthy anxiety can weaken the immune system and increase the risk of both acute and chronic psychosomatic illnesses.

### Symptoms of Anxiety Disorders

- Constant, chronic, and unsubstantiated worry that causes significant distress and disturbs your life or work.
- Avoidance of common social situations for fear of being judged, embarrassed, or humiliated.
- Repeated, random panic attacks or persistent anticipation of a panic attack, with feelings of terror or impending doom.
- Irrational fear or avoidance of an object, place, or situation that poses little or no threat of danger.
- Uncontrollable, repetitive, and unnecessary actions, such as washing your hands repeatedly or checking things over and over.
- Ongoing and recurring nightmares, flashbacks, or emotional numbing relating to a past traumatic event.

I believe that unhealthy anxiety is what most people think of when they hear the word *anxiety*. In fact, unhealthy anxiety is often too much anxiety—the pathological variety listed in the *Diagnostic and Statistical Manual of Mental Disorders*. This level of anxiety, whether genetically or psychologically based, is best treated through counseling or medication. It is well beyond the scope of this book. If you or someone you care about suffers from unhealthy anxiety, I strongly suggest that you seek professional help.

## A NEW MODEL OF ANXIETY

"Good leaders make friends with anxiety." So says Travelocity CEO Michelle Peluso. She speaks from experience. "Almost every step I've taken in my career, I've been very conscious of taking a risky move, of learning to live with a level of fear and uncertainty. In an odd way, I'm almost more comfortable when I know it's there than when it's not."

Not surprising. Michelle was raised in a family where risk taking was often its own reward. "I grew up in a family of entrepreneurs. My grandparents started a motel out in Montauk and had a fruit stand and a small grocery store. My dad started his own company. After he sold it, he missed the life so much that he started another company at the age of sixty-plus." Michelle caught on quickly. As a teenager, she earned her own money by babysitting and teaching neighborhood kids to swim. The desire to "control my own destiny, have some autonomy, and do something I'm passionate about, something I love" is in her genes.

Today, Michelle is passionate about building a winning company. When she took over at Travelocity, the company's market share was plummeting. It had an undifferentiated brand. And Expedia was breathing down its neck. She needed to turn a company known for cheap airline tickets into one known for its high-value travel solutions.

Michelle embraced the challenge. Her ability to face uncertainty, while managing her anxiety, enabled her to redefine the company as the preeminent travel advocate. Travelocity today is about helping people "experience the magic power of travel at their fingertips." Headquartered in Southlake, Texas, the company employs approximately 5,000 people in twenty-one countries. Its revenues in 2006 totaled $1.1 billion.

Michelle admits that managing her anxiety was not always so easy. "When you're going through it the first few times," she says, "you don't realize it. After a while, you become more conscious that anxiety is part of the process. You just have to focus on the goal and the passion you have for that goal. It's very hard to plow through anxiety if you're not really passionate about where you want to go."

Michelle understands that anxiety is part of leadership and life. "If you don't live with some level of anxiety, you're probably not taking enough risks in your life or stretching yourself. If you're sitting pretty and sitting happy, you're probably not pushing your own boundaries."

Nobody can constantly take risks and push boundaries without making mistakes. It's how you handle those mistakes that counts. JEA leaders like Michelle openly admit their mistakes to themselves and others. "None of us is perfect," she told me. "I remember when two technology teams had been working extremely hard. One of them missed its milestone, while the other team delivered. I really praised the team that delivered and was critical of the team that didn't. But when I actually dug underneath it, it turned out that the team that had delivered on time had sandbagged a lot of their estimates. The other team had a much higher quality standard in their code and had an aggressive time frame.

"Basically, I had rewarded the team that took no risk. And that's obviously not what I should be doing. When I found out, I was very public about it. 'I blew it,' I said. 'I should have looked deeper. And I want to be clear that meeting a time line is not the only criteria that matters. We all should be pushing ourselves a bit harder.'"

A lot of leaders surround themselves with people who tell them how great and infallible they are. And nobody likes to admit being wrong. But as Michelle knows, "If you think you are infallible, you're not learning enough. Still, admitting you're wrong isn't easy. Every time I go through it, it's still painful. But as a leader, it is sometimes important to acknowledge it publicly."

What gives Michelle the courage and confidence to push through difficult issues? It's her ability to confront her anxiety. She doesn't hide from it. As she puts it: "Difficult things don't go away. They're kind of under the rug, the big bulge in the corner. I'd rather just put it out on the table, and, at the end of the day, if we can't solve it, we can stick it back under the rug. Ball it up under the rug and put it back there."

Until she pulls it out again. "When I've been up a couple of times at night and I'm not sleeping well, my husband says, 'You're not here.' Or we'll be out to dinner and he'll say, 'Where are you?' I know that if I'm doing that, there's something bugging me. And the best thing I can do is figure out what it is."

Michelle is an ardent problem solver. A graduate in finance from the Wharton Business School of the University of Pennsylvania, she has a keen analytical brain. But she's also "very aware that abstract problem solving is only a piece of any good execution. The other piece is teamwork, the people side. To get anything done, you need to get people to use their discretionary effort, to feel passionate about what they're doing." It takes an emotional connection.

This is a woman who understands the power of intellect and emotion. She is using both her executive and emotional brains to solve problems and unleash the energy of Travelocity employees. Michelle is awake and alive in the world, comfortable with herself, her strengths and vulnerabilities. She is using healthy anxiety as a catalyst to grow the company.

The life of any leader is a recipe for anxiety. All the ingredients are there: complexity, uncertainty, change, and people. Some leaders get caught in unhealthy anxiety. They lose their creativity and resilience. They begin to experience stress in situations that normally wouldn't evoke such responses. Their anxiety manages them. Sooner or later, they burn out or burn up.

Other leaders, like Michelle Peluso, live and lead with a new understanding of anxiety. They embrace complexity, uncertainty, and change. They face problems head-on. They make friends with their anxiety. Self-aware, hearty, high-performing, and resilient, they are great examples of JEA leaders.

You, too, can be a JEA leader. You need only rewire your brain and change the way you think.

## REWIRING YOUR BRAIN

*Even when the brain suffers a trauma late in life, it can rezone itself like a city in a frenzy of urban renewal.*

—SHARON BEGLEY, "How the Brain Rewires Itself," *Time*

The human brain is remarkable. For years it was believed that our brains became fixed as we aged. Recent research, however, has revealed that the brain *never stops changing*. It continues to accommodate new information by modifying its internal structure of neurons and forming new connections between neurons. In fact, the brain is capable of creating new connections on a massive scale, at any stage of life, in response to anything new that is learned.

The capability to change the wiring and potential of the brain is called *neuroplasticity*. It means we can adapt to brain injury or trauma. It means that we can override unwanted habits and move from unproductive to productive responses to anxiety. It means we are never too old to learn something new. And it means we can refocus the way we think about things, including uncertainty, change, and anxiety.

It works like this. Our brains record our thoughts, experiences, and emotions in the form of neural maps. Just like any road map, our neural maps are made up of the intersections of many pathways—in this case, millions of dendrites and axons. Just like our everyday travels, the things we think and do over and over again become regular routes or superhighways, as do events that carry a significant emotional charge. Our occasional thoughts and behaviors, however, are less familiar hiking trails that take up little space. This is why it is so difficult to change our minds, to eliminate an ingrained habit, or to change our view of ourselves. We are "hardwired" to think and do what we already think and do.

The brain is also programmed to look for familiar patterns, a fact that often reinforces our resistance to something new. It compares incoming data with existing maps to see what fits and what doesn't. When it finds something familiar, it adds connections to an existing map or links similar maps together to form metamaps. When it encounters something entirely new, it creates a new map.

This is all good news. The brain's ability to form new maps of new thoughts and behaviors means you can reframe your experience of change, uncertainty, and anxiety. You can rethink your entire approach to managing anxiety. You might begin by asking yourself: What way of thinking about change and uncertainty serves me best? How has my anxiety helped or hurt me in the past? How can I approach anxiety—in myself and others—in a different way? What unproductive habits can I reframe into productive ones?

## Evidence of Our Adaptive Brain

- *The brain can reorganize itself in response to trauma and injury.* It can also "learn" to take over the functions of damaged parts following a stroke.
- *Talk therapy can be as effective as drugs.* Working with patients diagnosed with obsessive-compulsive disorder (OCD), Jeffrey Schwartz and colleagues at the University of California found that patients trained to reframe their obsessive thoughts improved significantly.
- *We can imagine our way to self-improvement.* Scientists comparing the brain activity of subjects practicing a piece of music on the piano with that of subjects practicing in their imaginations discovered a startling fact: The region of the motor cortex controlling the piano-playing fingers expanded for the people who imagined playing the music, just as it did in those who actually played it.
- *The way we think changes our brains.* Richard Davidson, a neuroscientist at the University of Wisconsin, compared the brain activity of Buddhist monks with that of novice meditators. Brain scans showed that the monks had a stronger link between thinking and feeling. Their brains were different.
- *Aging Japanese keep their minds active.* Based on research showing that people with active minds live longer and have a lower risk of developing Alzheimer's disease, Japan is helping its seniors stay healthy. Mental exercise programs, "brain" books, and trainers are a rising trend.

The goal is to get your brain to hardwire a new, more productive perspective on change and anxiety. You can accomplish this by paying more attention to who you want to be or where you want to go. Writing about it, talking about it, and taking action will all add to the map of your desired goal. In the words of David Rock, the author of *Quiet Leadership:* "If we literally put enough energy into the insight or idea, it will become a part of who we are. It's an attention economy in our brains, at a million connections per second."

The axiom "practice makes perfect" is applicable here. Like any athlete, artist, or musician developing a skill, your repeated practice of a new thought or behavior strengthens and expands that area of your brain. More practice, more brain connections, more skill. This is true whether you practice in real time or in your imagination, through visualizing the future or meditating on your desired outcome. Your brain treats both the same. Whatever you have done up until now, you can develop new habits of mind and action. You can override old circuitry based on limiting patterns, expectations, or beliefs. You can build your capacity to handle anxiety on your terms.

Your brain's ability to rewire itself provides the necessary mechanics. It's up to you to change the way you see the world. You need to learn to think differently.

## CHANGING THE WAY YOU THINK

*The voyage of discovery consists not in seeing new landscapes but in having new eyes.*

—MARCEL PROUST, French novelist

We have become prisoners of our own thinking. We have gotten locked into a narrow and negative view of anxiety by the very research designed to help us understand it. We have adopted Western views about change and uncertainty, while ignoring thousands of years of wisdom from Eastern philosophies. And we have bought into the notion that we are programmed solely to protect ourselves from danger, while overlooking our natural inclination toward growth and creativity. As a result, we have sought permanence and stability in our lives, while failing to see that permanence is an illusion and that stability can lead to stagnation.

These points of view are keeping us from embracing change and uncertainty as facts of life. They are making it impossible for us to live and lead with just enough anxiety. They are keeping us from evolving. It's time to change the way we think. We need to get beyond our limited—and limiting—perspective to embrace an expanded, more holistic point of view.

### Thinking from *Both* Eastern *and* Western Perspectives

Walk into the headquarters of Ping An Insurance Company, in the heart of Shenzhen, Guangdong Province, China, and you'll see a bust of

Confucius—not at all surprising in this Chinese company. But look again. Facing Confucius across the lobby is none other than Sir Isaac Newton. In fact, paintings of great Eastern and Western thinkers serve as a backdrop all the way down the entry hall to where Confucius and Newton peacefully coexist.

Chairman and CEO Ma Mingzhe, or Peter Ma as he is known outside China, is committed to blending the best of East and West. It's how he gains competitive advantage in a treacherous global market. "From the West, we've learned about professionalism and devotion to one's job and profession. But our values are rooted in the teachings of Confucius and in our history; we're very focused on relationships and social interactions. By integrating foreign expertise into the Chinese environment, we've created a highly competitive enterprise," he says.

Since founding Ping An in 1988, Peter has relied on Confucian principles to build the company. He has also hired Western consultants to upgrade systems and strategies. But he believes the company's future rests in the hands of its young, highly educated employees. "Young people are very smart and open to the principles of free markets, initiative taking, and adapting to change." More than 80 percent of Ping An's employees have college diplomas and higher degrees, 70 percent have insurance experience, and most are under twenty-eight years of age.

Ping An is doing something many other global companies are not. It is integrating its Eastern and Western perspectives. As a result, the company is growing steadily in an industry buffeted by agile foreign competition and precariously low interest rates. Its more than 210,000 sales agents, 50,000 staff, and more than 3,000 branch offices serve about 38 million retail customers and 2 million corporate customers. Company shares jumped nearly 23 percent in 2006. And analysts predict that the company's profits will advance 25 percent annually for the next three years, as net premiums climb 11 percent a year.

We can all benefit from both Eastern and Western points of view. But can these different beliefs and values help us live and lead with just enough anxiety? Let's take a closer look at each perspective to find out.

The Western perspective gives us logic and reason, planning and analysis. It celebrates individuality. Western minds see change and uncertainty as problems that can—and should—be managed and resolved. They strive to control nature, as well as their individual and corporate destinies. Generally optimistic, Westerners place a high value on winning and believe in people's ability to overcome the obstacles in their lives. Life in the West is about finding answers, working hard, fulfilling your potential, and reaping big rewards.

Eastern minds see things differently. They emphasize intuition and inward thinking. They celebrate community, loyalty, and respect for others. Because they see life as interconnected, they place less emphasis on trying to control nature or one another. Easterners embrace life's ups and downs. They see change and uncertainty as facts of life. Generally pragmatic, they place a high value on accepting life as it shows up for them. Life in the East is about learning to live in harmony with yourself, other people, and the world.

Not so fast. No country or culture in our rapidly shrinking world operates exclusively from only one point of view. The Chinese, for example, have a rich history of what we think of as Western ideals, especially capitalism. In fact, they were the first capitalists to use paper money—more than eight centuries before European countries. You need only to take a walk down a Shanghai street to see that China is well on its way to becoming the world's largest economy. Yet it is still grounded in Taoism and Confucianism, which influences how business is done, as well as life in general. Almost everything in China revolves around relationships. Even the Chinese word for "self" carries a negative connotation because the group generally comes first.

In the United States, the individual reigns supreme. Solo performance is celebrated, even glorified. Americans believe that anyone can become whatever he or she wants to be—at least in theory. Their can-do spirit shapes a diverse nation of entrepreneurs and big business oriented toward achievement, problem solving, growth, and the accumulation of wealth. At the same time, there is a pervasive search for spiritual meaning. Millions of Americans spend billions of dollars on self-help books and events and talk therapies to better understand and improve themselves. And many of the most popular American sports are those played by teams.

Several years ago, I interviewed CEOs around the world about the emergence of global leadership. What became clear to me in talking to these folks is that there is an evolving model of leadership that is common throughout the world. Principles like trust, respect, execution, participation, and teamwork are universal. Fostering these in your group is simply good leadership. Yet each culture seems to understand and express these leadership qualities in its own unique way. That's what makes the world so interesting—and so complicated.

*By thinking from both Eastern and Western perspectives, you can better live and lead with just enough anxiety.* You can see change and uncertainty as facts of life while handling whatever comes your way. You can learn to trust your inner voice while thinking through problems logically and systematically. You can discern and accept what you can't control while controlling what you can. This both/and perspective gives you an understanding of the present and the promise of dreams come true.

Ask yourself . . .

- How well do I integrate Eastern and Western thinking into my life? My leadership?
- What more can I do to lead from this both/and perspective?

### Balancing Your Drives for *Both* Protection *and* Growth

"I first became aware of how important growth and protection behaviors are in the laboratory. When I was cloning human endothelial cells, they *retreated* from toxins that I introduced into the culture dish, just as humans retreat from mountain lions and muggers in dark alleys. They also *gravitated* to nutrients, just as humans gravitate to breakfast, lunch, dinner, and love. These opposing movements define the two basic cellular responses to environmental stimuli."

This is the story told by cell biologist Bruce Lipton in *The Biology of Belief.* His findings prove that we are programmed—at a cellular level—for both protection and growth. We move toward life-sustaining elements and away from life-threatening ones. It's who we are.

These inherent drives for protection and growth apply to individuals and organizations. They compete for our attention every day—part of the battle between our emotional (protection) and executive (growth) brains. As individuals, we want to protect ourselves from pain and suffering, while striving to learn, improve ourselves, or create something new. Our companies work to protect their assets, competitive position, reputation, brands, identity, and employees, while growing the business and advancing in the marketplace. Both drives are vital to our success.

What complicates this balancing act is the changing relationship between companies and their employees. How much do companies protect employees with tenured jobs, health benefits, and pensions? How much loyalty do employees give to companies in return? Understanding these issues around growth and protection helps leaders and employees make smart decisions.

The turnaround success of GlaxoSmithKline (GSK) is a great example of how balancing protection and growth can create just enough anxiety to build a winning company. Five years ago, the U.K.-based company had one of the worst R&D pipelines in the industry. Today, it is the most admired company in its class.

You met GSK CEO J. P. Garnier in Chapter 1. He talked about stretching people beyond their comfort zones and pushing them to change, while giving them the support and guidance they need. Here's what Robert Carr, vice president and corporate medical director; Adrian Machon, director of leadership development; and Sue Cruse, director of leadership health and sustainability, have to say about executing J.P.'s strategy: "The goal is to create an environment in which people feel safe and protected while they learn and grow. If people try to protect themselves against their anxiety, they do the same old stuff. They keep themselves safe. But if we can get people to work with their anxiety as energy, then they will be innovative and take themselves and the organization forward."

People act just like the cells in Lipton's petri dish. Their drive for protection causes them to disengage. But their drive for growth allows them to move toward positive change. Aware of this, GSK is making it safe for people to talk about their anxiety. It is educating leaders to get comfortable with their own anxiety. And it is helping people at all levels to channel their anxious energy toward creating something new.

It's all about energy. At GSK, anxiety is seen as energy that can be directed toward protection or growth. GSK leaders understand that there's a time for stretching and learning and a time for rest and rejuvenation. Their ability to incorporate both is the secret behind the company's recent success.

By balancing protection and growth, GSK is building a resilient organization—one that can devise and manage its own pace of change. "Everyone knows their thread of activity and where it leads. They feel fully supported through guidance and intellectual support as well as resources, incentives, feedback, and recognition. They're encouraged to experiment, try things that haven't been done before. That leads to innovation and self-fulfillment. It gives people the feeling that they're in control of their own situation. This allows them to take risks and manage change." It builds resilience.

J.P. sums up GSK's philosophy: "I look for people who stand straight no matter what happens. If you are not resilient, if you fall apart easily, if you don't show calm under pressure, you're not going to be an effective leader. It's that simple. People who are resilient manage to internalize their anxiety, and then release it in appropriate doses as they move the company forward."

*By balancing both protection and growth, you can increase your capacity to handle change and uncertainty with just enough anxiety.* You can avoid taking unnecessary risks while taking advantage of promising opportunities. You can maintain what's important to you while venturing into new territory. You can take time to replenish your strength while putting forth that extra effort when it's needed. This both/and perspective offers you the security you seek and the stretch you desire.

Ask yourself . . .

- To what extent am I driven by the need for protection? The need for growth?
- What more can I do to balance these two drives as a leader? In my personal life?

## Embracing *Both* Personal Power *and* Uncertainty

Over the years I've observed two kinds of leaders. There are those who rely heavily on their personal power. Confident and courageous by nature, they believe in their ability to master their environment and create the outcomes they desire. They have what scientists call a high degree of self-efficacy—one of the most important predictors of what people will do and how successful they will be. These leaders are usually high achievers, top performers. They accomplish a lot and are widely admired. But they can also overlook key factors beyond their control or end up manipulating people to their own ends. They tend to ignore life's mysteries.

Then there are those who embrace the uncertainty and mystery of life. Recognizing how much of life is out of their control, they rarely try to predict the future. They are agile and flexible thinkers, and good listeners. These leaders tend to seek out and adapt well to changing circumstances. Little seems to upset them. Like a willow tree bending in the wind, they are able to accommodate the forces around them. And they are often just as successful as their personal power–minded counterparts. However, they can become cynical or feel tossed about by fate. They tend to ignore their own power.

These two kinds of leaders have totally different worldviews. Their belief about the world, and their relationship to it, shapes their behavior. It has an especially profound effect on how they accept and respond to change and manage anxiety.

As we grow older and wiser, most of us realize that both of these worldviews are true. Life is filled with uncertainty *and* we each have the power within us to choose how we navigate its ups and downs. To me, this is what just enough anxiety is all about.

I've come to see that each of these worldviews exists on a continuum. The more comfortable you are with one, the less comfortable you are with the other. In the table below, I've condensed my idea into four distinct types: Controllers, Victims, Fatalists, and JEA Leaders. While people are a lot more complicated than this, the table shows the directions in which a leader's thinking might go. Which description fits you best?

You are a Controller if you have a strong sense of personal power and a low acceptance of uncertainty. You believe you are the master of your own fate because life is relatively stable and predictable. Preoccupied with gaining control, however, you tend to fall apart when something bad happens.

You are a Victim if you have a weak sense of personal power and a low acceptance of uncertainty. You tend to do the minimum to get by, since everything is inevitable anyway. Change is just par for the course. And you don't think you can do anything to change the course.

You are a Fatalist if you have a weak sense of personal power and a high acceptance of uncertainty. You grumble about everything that happens to you, and, to hear you tell it, everything that happens to you is out of your control. You tend to take uncertainty and change very personally.

You are a JEA Leader if you hold both worldviews (personal power and uncertainty) simultaneously. You know that life is unpredictable. Just when you think you're on top of the world, something or someone arrives

|  | Low Acceptance of Uncertainty | High Acceptance of Uncertainty |
|---|---|---|
| **Strong Sense of Personal Power** | CONTROLLERS BELIEVE . . .<br>• I can control my life and destiny.<br>• Things don't change much.<br>• People follow my lead.<br>• I can create what I desire.<br>• I can predict and control what happens. | JEA LEADERS BELIEVE . . .<br>• I accept what I can and can't control.<br>• The world is constantly changing.<br>• People do the best they can.<br>• I can shape my future.<br>• I'm comfortable with uncertainty. |
| **Weak Sense of Personal Power** | VICTIMS BELIEVE . . .<br>• I have little control over my life.<br>• Things tend to stay the same.<br>• People disappoint and hurt me.<br>• I rarely get my needs met.<br>• Life is predictably negative. | FATALISTS BELIEVE . . .<br>• Many things are beyond my control.<br>• Everything changes constantly.<br>• I have trouble counting on people.<br>• I often can't get what I want.<br>• Nobody can predict the future. |

to mess it up. And just when things are going south, a new opportunity shows up on your doorstep. At the same time, you understand the need to take charge of your own destiny. You know from experience that you can shape and influence your future by the everyday choices you make concerning your health, career, goals, and performance. You embrace change and uncertainty as opportunities to learn and grow.

Nobody understands how to use personal power to live with uncertainty better than General John P. Jumper. As the senior officer in charge of the U.S. Air Force's 700,000 enlisted men and women, General Jumper became one of the top military advisers to the president and the secretary of defense in the wake of 9/11. With more than thirty years of active duty service, including two combat tours in Vietnam, he was the right man to transform the air force from its cold war focus to a more agile, innovative, and forward-looking organization.

"When we fought Desert Storm in 1991, I watched all the services—not just the air force—respond to the crisis. Our reaction was anything but agile. This big machine we call the U.S. military was very ponderous and slow. Then, in 1994, when I became the 9th Air Force commander, we took the entire U.S. Air Force, which is organized around static bases, and reorganized it into Ten-Force packages. These packages can go wherever you need them to go, and in whatever size.

"Now your base is your fighting position, like an aircraft carrier or a foxhole. You have to treat your base as the place you're fighting from. What makes this possible is the fact that skill sets are interchangeable."

Jumper dubbed this innovative approach the Air Expeditionary Force (AEF). But selling the idea to the Pentagon was tough. To do it, the general crafted a philosophy that laid the foundation for the AEF and other changes he would introduce. The essence of his philosophy: Prepare for the unexpected, build courage and confidence, embrace change and uncertainty, be agile and adaptive, and live with just enough anxiety. With this approach, Jumper transformed not only how the air force operates but also the hearts and minds of the 700,000 people behind those operations.

So how is it working? "The best example of the transformation is 'Enduring Freedom' in Afghanistan. During the first wartime moves into Afghanistan, we had airmen on the ground with U.S. Special Forces. We hooked them up with a satellite data link, enabling them to communicate directly with B-52 bombers. Our people on the ground with these satellite dishes were enlisted sergeants, riding horses and equipped with laser range-finding devices that could get exact coordinates of enemy positions and beam them to B-52s.

"The B-52 was built in the 1950s to fly into the heart of the Soviet Union with nuclear weapons. Now they're up there carrying satellite-guided bombs for conventional purposes. The bombs are essentially World War II designs. We strap a global positioning system (GPS) kit on them to make them very accurate. So a kid on the ground in Afghanistan is able to spot the enemy across a valley, get the precise coordinates to the B-52. Airmen in the plane program the GPS and lay down a string of bombs that kill a hundred bad guys at a time.

"When you adapt, you need to take things that were never intended for one purpose but that fit perfectly into a brand-new scenario. It's the agility of the people on the ground who are willing to put things together in completely new and different ways that gave us the edge over the Taliban."

It used to be that agility and adaptation didn't matter so much. But uncertain times call for different measures. "The world may be unpredictable in the future. But we shouldn't be afraid of that. We have to find the courage to deal with change, and to stretch our imagination beyond what's possible.

"We have to be able to imagine the things that would be unimaginable. If I had told the president on the tenth of September that, sir, on the eleventh of September, I am very fearful that someone's going to crash an airplane into the World Trade Center, so I've got to teach my air defense pilots to shoot down U.S. airliners, then they would have carted me off in a white truck. Until it happened it was an imponderable event."

Because of Jumper's AEF, adjustments after 9/11 were easy to make. "Even the day of, we were able to change our mind-set quickly, so that if any more airplanes were up there we would have been able to take appropriate action. The day before 9/11 we couldn't even have thought about it."

*By embracing both personal power and uncertainty, you can learn to modulate your anxiety in the face of change.* You can take charge of your life while remaining open to the unexpected. You can create specific goals for yourself and your organization while being willing to modify them when necessary. You can anticipate the future, and act with courage and conviction in the present, while remembering that some things are just beyond your control. This both/and perspective provides you with sustainable self-confidence and a sense of wonder about the nature of life.

Taken together, these three both/and points of view give you what you need to embrace change, uncertainty, and anxiety as facts of life. They

## BOTH/AND THINKING

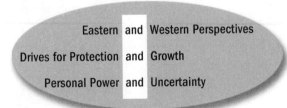

Eastern and Western Perspectives

Drives for Protection and Growth

Personal Power and Uncertainty

make it possible for you to create just enough anxiety to live and lead in our complex world by using your healthy anxiety as a positive force for growth.

Ask yourself . . .

- How do I see the world and my relationship to it?
- What beliefs are getting in the way of my embracing both my personal power and uncertainty as a leader? In my personal life?

## ANXIETY AS THE CATALYST FOR GROWTH

If you've ever taught a child to ride a bike, you know all about anxiety. You know it's up to you to help the child conquer her fears. After all, you're the adult. But you've got fears of your own. You want to help her become more independent, to build up her self-confidence. But what if she falls? What if she gets hurt? You see the hesitation, fear, and excitement on the child's face. But she says that she wants to do it so you let go of the bike. That's my idea of leadership.

But being a leader is tough. You have to modulate your own anxiety while alleviating the anxiety of the people around you. You need to turn healthy anxiety into a catalyst for growth—for yourself and your organization. You need to let go of the bike.

Change and uncertainty are facts of life. Anxiety is natural. Our brains are hardwired to protect us in the face of potential danger, including the unknown. But not all dangers are cause for fighting or fleeing. Not all anxiety is unhealthy. In fact, most of the anxiety we feel on a daily basis is natural and healthy. It provides the energy we need to help us handle whatever we're facing. As it is for every four-year-old learning to ride a bike, our anxiety is the catalyst for growth. As leaders, it's the catalyst for stretching ourselves, challenging others, and building winning organizations.

Think about the leaders you've met in this chapter. Manny Pangilinan used an external threat to befriend his anxiety and unleash his people's creativity at First Pacific Company. Peter Ma's motivation was internal. He capitalized on Eastern and Western values to make Ping An Insurance a world-class player. Michelle Peluso confronted her anxiety head-on to redefine Travelocity. She understands that anxiety is an integral part of life and leadership. At GlaxoSmithKline, J. P. Garnier and his colleagues transformed the anxiety created by the merger of SmithKline Beecham and Glaxo Wellcome into a resilient organization. And General John Jumper used the anxiety generated by 9/11 to create agility in the U.S. Air Force. His Air Expeditionary Force now enables the United States to be much more responsive in a world of escalating uncertainty.

Each one of these leaders uses healthy anxiety as a catalyst for growth. Whether they employ just enough anxiety as a positive motivator and source of productive energy, a path to creativity, or a tool for leading change and mobilizing people, they all consider it a vehicle for understanding and challenging themselves and their organizations. They set the standard for JEA leaders.

Whether you are a top executive or a project manager, you can make just enough anxiety your tool for top performance. It all depends on how well you understand your anxiety and use it as a catalyst for growth. I promise: It will help you get from where you are to where you want to be.

# 3

# LIVING IN THE GAP

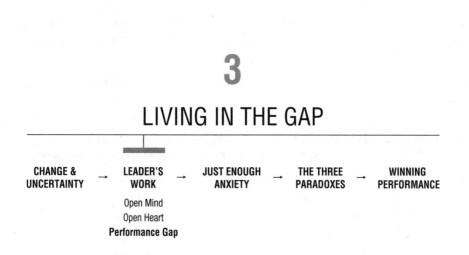

CHANGE & &rarr; LEADER'S &rarr; JUST ENOUGH &rarr; THE THREE &rarr; WINNING
UNCERTAINTY     WORK     ANXIETY     PARADOXES     PERFORMANCE

Open Mind
Open Heart
**Performance Gap**

I love Italian piazzas, open expanses of cobbled bricks surrounded by historical stone buildings, often with a beautiful fountain in the middle. They bustle with energy as people come from every direction. Some people meet and greet each other and engage in lively conversation, while others scurry through, their attention on where they've been or where they're going. Others, like me, like to linger and soak up the ambience. The vibrancy of life is palpable in a piazza.

Imagine a piazza-like place in your mind. Instead of attracting people, this place attracts your dreams for the future and your sense of where and who you are now. It is where your desire to learn and grow comes face-to-face with your desire for stability and protection. This place in your mind is where your thoughts and emotions—both positive and negative—vie for your attention. It is where your emotional and executive brains each grapple for control, as your ancestral instinct for survival meets your capacity for reason and analysis. Like the Italian meeting place, this part of your mind is full of energy and life.

The piazza is a metaphor for the place in our minds where we find ourselves in the midst of change and uncertainty. It represents the disparity we see or feel between who we are and who we want to be as the world around us—and within us—changes and evolves.

# THE GAP IN OUR MINDS

*After you've done a thing the same way for two years, look it over care-fully. After five years, look at it with suspicion. And after ten years, throw it away and start all over.*

—ALFRED EDWARD PERLMAN, twentieth-century
business visionary

I think of this place in our minds as a *gap*. Webster defines a gap as an "opening," "empty space," or "wide divergence or difference." As I see it, the gap in our minds is the difference between how we currently see ourselves and how we want to see ourselves. It is part of our consciousness, shaped by our experiences and beliefs. The gap is where we "go" in our minds when we sense things are changing.

We enter the gap every time we stretch ourselves or solve problems. It is our personal laboratory for change, where anxiety lives and flourishes. We live in the gap as long as our current reality is out of sync with our desired future.

Psychologists often portray the gap as the difference between our real self and our ego ideal. Experts in adult development say the gap is where we deal with our ambitions and our desires to achieve. Leading thinkers in personal transformation describe the gap as the "neutral zone," where we go in the midst of life transitions. In business we talk about the gap between our organization's current reality and its desired outcome, or between the status quo and real change. Change experts say the gap is where we adapt to new circumstances in our search for stability. Some leaders refer to the gap as the distance between their burning platforms and their defined goals. In each case, the gap symbolizes how we see ourselves now compared to how we hope to see ourselves in the future. On a personal level, it sets the course for our development. In business, it defines our strategy for growth.

We are *pushed* into the gap whenever we face something in our lives that we want to fix or change. We are *pulled* into the gap whenever we seize an opportunity or dream of a better future.

As individuals, we can enter the gap intentionally or unintentionally. We create our own gap by deciding to be a better person, strengthen our relationships, make more money, improve our health, start a new job, or

## THE ANXIETY GAP

Leaders feel anxiety when forces both push and pull them
into the gap between the present and the future.

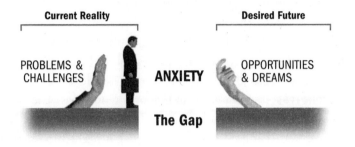

deepen our spiritual practice. We are thrown into the gap by unforeseen circumstances, such as when we or someone we love is diagnosed with a serious illness or a storm wreaks havoc with our homes and lives.

Organizations are no different. They enter the gap willingly whenever they envision new possibilities, seek to build better teams, implement a new technology system, or tackle a reorganization, merger, or acquisition. They fall into the gap when faced with unexpected consumer demands, loss of revenues, threats from increased competition, or corporate misconduct.

As we look at where we are in the present—as individuals and organizations—we judge whether that position is acceptable or unacceptable, changeable or unchangeable, pleasurable or painful. Similarly, as we imagine our future, we assess whether the image is anticipated or dreaded, predictable or unpredictable, and achievable or unachievable. Our decisions drive the choices we make and the emotions we feel.

Sometimes the gap is well illuminated. You can see clearly across it to the other side. At other times the gap is dark and mysterious. You can't see how wide or deep it is. So you experiment by testing your assumptions, taking small steps, and looking for evidence that you're on the right course. It's like sailing on a foggy night with no visual cues to guide you. You must use your experience, and whatever data you can gather, to assess the risks and to course correct along the way.

Your entry into the gap can happen gradually or in the blink of an eye. You can even find yourself in several gaps at the same time. For example, you might be living in the gap between your real and ideal jobs, leading your business through a difficult change, and working to bridge the gap between the relationship you have and the one you want. In today's fast-paced and rapidly changing world, it's impossible to know in advance what your next gap will be.

Sometimes the gap finds you. Take PricewaterhouseCoopers, for example. After decades of self-regulation and status quo, PwC was forced to redefine its business because of the passage of the Sarbanes-Oxley Act in 2002. Highly publicized scandals at Enron, WorldCom, and Tyco had eroded public trust in accounting and reporting practices. The new legislation established new standards that created a huge disconnect between the way PwC was doing business and the way it needed to operate. The firm was turned on its head.

Dennis Nally, PwC's U.S. senior partner, talked openly with me about the experience. "The amount of external change that we've had to deal with in such a compressed time period is more than we've ever had to deal with before. As everybody knows, the accounting profession has been steady as you go. Sure, it's evolved and there have been changes, but they've all been gradual. This was a showstopper, a massive change in short order. Every part of our organization felt it."

Like Dennis Nally and PwC, once we find ourselves in the gap, our first thought is: How do I get out? Whether we are motivated to protect ourselves or to improve our situation, we are eager to "close" the gap. But how can we turn our anxiety into the productive energy we need to get to the other side?

Dennis Nally faced PwC's challenge head-on. "You can sit there and hound yourself and say, 'How am I ever going to deal with all this change? Can't we go back to the way things were five years ago?' Or you can create an environment where you expect more change to come down the road, and you can embrace it all as opportunity. If you can get people to look at challenge as an opportunity, you can get much more positive energy around what you're trying to accomplish. The organization that embraces change as an opportunity will move toward distinction."

Sometimes you create the gap from your desire to grow or be the best. Like Ken Samet, the CEO at MedStar Health, a seven-hospital, acute care health system serving the Baltimore–Washington, D.C., metropolitan area. Ken had been handed the reins by John McDaniel, who had successfully shepherded MedStar for twenty years. At the time, MedStar was the largest health care employer in the region, with 23,000 employees and revenues of $2 billion. In fact, it was already a winning company when Ken began his drive to move the company from "good to great."

"It's easy to say that we are this high-quality, wonderful place," Ken told me when we first met. "We've got some world-class services and the biggest volume in the region. But when you really stare at some of the data, you realize we're not as good as we could be. And our excellence isn't consistent across the organization." MedStar's good-to-great vision: "To be the trusted leader in caring for people and advancing health."

Motivating people to make changes when things are going well is tough. "It's like fixing the train while it's running down the track. If we could just step into the future state, it would be easy," said Ken. "If it happened that way for everybody at the same time, people would be on board, and we'd be over it. But that's not the way change occurs."

Hospitals are high-stakes businesses. Time is money; risk and pressure are everyday occurrences; and many decisions are life and death. To bridge the gap between where MedStar was and where Ken wanted to take it, he had to develop and execute a strong change strategy. The health care industry was already in a state of constant flux—some would say crisis. There was growing competition for skilled health care workers, increasing pressure for clinical quality, and the ever-present need for service excellence. Plus, employees and associates at the not-for-profit organization were motivated by its higher purpose to deliver superior service to patients and their families. Tinkering with something so fragile and important could escalate people's anxiety, causing them to resist or resent the change. With this in mind, and in partnership with his leadership team, Ken began to create a culture of change that would inspire people to help move the organization to the next level.

Ken was raising the bar. He focused first on what MedStar was doing well. "We are a good company," Ken told his team. "You are doing important work, and we have much to be proud of." Then, Ken and his top thirty leaders jumped willingly into the gap by developing a compelling vision and positive platform for change that everyone could embrace. With the "good-to-great" approach, nobody felt they were part of a losing team. Says Ken, "People really look for direction, for communication, for an aspiring vision. And when they see we are putting our resources where our mouth is, they are willing to do the work."

Though still in the early stages of its multiyear plan, MedStar is already enjoying real success. The level of engagement across the organization has improved. Senior leaders are addressing key strategic issues with trust, openness, and optimism. Metrics on three system-wide, core medical processes have improved substantially. And the company is experiencing record financial performance, including an upgrade in its bond ratings. Ken recently told me, "We finished 2006 with the strongest year we've ever had."

Ask yourself . . .

○ What gaps have I experienced in my life?
○ Do I tend to be pushed or pulled into the gap?
○ What gaps am I in right now, at work and in my personal life?

## NAVIGATING THROUGH THE GAP

*The greatest barriers to change come from within; so do our greatest opportunities.*

—ROBERT KEGAN, Harvard School of Education

Each of us has a personal strategy for navigating through uncertainty and change. Developed over a lifetime of experiences, this strategy is mostly automatic. Think about it. How do you navigate the gaps in your life? Do you relish every opportunity to learn and grow? Or do you enter the gap only when compelled by circumstance or crisis? Do you believe life is all about the destination? Or do you live one day at a time?

Whatever your strategy, timing is critical. If you don't enter the gap with your eyes open, or are not ready to do the work required in the gap, you let opportunities pass by. You stick with things as they are. But if the timing is right, you see challenges and opportunities everywhere. A conflict with a coworker, some provocative customer feedback, a fight with your spouse, a chance meeting, a moment in prayer, or a checkup at the doctor's can inspire you to leap into the gap. You're ready for change. You're ready to see yourself in a new light and take on the anxiety that lives in the gap.

Navigating the gap is a lot like finding your way through the Land of Oz. It involves digging deep to discover who you are and what you truly desire. It requires that you face unexpected challenges along the way, while staying on the right path. If you're lucky, you will have friends and colleagues to help you on your journey. And yet you need to trust yourself, to know that the answers lie within you. Here are a few guidelines to help you as you navigate the gaps in your life and your organization.

### Know Anxiety When You See It

In the words of Daniel Vasella, the chairman and CEO of Swiss pharmaceutical giant Novartis AG: "You know you're stretching yourself when you have an empty feeling in your stomach and don't really know if you'll be able to make it—you know it's not impossible but that you can't achieve it just sitting down."

When the space between where you are and where you want to be is too large, you feel too much anxiety and have trouble taking action. When it's too small, you feel no desire to act. In both cases, you shut down learning, growth, and performance. But when the distance between here and there is big enough to make you stretch, yet small enough to be surmounted, you experience just enough anxiety to live and to thrive in the gap.

Effective leaders are able to manage their own anxiety and reshape or resize the gap—or people's perception of the gap—to create the right amount of anxiety for the situation. The result is a greater capacity to lead and achieve results.

It's about knowing how much anxiety is just enough. Says Vasella, "Between my ideal of where we should be and the reality of where we are, there's always tension—and I'm somewhere in between. But I can't stay where everyone is; I have to lead. It's important to put stretch goals out there and create enough healthy anxiety so people are leaning into the future. If you go overboard, you create paralysis, and if you go too slow, it's too cozy. So the question is: How far can you go?"

### Treat Success as a Moving Target

Life in the gap is complex, nonlinear, and ever changing. We are constantly moving from too much to too little to just enough anxiety. We bounce between equilibrium and disequilibrium and back again as we take risks or stretch ourselves and then step back to replenish our energy. Sometimes our level of anxiety propels us forward, while other times it holds us back. We're like the strings of a guitar: We need the right amount of tension to function properly. If we're wound too tight, we break; too loose and we're unable to perform. We need just enough anxiety to make our way through the gap.

But the right amount of anxiety is a moving target. Even your desired outcome may change as you face new challenges. Nothing stays the same, and this is particularly true in the gap. While here, you need to focus on what you can learn, not on what you already know. You need to ask yourself hard questions, examine yourself deeply, seek and listen to feedback, and reinvent yourself and your strategy—in real time—to move forward. You may yearn for an easy passage. But if you're honest with yourself, you know that it is through your struggle and stretch that you become your best self.

Adaptability is the name of the game. In the words of MedStar CEO Ken Samet: "Sometimes you have to take a half step backward on a short-term goal to spring forward on a bigger, longer-term issue. That's when you're really on your game as a leader. You have to be able to see the need to turn left for a little bit, even though you need to get back to the right. You need to assess the general feel of your management team and of the organization. Otherwise, you look back over the course of a month, and it's very easy to see how the urgent has always pushed out the important."

## Listen to the Competing Voices Within You

The image of a devil whispering in one ear, while an angel whispers in the other, is one we've all seen in the movies. The image illustrates our human tendency to have conflicting desires. It represents the two opposing voices in our minds that tell us "yes" or "no," "stay" or "leave," or "go for it" or "forget it."

Life is complicated. So are our ideas about the world and our place in it. We all hold conflicting beliefs, expectations, feelings, and assumptions that give rise to the competing voices in our minds. These internal voices can be negative or positive. They can help or hinder us as we strive to close the gaps in our lives and our businesses.

The voice of fear is usually the loudest. It's the one telling you to wait when opportunity knocks at your door. Or run at the slightest possibility of failure. It's also the one most likely to deceive you. It keeps you from taking risks, learning new skills, or following your heart. Fear is the voice that will keep you poised on the precipice—or stuck in the middle—of a gap.

But fear is a trickster. It focuses your attention outside of yourself, causing you to blame some external factor for your decision to stand still or give up your dream. It reminds you of prior failures. It brings to mind previous emotional pain. It plays negative "what if" scenarios over and over. Fear does whatever it can to bind you to itself.

You can take control. By understanding your own motivations—the devils and angels inside of you—you can begin to confront your fears. By uncovering your assumptions and beliefs about the world, you can better manage your personal experience of the world. By learning to recognize how and when you are undermining your own success, you can override unwanted reactions. You can make positive choices. The power to succeed lies within you.

---

### Tips for Getting Through the Gap

- Continually assess your strengths, weaknesses, opportunities, and threats.
- Be open to the thoughts and feelings that speed up or slow down your journey.
- Shine a bright light on the questions you are grappling with to understand your motivation.
- Experiment with new behaviors and ways of thinking.
- Look for and apply new lessons.

---

## Trust Yourself

Remember jungle gyms? I used to love hanging from those horizontal bars, where you had to reach out with one hand to grab the next bar while your feet dangled in midair. If I slowed down too much or doubted my ability, I fell to the ground. If I swung from bar to bar with confidence, I always got to the other side. This is the epitome of leaning into uncertainty. I had to think "off my feet," connect with what I was feeling, draw on my past experience, test my capabilities, and reach for the next bar.

Navigating the gap requires a similar combination of self-confidence and momentum. We have to be willing to let go of what's behind us to grab hold of what's next. If we cling to our ideas of who we are or what we have, we will continue to dangle from where we are. We will never move forward.

Then again, sometimes we need to wait for the next bar to appear. There are times in the gap when we don't know what our next move is. There are no battles to fight or problems to solve. There is just quiet. When this happens, it's tempting to reach for the bar behind us. Movement in any direction feels better than none. We would rather have what we know than hang out in the unknown.

Whether you are actively battling or quietly facing your challenges in the gap, it's important to trust yourself and the process of moving through. Trust your decision to enter the gap and your ability to reach the other side. And trust the timing. It helps to ask yourself, What do I need to let go of to move forward? Perhaps you're holding on to unrealistic expectations. Perhaps you're still using old mental models for solving problems. Or perhaps your fears are hijacking your dreams. As you identify and release the bars behind you, you will be able to see more clearly and grab the bars ahead.

## Learn from Your Successes and Failures

We are conditioned to value success and fear failure. So we sometimes set low goals to avoid failure, rather than give ourselves the chance to shine. Aiming high is too big a risk, we think. But the real risk is that we will fail to realize our full potential.

If you find yourself backing away from what you truly desire, stop. You're about to short-change yourself. Consider setting a series of smaller goals that lead to your heart's desire. Or give yourself more time. More important, learn to find the lesson in your mistakes. Allow yourself to reach for the stars.

Life is about learning and growing. You've already learned and grown from your mistakes and failures, as well as from your successes. You are who you are today because of the many gaps you've closed behind you and the ones you couldn't close. And you will be who you will be because of the gaps yet to come. The gaps you navigate in your lifetime—whatever the outcome—are your pathways for self-discovery and development. They enable you to evolve.

## OUR BUILT-IN HUMAN ENERGY SYSTEM

*The gap between vision and current reality is a source of energy. If there was no gap, there would be no need for any action to move toward the vision.*

—PETER SENGE, author of *The Fifth Discipline*

Imagine that you are about to give a big presentation. Normally, you have no trouble with public speaking. Today, however, you're being evaluated for a promotion. As you step onto the stage, your body is coursing with stress hormones, unleashed by your brain. You see your boss in the audience, and your anxiety shoots way up. You think, I'm a nervous wreck.

If you allow yourself to be hijacked by your anxiety, your energy will become too chaotic to manage and you will have trouble focusing on what you are saying. Your mind will start playing worst-case scenarios. Just when you need them most, your cognitive capabilities will be shut down so your body can send blood to your legs, making a quick escape possible. But escape is not a real option here.

On the other hand, if you try to repress your anxiety, you will need all your energy to hold it at bay. Your presentation will be boring or lackluster at best. You will put your audience, including your boss—and your promotion—to sleep.

Fortunately, there's another way. If you can manage your anxiety, you can turn it into productive energy and use it to motivate your best performance. Instead of labeling your feelings as negative, you can think of them as energy boosters that are keeping you alert and focused. You can use deep breathing to calm yourself down while you imagine your boss congratulating you on a job well done. Or better yet, imagine being told you got the promotion. Tell yourself "I can do this" until you believe it.

Remember that the athlete who sees anxiety as detrimental, who says he is "tied up in knots," performs poorly. The athlete who believes that anxiety facilitates top performance, who says she is "psyched up," performs well. The point is that you can learn to use your cognitive abilities—your executive brain—to override, or at least manage, the anxiety you feel when your emotional brain tries to take control.

As I see it, the gap is more than a chasm to be crossed. It is part of a dynamic process that enables us to protect ourselves while expanding our

## THE ANXIETY GAP

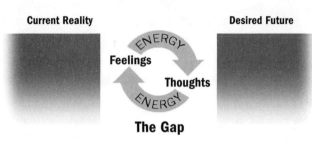

capabilities. It is a human energy system. Through this system we can transform our anxiety into productive energy.

It works like this. Incoming information activates the physiological processes within the brain programmed to alert you to potential dangers and excite you to potential opportunities. Stress hormones released through the emotional brain (amygdala-hypothalamus connection) prepare you for an approach-avoidance response, in the form of energy. When you notice the shift in your energy, you assign meaning to what you're feeling, through your executive brain (prefrontal cortex). You call it anxiety or fear, anticipation, or excitement. The label you attach to your bodily sensations influences the quantity and quality of energy available to you. Your interpretation of your feelings affects the action you take. The process becomes an energy-emotion-thought cycle of sorts, as your emotional and executive brains keep sending signals back and forth. The longer it goes on, the stronger it becomes.

Anxiety is energy that propels us through the gap. When we have too little, we lose momentum. We stall out. When we have too much, we spin our wheels and create chaos. In either case, we take longer than necessary to reach our goal, if we get there at all. When we have just enough anxiety, however, we have the productive energy we need to turn our thinking and feeling into action. We are able to move forward through the gaps in our lives, one step—or one rung—at a time.

Dave O'Reilly at Chevron Corporation knows a lot about energy. When I met with him, oil prices were near record highs. The increasing cost of energy was making Wall Street investors beam, but it was also causing public outcries, intense media scrutiny, and congressional hearings. The general mistrust of energy companies was rising as fast as the price of gas.

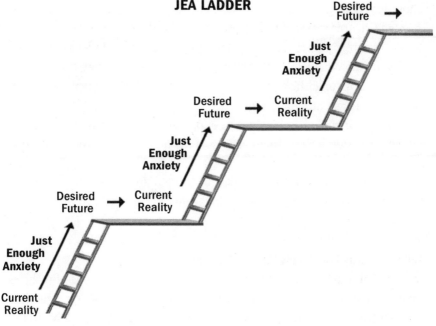

**JEA LADDER**

The situation was enough to worry any CEO. But as I talked with Dave at the company's main office near San Francisco, I learned that this CEO saw the situation as an opportunity to look toward the future and accelerate and globalize the company's leadership—the human energy of Chevron. "Human energy is an engaging way to remind the organization of how important its people are to our success. We're in the business of delivering energy. But we're doing it with humans. So it's the human energy that's really fueling the company and making it possible for us to deliver energy to our customers." Dave knows that by emphasizing leadership, he can help people convert their anxiety into productive energy. He can then focus that energy on getting access to energy supplies and developing the technology necessary to find new energy sources.

With the demand for energy expected to increase by 71 percent over the next twenty years, Dave is making progress on both energy fronts. The company recently shelled out $18.4 billion for Unocal. The acquisition catapulted Chevron ahead of Total as the world's fourth-largest oil-producing company, and ahead of Royal Dutch Shell as the third-largest reserve holder among international oil companies.

As for the human element, Dave was quick to reach into his wallet to show me "The Chevron Way." Here on one small laminated card were printed Chevron's values, goals, and strategies. He told me, "It's important to have people internalize the values and strategies and to let them know how you want them to perform and behave. But once they are set, you need to give people the freedom to lead their part of the business. That's how you unleash human energy."

Dave is turning a crisis into an opportunity by creating just enough anxiety to unleash the human energy of his organization. Today, he continues to close the gap between current and future realities with his inspiring leadership. With more than 62,500 employees in 140 countries, you can bet Chevron will be at the forefront of energy—both human and otherwise—for a long time to come.

## Human Energy Is a Deeply Personal Experience

We differ in our ability to manage our energy in the gap. Some of us have an extraordinary capacity to live with tension, pain, discomfort, and disequilibrium. We love living on the edge, creating "adrenaline highs." Others of us are too busy or too scared to look inside ourselves. Shackled by past experiences, traumatic circumstances, or old habits, we resist or reject our anxiety and spend as little time as possible in the gap. Most of us fall between these two extremes.

There are many factors that affect our experience in the gap. Our relative desires for stability and growth make a real difference here. Our genetic makeup, personal development, beliefs and expectations, and life experiences all contribute to the size of the gap we see. These factors, plus our learning styles, motivation, and personalities influence what we typically do to close the gap. It all comes together to influence how we feel.

Sometimes the drive for just enough anxiety is imprinted in early childhood. "Good enough isn't good enough" is what Linda Rabbitt, founder of Rand Construction Corporation, learned from her father. "The desire to be better tomorrow than I was yesterday is really important to me. My ultimate goal is to be successful in life," she admits. "That means accomplishing things I want to accomplish, pushing my envelope, raising my bar, being the most I can be, and helping people around me." Her drive for success creates a perpetual gap at Rand Construction, now one of the country's more successful entrepreneurial companies. "When you walk down the hall and see all the projects that we've won awards for, you can't help but feel that somebody around here has had very high expectations."

At other times the gap shows up unexpectedly and is relatively short-lived. When Eli Lilly's Prozac patent was about to expire in 2001, the Indianapolis-based drug company faced a tremendous challenge. At the time, the antidepressant blockbuster drug accounted for approximately 25 percent of the company's sales, close to $3 billion. No company in the pharmaceutical industry had ever survived a challenge of that magnitude as an independent entity.

With the expiration date looming, CEO Sidney Taurel did not make a splashy acquisition or look for a white knight to rescue the company. His strategy for closing the gap was to renew the company from the inside, with strong values and more anxiety. "We had always been successful—for about 125 years—and we were a little too comfortable. My first priority was to reengage the hearts and minds of employees," Sidney admits. "We were working in a very tough environment, and I felt we needed to reinstill in our employees the pride of working at Lilly—to save people's lives and work in a very ethical company. We needed to build a company that could renew itself all the time."

Sidney's strategy has paid off handsomely. The company's top-line growth in 2004 increased 10 percent, and its one-year net growth in 2006 was 34.5 percent. Instead of watching its market share erode, Sidney turned up the heat, sought out new markets, and increased spending on R&D. Lilly has since clinched the number-four spot on the pharmaceutical industry list of *Fortune* magazine's "Most Admired Companies"—ahead of global rivals Pfizer and Merck.

Whatever our predisposition or situation, the gap is where we deal with the uncertainties in our lives. We bounce between excitement and disappointment and between being stuck and moving full speed ahead. Our images of ourselves constantly bump up against the images we have of the outside world. And we are continually rethinking our desires, reassessing our positions, and reinventing ourselves.

Leaders who know how to navigate the gap are better able to live with and lead with just enough anxiety. Like Dennis Nally, Ken Samet, Dave O'Reilly, Linda Rabbitt, and Sidney Taurel, they understand that only by pushing ourselves beyond our known limits can we grow personally and professionally. They accept change as a part of life. They remain confident in their ability to manage uncertainty. They draw upon their intellect and their intuition to make effective decisions, while being open to learning and growth. And they imagine the future, while assessing the present, without getting too attached to either one. These successful leaders operate at 30,000 feet able to look dispassionately at themselves and their organizations. They are participant observers.

Ask yourself . . .

- What life experiences, beliefs, and expectations have shaped my perception of the gaps in my life?
- How well do I manage my anxiety when moving from here to there?
- As a leader, do I help or hinder others in navigating the gap?

## Becoming a Participant Observer

As humans, we have the unique capacity to be witnesses to our own lives. We can remember where we've been, recognize where we are, and envision where we're going. Our amazing brain is able to sort through, select, coordinate, and evaluate the cognitive abilities we need to do this. It enables us to be our own travel guides through the gaps in our lives.

Elkhonon Goldberg, in *The Executive Brain,* describes how this process takes place in the executive brain. Our prefrontal cortex creates neural models of our past, present, and future experiences and desires. It then organizes our actions over time to manifest our vision in alignment with our "memory of the future." It also allows us to think about our thinking— to reconfigure or manipulate the future we're designing—as our circumstances and our desires change.

This thinking about thinking is called *metacognition.* It's like having an "objective" bird's-eye view of our lives and how we're moving through them. Unlike any other primate, we can see patterns, assess our effectiveness, and measure our progress. We can ask ourselves, How am I doing? Is this strategy working? What can I do differently? We can control our actions, even our thoughts. This enables us to learn, adapt, and improve ourselves.

Whatever you have done up until now, you can learn to manage change and uncertainty and effectively close the gaps in your life. You can live and lead with just enough anxiety. But you need two essential ingredients to succeed. You need an open mind and an open heart.

## AN OPEN MIND SHINES A LIGHT

*Chance favors the prepared mind.*

—LOUIS PASTEUR, nineteenth-century French chemist

My mind raced as the ambulance sped through traffic. Lying on the gurney and listening to the siren, my heart pounded and my anxiety skyrocketed. I was a healthy forty-five-year-old guy. I was the CEO of a successful company. I worked out. This wasn't supposed to happen. But there I was, headed for the hospital and a diagnosis of atrial fibrillation.

I struggled to understand what was happening to me. My beliefs about my health and my ability to handle any situation were shattered in that ten-minute ride. I worked hard over the ensuing months to expand my thinking. I struggled to make peace with my own mortality while doing everything in my power to stay healthy.

A year or so later, I was hospitalized again—not once, but twice—for a bowel obstruction. Soon after, I underwent surgery to correct a congenital growth in my small intestine. And as I write this, I am recovering from an unexpected surgery to repair a herniated disk that ruptured while I was sitting on a Canary Islands beach.

With each health crisis, I found myself face-to-face with the uncertainty of life and my fears of illness and death. Each time I had to make a choice: Was I going to let my emotions shut me down or could I find a way to understand and manage them? I decided to confront my fears.

I exercised both my brain and my body to gain control over my anxiety. You might say I strengthened my relationship with my executive brain, even as I was strengthening my heart at the gym. I thought about how I wanted to live my life and developed new goals for myself. I meditated more often and for longer periods of time. I imagined my body at its healthiest. As I opened my mind and got more honest with myself, I got clear about what really matters to me. And I gained deep insights into what it means to be truly alive. In fact, it was during this time that the concept of just enough anxiety began to take shape.

I also used my deeper understanding of myself to help me close the gap between where I was and where I wanted to be. Always an eager student, I began to do research on atrial fibrillation and my other health issues. I talked things over with my family and close friends. Over time, I learned to let go of my old image of myself and created new healthy habits. With knowledge and experience came increased confidence that I could manage my health—an ongoing exercise of mind over matter. I now continually monitor my progress and adjust my behavior to keep myself on track. And I'm happy to report that I am healthier than ever before.

My experience taught me that to live in the gap we need to cultivate an open mind. Without it, we remain slaves to the past. We easily become hijacked by our fear of anxiety—or by anxiety itself—which limits our ability to navigate through uncertainty. Unless we find a way to open our minds to new possibilities, we are forever fixed in our current concepts of ourselves and our world.

An open mind allows you to see where you're going and understand the terrain and roadblocks along the way. It enables you to understand yourself and others at deeper levels. With an open mind you can face challenges with insight and courage. You can embrace growth and change with excitement, inspiration, and resilience.

## The Three Keys to Opening Your Mind

We come into this world with insatiable curiosity. Over time, as we become successful adults, we often close ourselves off to new ways of thinking. We get locked in by our mental models, shackled by our biases and prejudices, and blinded by our perceptions of ourselves and our perceptions of others. We become immune to new ideas. To keep our minds open, we must deepen our self-awareness, make learning a lifelong priority, and practice nonattachment. Let's take a close look at each of these qualities.

**OPEN MIND**

Self-Awareness
Lifelong Learning
Nonattachment

### Self-Awareness

Self-awareness forms the foundation for living in uncertainty. It enables us to play to our strengths and compensate for our weaknesses in the midst of change. It allows us to be cognizant of what is going on around us—and within us—from moment to moment. When we are self-aware, we are able to read and manage our emotions. We know how change and uncertainty affect us. We understand what makes us anxious and can manage our anxiety.

Leaders who possess deep self-awareness are honest with themselves and others. They value authenticity. Rand Construction Corporation founder Linda Rabbitt lives this every day. "You can't really be successful without this self-knowledge. I have watched too many people try to lead organizations with lots of intellectual dishonesty, and it eventually catches up with them." But knowing who you are is only half of the equation; you need to be true to yourself and transparent to others. "I have a philosophy that everything counts," admits Linda. "You're the same person everywhere you go—at home, at work, at church, and at school—in your personal life and in your public life. If you're a person of integrity, it shows up in all aspects of your life." And so it does. The *Washingtonian* magazine named Linda "Washingtonian of the Year" in 2004. And *Working Woman* magazine has ranked Rand Construction among the nation's top 500 women-owned businesses.

Telling the truth *about* yourself begins by telling the truth *to* yourself. Self-awareness requires conscientious attention, discernment, emotional intelligence, and sincere internal scrutiny. But only by being awake can you be true to yourself. And only by being true to yourself can you navigate your way through the gaps between who and where you are and who and where you desire to be.

### Lifelong Learning

Learning is a lifelong endeavor that feeds the mind and the soul. It helps us solve problems and handle adversity. It enables us to grow, to let go of fears and behaviors that don't make sense anymore. Without learning we can never cross the gaps in our lives. As Henry Ford said, "Anyone who stops learning is old, whether at twenty or eighty."

Learning is behind real change and development within every successful organization. To lead in a world of uncertainty, you have to be able to learn in real time on a public stage. You need to admit your mistakes, ask difficult questions of yourself, have the courage to change patterns that don't work, and avoid rehashing the past or rehearsing the future. You need to develop a learning environment where people feel safe to try new ideas and expand their knowledge and skills.

The successful leaders I know all have a deep commitment to learning—for themselves and their companies. At PepsiCo, CEO Steve Reinemund made it his mission to "light the fire in every individual on what he or she needs to do to grow as a person. If learning isn't built person by person and from the inside out, there isn't anything there. Programs are interesting, but people make the difference."

When he turned over the reins of PepsiCo to Indra Nooyi in 2007, Steve knew that learning and development would remain high priorities. Indra, the company's former senior vice president of corporate strategy and its CFO since 2000, had worked side by side with Steve to grow the business. By paying attention to changing consumer interests, they kept pace with the trend toward better nutrition and healthier lifestyles. They diversified. PepsiCo's acquisition of Quaker Oats brought them solidly into the emerging market, with nutritious cereal bars and the Tropicana and Gatorade brands. The deal, along with strategic global expansion, helped PepsiCo consistently outperform its competitors, including Coca-Cola.

The long-held tradition of growing leaders within the company sets PepsiCo apart. It also pays off. During Steve's five years as CEO, the company's sales increased by more than $9 billion, net profits climbed more than 70 percent, earnings per share went up by about 80 percent, and the annual dividend doubled. Today, seventeen of the company's brands, including Lay's, Pepsi-Cola, Quaker, Tropicana, and Gatorade, each generate $1 billion or more in annual sales.

Steve and Indra understand the value chain between individual and business growth. It's a straightforward formula: Personal growth leads to professional growth, which leads to organizational growth, which in turn leads to financial growth.

PepsiCo's success demonstrates that learning enables us to reinvent ourselves—and our businesses—to meet new challenges. It helps us take advantage of opportunities. Learning propels us forward. It makes it possible for us to adapt to what's going on around and within us. Our commitment to lifelong learning is what shapes the future.

### Nonattachment

Many Eastern philosophies extol the virtue of nonattachment. This involves letting go of any preconceived notions we have about who we are. It requires that we avoid hanging on to negative habits and frozen behavior patterns. That we stop telling ourselves what we want to hear about ourselves and our lives. Nonattachment means giving up our psychological attachments to people and things, as well as our overidentification with our emotions. When we cling to strong emotions like fear and anger, we lose our true selves. We allow our feelings to possess our thoughts and obscure our view.

When we become attached to the way things are, we sabotage our efforts to live with uncertainty. We end up denying reality—and forfeiting our ability to manage change—if we become attached to pleasure and try to avoid discomfort, if we become attached to praise and try to avoid criticism, or if we become attached to getting what we want and try to avoid losing what we have. It is our attachment to stability that causes us to magnify or suppress our anxiety when circumstances start to change, as they always will. Only when we allow ourselves to feel our insecurity, discomfort, confusion, and pain can we moderate our level of anxiety. And only then can we make the most of change.

This can be a tough concept to embrace. But to cultivate a truly open mind, we must detach ourselves from any particular truth. We must be willing to accept a new truth, especially one that contradicts what we thought we knew. Remember: If you cling to nothing, you can handle anything.

Ask yourself . . .

- How can I better use my understanding of myself to cross the gaps between who or where I am and who or where I want to be?
- What more can I do to learn and grow in my life?
- What limiting thoughts, beliefs, and expectations am I attached to?
- What stories am I telling myself about who I am and what is or isn't possible?

## AN OPEN HEART FUELS THE FIRE

*To measure a man, measure his heart.*

—MALCOLM STEVENSON FORBES,
former *Forbes* magazine publisher

I was on my way to my first CEO interview. It was 1988. As I walked into the auditorium of the midwest Michigan company, I saw a woman meticulously organizing rows of chairs. Curious about her motivation, I asked her why. "I'm committed to doing a good job," she said, "because the people who run this place are committed to me." Later that day, I met with Max DePree, chairman and CEO of Herman Miller, a global manufacturer of office furniture, who described leadership as "a condition of the heart." His words really struck a chord and had a lasting effect on me. In fact, both conversations still echo in my mind.

Max understood that the heart of leadership is, literally, the heart. And the heart is all about how we feel about ourselves and the people who work for us. To say that someone has heart is to comment on his ability to live his values and touch deeply the lives of others. It's what enables great leaders to inspire and engage people. The heart is the seat of passion and purpose. Unfortunately, many of us have lost touch with our hearts, especially in business.

An open heart is an open door for the energy you need to move through the gap. The energy comes from your emotions—fear, anger, love, compassion—and can slow you down or speed you up. Your level of anxiety is the master key. If you try to navigate the gap with too much anxiety, your emotions will overwhelm you. They will hold you hostage and misguide you. If you reach for the other side with too little anxiety, you will be afraid of your emotions. You will become too detached and live in denial of your feelings. But if you proceed through the gap with just enough anxiety, you will fully experience and skillfully manage your emotions. You will stay focused until you reach your goal.

### The Three Keys to Opening Your Heart

There are three keys to opening your heart: emotional honesty, empathy and compassion, and emotional resilience. Let's take a close look at each one.

## OPEN HEART

Emotional Honesty
Empathy & Compassion
Emotional Resilience

### Emotional Honesty

I consulted once with an organization completely averse to conflict. Most folks were courteous, which created a pleasant enough work environment. But the polite atmosphere kept leaders and employees alike from raising controversial and important issues. The few people willing to have difficult conversations held them behind closed doors and were frequently targeted as naysayers or troublemakers. The overall lack of emotional honesty constipated the organization. It also limited its executive team's capacity to hear bad news. The company eventually went bankrupt.

Without the ability to express our feelings—freely and flexibly—we are forced to ignore or hide what we feel. The energy of our emotions remains inside of us. We end up exploding in anger, imploding in resentment, or sinking into depression. We may even make ourselves physically ill. A workplace that inhibits emotional honesty is a disaster waiting to happen. It will either be pummeled by waves of anxiety or, like the organization I mentioned above, buried in a sea of denial.

Emotional honesty is critical to living in the gap, for leaders and organizations. When you are emotionally honest, you are able to feel your emotions without being hooked into them. You recognize feelings of anger, frustration, and fear, as well as feelings of gratitude, joy, and love—and you express them in healthy ways. This, in turn, serves to turn the energy of your emotions into productive energy. It enables you to live with uncertainty, face change, and manage your anxiety. Conversely, your ability to live with uncertainty and change enables you to feel your full range of emotions.

Not all people have the same set point for expressing their emotions. Some operate with a brutal level of honesty, valuing directness above all else. Others tell the truth indirectly, taking care to respect the feelings of everyone involved. Some gravitate to positive emotions; others to negative ones. Most are influenced by the cultures that surround them. Italian,

Jewish, and Latin cultures, for example, are highly expressive cultures, while the Japanese and Swedish are more stoic by nature.

One leader stands out in my mind when I think about leading with emotional honesty: Baron Philippe Bodson, the CEO of Tractebel during the 1990s. During his tenure at the Belgium-based utility and industrial-services company, Baron Philippe thrived on the energies and anxieties of teamwork. Open and direct himself, he built a global-management team that could argue, handle conflict, and build consensus in the midst of uncertainty. "If debate doesn't take place, then I make it happen," he told me. "I push until they react. I want people to speak their minds. My job is to unveil truth around the table." Baron Philippe's leadership style was truer to his university upbringing—he had degrees in engineering and metallurgy—than even he realized. Like the metal and ideal gases he had worked with in school, his team was made stronger by being forged in heat—in this case, the heat of confrontation and emotional honesty.

### Empathy and Compassion

In many companies, values are like wallpaper—nice to have, but not part of the foundation. Not at Four Seasons Hotels. From the opening of the first hotel in 1961 to the increase in business following 9/11, Four Seasons built its success on its commitment to the Golden Rule. This value is hardwired to everything the company does, from hiring staff to dealing with the world's most demanding customers. Company founder Isadore (Issy) Sharp tells people at all levels of the company, "Whatever you have to do, however you act, however you want to come to a decision, just put yourself in the other person's shoes and use your common sense. It's no big deal. Business is just a small part of our lives, so go ahead and make the decision. You the housekeeper, you at the front desk, you the doorman, or you the waiter. Just use your common sense."

Issy's story reminds us of the importance of caring about the people we lead, especially in the midst of change and uncertainty. Everyone may go through the same four stages: denial, resistance, exploration, and commitment. But they do it in their own way and at their own pace. Good leaders are sensitive to where people are at any moment in time. That takes empathy and compassion.

*Empathy* is the ability to put yourself in another's shoes and understand her feelings. *Compassion* is a sense of shared experience—the ability to understand the suffering of another, to identify with that suffering inside yourself, and to reach out to help others. The Golden Rule, in its various forms, is rooted in the concepts of empathy and compassion.

Compassionate leaders assume goodwill. They respect and see the good in others, and in themselves. They honor people's feelings as true for them. And they try to minimize people's pain and fear while maximizing their sense of well-being. In the words of George Washington Carver: "How far you go in life depends on your being tender with the young, compassionate with the aged, sympathetic with the striving, and tolerant of the weak and strong. Because someday in life you will have been all of these."

Ultimately, empathy and compassion are about being part of something bigger than ourselves. They stem from the belief that all of life is interconnected. As Albert Einstein put it, "A human being is part of the whole, called by us 'the universe.' Our task must be to widen our circle of compassion to embrace all living creatures." This belief in something beyond ourselves can express itself in many ways—through spiritual practice, religion, philanthropy, volunteerism, or simple acts of kindness.

### Emotional Resilience

I turned fifty atop a mountain in Angkor Wat, Cambodia. Embraced by the natural beauty of the rain forests around me, and awed by the man-made beauty of the Hindu and Buddhist temples below me, I sat reading *Comfortable with Uncertainty* by Pema Chödrön, a Buddhist nun who lives in Halifax, Canada. Her words spoke to me in the silence. Instead of trying to "control the uncontrollable by looking for security and predictability, always hoping to be comfortable and safe," I should "learn how to relax in the midst of chaos." I should "learn to be cool when the ground beneath [me] suddenly disappears." After all, according to Chödrön, "We can never know what will happen to us next."

Pema Chödrön's words had a profound effect on me. Whether it was because of the location or the timing—or both—I took to heart the importance of learning to see uncertainty and change as part of life, while believing in my ability to manage it. That's where emotional resilience comes in.

Sometimes timing is perfect. We're ready to truly see what shows up in our lives. At other times we're simply too busy or too blind to take in what the world is offering. But when we're open to these special moments of discovery, as I was at Angkor Wat, we can learn some of life's most enduring lessons. When our mental defenses are down and our hearts are receptive, we can see things differently. Striving to stay open to new ideas and possibilities is one of the best ways to develop emotional resilience.

Emotional resilience is the ability to navigate and recover from the inevitable emotional ups and downs of life. It is what enables us to pick ourselves up after our failures and it gives us energy for our successes. Emotional resilience involves our thoughts, feelings, and actions. We need it to address unexpected challenges and cope with change and uncertainty. We need it to solve problems, take on extra work, and bounce back from setbacks. We also need it to learn from our mistakes, to dust ourselves off and move on.

Emotionally resilient leaders take time to reflect during challenging times. They get help when they need it, from friends, coworkers, partners, or professionals. They take vacations, meditate, or find other ways to rest and renew themselves. Such renewal, according to Richard Boyatzis and Annie McKee in *Resonant Leadership*, arouses "a different part of (the) limbic brain than that involved in stress responses," which leads to the body's activation of the parasympathetic nervous system. This produces hormones that lower blood pressure and strengthen the immune system. It also creates a sense of well-being, in which we are "more likely to perceive events as positive." Emotionally resilient leaders are also more likely to be physically healthy—eating right, exercising, monitoring their blood pressure and cholesterol, and not smoking—than their less resilient counterparts.

Only emotionally resilient leaders can foster emotional resilience in others. Their capacity to move through life's highs and lows with grace shapes their organizations' ability to do the same. This quality unlocks the productive energy needed to navigate the hallways of uncertainty.

Not long ago I was coaching a top leader at a large financial institution. The organization's accounting and reporting practices were under investigation. Unfortunately, the executive personalized the situation, believing it was her fault. She lived alone and had few social supports. She pulled away from the people at work. Not surprisingly, she felt overwhelmed by events and was unable to bounce back, even after the investigation was completed and the company moved forward. She left the company shortly thereafter.

Emotional resilience requires deep self-awareness. You need to know how much you can do before reaching a breaking point. You need to know what attitudes and behaviors make you vulnerable. Where in your body does stress appear? What are the signs that indicate it's time for renewal? As you strengthen your emotional resilience, you need to be patient and gentle with yourself. Don't take anything too personally.

Ask yourself . . .

- How honestly do I express my emotions at work? In my personal life?
- What can I do to be more empathetic and compassionate?
- Am I emotionally resilient? Why or why not?

## AN ALIGNED HEAD AND HEART

The partnership of head and heart reflects the relationship of the executive brain, the seat of higher thinking, and the limbic system, or emotional brain. "When these partners interact well," says Daniel Goleman, "emotional intelligence rises—as does intellectual ability."

But it's not just the brain at work here. Recent research has confirmed what philosophers and poets have known for centuries: The heart is more than a mechanical pump controlled by the brain. In fact, the heart has its own nervous system—its own brain—that communicates with the executive and emotional brains as well as with other parts of the body. This communication takes place on neurological, biochemical, biophysical, and energetic levels.

Research conducted by the Institute of HeartMath shows that messages from the heart have a strong influence on brain activity. "As we perceive and react to the world, messages sent by the brain affect the heart's beating patterns. At the same time, the heart's rhythmic activity generates neural signals that travel back to the brain, influencing our perceptions, mental processes, and feeling states," say Doc Childre and Howard Martin in *The HeartMath Solution*.

What does it all mean? I see this research as evidence that our best selves arise out of having an open mind and an open heart. We think clearly and communicate effectively. We are creative. We feel our full range of emotions and enjoy more fulfilling relationships. We perform at the top of our game. We are vibrantly alive.

Great leaders know intuitively that, as Max DePree told me nearly twenty years ago: "Leadership is a condition of the heart." Whatever intelligence and wisdom leaders bring to their organizations, it all begins with the heart. When the head and heart are aligned, anything is possible.

## Living in the Gap with an Open Mind and Heart

Eric Schaeffer lives in the gap. In fact, he lives in one gap after another. As the artistic director of the Signature Theater near Washington, D.C., he enters this fertile space each time he starts rehearsal for a new play. What does he have to work with? What is his vision? How will he achieve it? Can he get everyone else on board?

"I think the whole anxiety thing is about not knowing," he told me. "But I'm a firm believer that the only way you're going to grow as a person, as an artist, is to take these risks. You may be stepping into a black hole and not know you're stepping into it, or there may be a warning, but you'd better be able to swim."

Eric thrives on creating gaplike journeys for his audiences as well. "Whether it's dealing with hard issues, like incest or sexual relationships or social questions, I always try to push the envelope, to make us look and laugh at ourselves. I want the audience to feel like they are going on a journey. They might not understand it, but they want to talk about it. Why else are we sitting in a dark room for two and a half hours? If we are not challenging ourselves, if we are not learning something, then there is no point in doing it."

Using the theater as a social catalyst, Eric gives people the chance to think about themselves in new—and sometimes uncomfortable—ways. This allows them to travel into the gap between who they are and who they want to be. "The theater lets you look at what you normally couldn't look at, and admit what you see without saying it out loud. Whether it's right or wrong, you get to see yourself in a way that maybe you never have."

How does Eric do it? He leads with an open mind and an open heart. He is self-aware and committed to his own learning. Every new play is fertile ground. "I think that every show that I've done, I've learned something from the actors and, hopefully, they've learned from me as well."

At the same time, Eric is willing to exert his authority to bring out the best in people. He is comfortable with his personal power, expects a lot, and pushes people to deliver. "I don't think you should ever lower your expectations," he says. "If anything, we push harder and sometimes we reach further than we should. I think that's the most important thing."

The award-winning director balances his artistic vision with emotional support and guidance. "The theater deals a lot with raw emotion. And you have to be able to have trust; actors have to trust me and I have to trust them. We're in a marriage, in a sense, where you have to become naked. I will say, 'We've got to get naked here, guys,' and it's an emotional naked. We need it to get the physical connections, as well as the emotional connections, to whatever the characters need to tell the story."

Eric's comfort with the range and depth of human emotion enables him to tap into the emotional energy of actors to create emotional journeys for audiences. This skill, combined with his ability to monitor where people are and modulate their anxiety, helps make Signature performances big hits. By acting as an emotional barometer, Eric provides the cast and crew with what's needed to create a safe, creative environment. "If I get to the theater and all of a sudden I'm throwing a fit and saying, 'This isn't working, we're screwed,' then everyone starts panicking. If I'm in there saying, 'You know what? It's a mountain, but we're going to climb it—let's go,' then everyone joins in."

It's not always smooth climbing, however. Occasionally Eric has to deal with an actor who just doesn't get the picture or who turns out to be wrong for the part. "It's like a cancer in there, because you are in an incubator. If there is one bad seed in there, it affects the whole thing," he says. "So I talk to that person and if things don't improve, I make a change. I try to put it on me, not on the actor. I say, 'You know what? I made a mistake. I am doing you a disservice as an actor, and this role is not going to make you look good.' It's hard enough firing someone, so I approach it as if I'm the one who screwed up."

Eric's capacity to absorb and bounce back from negativity is essential in a business that pushes people's buttons. He models emotional resilience for everyone else. "I remind everyone that we have done something great here. I know that everyone gets frustrated when we get negative comments. But 'Don't forget the positive,' I say. 'Look at everything that we've done. Six months from now we will be laughing about this, so don't let it get you down.'"

Eric Schaeffer is successful because he understands the experience of living and leading in the gap. He is a master of just enough anxiety. With an open mind and open heart, he has become one of the most successful producers of Broadway musicals in the world.

## CLOSING THE GAPS IN YOUR LIFE

As you enter and travel across the gap, you will feel energized. You will see your choices unfold. Things will fall into place, eventually. Although you may be stretched beyond your expectations, you will find you have—or can develop—the skills you need. You will feel confident and a true sense of personal mastery. You will be in the flow of your life at its best.

Occasionally, you may feel considerable discomfort. You may feel out of balance or unsure of yourself. You may struggle to answer hard questions and be uncertain about what to do. Feeling bewildered, maybe even scared, you may think about turning back. You may think you're in no-man's-land and it's not worth the effort.

Expect both experiences. Each one is part of living and leading with just enough anxiety. In your search for comfort, you want to retreat. In your striving for more, better, or different, you want to forge ahead. You can create balance between these two desires by pushing and pacing yourself and taking time for rest and renewal. Remember to keep an open mind and an open heart.

---

### Five Steps to Closing the Gap

STEP 1: Identify your target of change. Pinpoint what you are choosing to change or achieve. What problem are you solving? What opportunity will you seize? What is your dream?

STEP 2: Imagine your desired outcome. Get clear about what the other side of the gap looks, sounds, and feels like. Make sure you really desire to be "there."

STEP 3: Assess your current reality. Gather data about your current situation. Be honest with yourself about where or who you are now. Clarify what it's like to be "here." What inside of you is scaring you, blinding you, or holding you back? What is pulling you forward?

STEP 4: Analyze the gap and your ability to close it. Determine its size and scope. Why does it exist? Assess your level of anxiety and your willingness to do the work. Think about how you will navigate from here to there and what resources and support you will need.

STEP 5: Take action. Take one step at a time and stay focused. Assess your progress periodically and make adjustments as necessary—to your goal, expectations, strategy, or attitude. Extract the lessons and celebrate your successes. And amp up or tone down your anxiety to maintain your momentum.

Without the gaps in our lives we would never grow. We would be unable to fulfill our potential. We would be bored. The gaps between where we are and where we desire to be keep us alive. They give us hope and offer promise. They inspire us to do great things, to engage and challenge people, and they help us to build winning organizations.

# 4

# THE THREE FACES OF ANXIETY

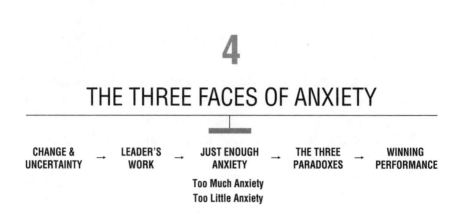

| CHANGE & UNCERTAINTY | → | LEADER'S WORK | → | JUST ENOUGH ANXIETY | → | THE THREE PARADOXES | → | WINNING PERFORMANCE |
|---|---|---|---|---|---|---|---|---|
| | | | | Too Much Anxiety | | | | |
| | | | | Too Little Anxiety | | | | |

Milo of Croton dreamed of becoming the strongest man in the world. According to Greek legend, he started training as a young boy by carrying a newborn calf on his back every day. He walked from his family's farm into the town square, the calf stretched across his shoulders with its feet projecting stiffly forward. By the time he entered the Olympics around 550 B.C., Milo was able to carry a four-year-old cow. Some say he entered the Olympic arena carrying the animal. And his strategy paid off. Milo became a six-time Olympic wrestling champion.

Carlos Berio, an exercise physiologist and my personal trainer of three years, told me this story one day at the gym. We were talking about the similarities between just enough anxiety and physical training. "Milo overloaded his system progressively so he could bear the weight of the growing calf. In the beginning, the calf was not that heavy, but a full-grown cow probably weighs more than a thousand pounds. By carrying the animal every single day, he was able to increase his capability incrementally. He provided his body with just enough stress to force it to adapt.

"When I'm working with you," Carlos said, "I'm always thinking about what we're doing in the form of progressive overload. On a molecular level, all muscle is the same, whether it's in your heart, your legs, or your back. When you stress it, you cause a microtrauma—a microscopic tear in the muscle tissue. Then, provided you have enough rest and the proper nutrition, your muscle will adapt in the right direction. It will repair itself. You will be stronger than you were before."

Carlos's objective is to break down muscle just enough so that it regenerates itself into a stronger muscle. In essence, he's creating a gap between what the muscle is capable of and what he wants it to do. The muscle bridges the gap by increasing its capability. But this works *only* when the intensity of the exercise is just enough to create tiny tears, followed by relaxation. Too much intensity and the muscle will not be able to recover. Too little and it will remain unchanged.

My workouts with Carlos are all about just enough. He pushes me just beyond the limits of what my body can do, to force my muscles to adapt and get stronger. He monitors my mood and motivation to find the right moments to teach me what I need to know. Because he understands how much pain I can tolerate and when I need to rest, he keeps me poised on the edge of my discomfort. His encouragement and belief in me—and his humor— have helped me build both muscle and confidence over the years.

The importance of just enough is evident in multiple disciplines— from the arts and education to sports, and even religion. In business, we are always seeking middle ground. We need to generate revenue while cutting costs. We need to be innovative and create new products while exploiting our cash cows. Finding the right balance between long- and short-term goals is always a challenge, and all companies operate in the tension between making enough changes to stay competitive and jeopardizing success by changing too much or too little.

Even our brains benefit from just enough. Cognitive research reveals that the executive brain slows down when under- or overaroused. With the right amount of arousal, however, our higher mental faculties operate at peak efficiency. We hold a clear vision of what we want to accomplish and become totally involved in our task. We are motivated.

Remember the anxiety that came with college exams? A study of students preparing for exams confirms the importance of just enough. Students with too little anxiety failed to study enough, while those with too much anxiety had insomnia and poor concentration. Only students with just enough anxiety developed effective studying habits and performed well on their exams. The Yerkes-Dodson law, shown on the next page, illustrates the effect of too little and too much arousal on performance. This

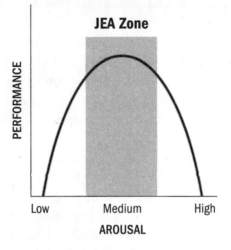

## YERKES-DODSON LAW

**JEA Zone**

*(Vertical axis: PERFORMANCE; Horizontal axis: AROUSAL — Low, Medium, High)*

psychological principle applies not only to academic achievement but also to business, art, music, and sports.

Great athletes understand the importance of arousal. They enter an optimal performance zone whenever their thoughts, intentions, feelings, and senses are all focused on the same goal. With no distractions, their energy is fully available to complete the task at hand. They experience pure concentration and a sense of well-being.

You enter the JEA zone when your body, mind, and emotions are focused, activated, and aligned. It happens most frequently when you are stretching yourself just beyond your proven ability. Stretching too far overtaxes your systems; too little shuts you down. You need just enough anxiety to enter the JEA zone and perform at your best.

### How Champion Athletes Enter the *Zone*

- *They see the end from the beginning.* Baseball legend Hank Aaron described it this way: "You visualize. You see it in your head. I used to play every pitcher in my mind before I went to the ballpark." Aaron had one of the most consistent offensive careers in baseball history. In addition to his 755 home runs, he holds the major league record for total bases, extra-base hits, and RBIs, and he was named to a record twenty-four All-Star squads.

- *They persevere against all odds.* When Lance Armstrong was diagnosed in 1996 with testicular cancer, which doctors said had spread to his lungs and brain, he was given a 50 percent chance of survival. But Armstrong defied the odds. Not only did he beat the disease, he resumed his training and won his first Tour de France in 1999, just three years after the diagnosis. He then added six consecutive Tour victories to set a new record. As Lance sees it, "One of the redeeming things about being an athlete is redefining what is humanly possible."

- *They ooze self-confidence.* "Some people say that I have an attitude. Maybe I do. But I think that you have to. You have to believe in yourself when no one else does—that makes you a winner." Venus Williams has every reason to be confident. Making her U.S. Open debut at age seventeen, she was the first African American women's finalist since Althea Gibson won the title in 1958. She won the U.S. Open title in 2000 and 2001. Williams is the most highly endorsed female athlete ever, owns her own interior design company, and holds twenty-eight career singles titles.

## JUST ENOUGH ANXIETY IS THE MIDDLE WAY

*The happiest among us keep the pressure turned up or down to that point where we have a challenge we believe we can manage.*

—GILBERT BRIM, *Ambition*

Anxiety has three faces. Each one has distinct characteristics and consequences.

- *Too little anxiety* is grounded in contentment. If you have too little anxiety, you avoid change. You value the status quo and believe that everything will be okay as long as nothing changes. Your minimal level of anxiety creates boredom and stagnation in your organization.

- *Too much anxiety* comes from negative thinking. If you have too much anxiety, you attack change. You become combative or controlling as you try to ease the pain you feel. Your over-the-top level of anxiety creates frustration and chaos in your organization.

• *Just enough anxiety* grows out of the ability to be comfortable with discomfort. If you have just enough anxiety, you embrace chance. You reach for opportunities to learn and grow. Your "just enough" level of anxiety unleashes human energy and creates hope and momentum in your organization.

Just enough anxiety is the middle way. It is not about passivity or compromise. It is about maintaining your balance in the midst of opposing forces. Like a champion skater, you can round any corner with the right mix of speed and balance.

There is no single point of just enough anxiety. It exists on a continuum and encompasses the full range of healthy anxiety. Like your other emotions, your range of just enough anxiety moves along the continuum—between too little and too much—over time and as your circumstances change.

For example, you may lean toward too little anxiety when things are going well. You may jump into too much anxiety when facing a major challenge. But as long as you are in the range of anxiety that's healthy for you, you are using just enough anxiety for the situation. Remember: The goal is to use just enough anxiety within yourself to maximize your learning, creativity, achievement, and performance—at each moment in time.

This healthy range of anxiety differs from person to person and company to company. One leader's "just enough" may be "too much" for someone else. Mature organizations may have a higher tolerance for anxiety than start-ups, either because they've found ways to protect people from anxiety or developed ways of handling it. Or they may live dangerously close to too little anxiety, because they are mired in bureaucracy or content with their history of success. On the other hand, new companies may find that a high level of anxiety is their "just enough." There is no one-size-fits-all definition of anxiety that applies to every situation. Just enough anxiety is a moving target.

Hitting the just-enough-anxiety target in the midst of change is tough. But this middle way is the only proven passage through the gap. Too much and too little anxiety are both dysfunctional and destructive. They hold you back or send you in the wrong direction. Just enough anxiety gives you the energy you need for optimum performance.

## YOUR ANXIETY CAN MOBILIZE OR DESTROY

As a leader, you are the steward of anxiety inside your organization. Your ability to manage your own anxiety directly affects your ability to help others manage theirs. It determines how effective you are in unleashing and mobilizing the creative energy inside your organization.

Your anxiety plays out in what you see, how you think and feel, what you say, and what you do. Through your attitudes and actions you influence the people around you on a daily basis. If they sense too little anxiety, they lose their enthusiasm. Their level of engagement and productivity declines. If they sense too much anxiety, they lose their focus. They begin to make mistakes and bad decisions. But if you bring just enough anxiety to the table, your people feel excited, hopeful, and challenged to do their best.

Several years ago I spent the day with world-renowned conductor James DePriest. What a treat it was to watch him conduct the Oregon Symphony, and to discuss his views on leadership. A tall man who walks with crutches from polio, he sounds a little like James Earl Jones. Although both his size and voice can be intimidating, almost everyone calls him Jimmy.

To Jimmy, leadership is a deeply personal experience. "You're doing things that impact people's lives. You impact their monetary future, their psychological well-being, and their families, as well as their performance. You have to be really circumspect, because an idle word or an ill-chosen gesture carries the cumulative effect of all the baggage they see you possessing.

"I try to be conscious of the impact of my position, never being cavalier, never being thoughtless. And if by some accident I forget to acknowledge a person's contribution, or just forget something that could be interpreted as a slight, it's very important to make clear to everyone that it was unintentional, and that I accept responsibility for it. I can't assume the person will get over it."

Jimmy DePriest understands the magnitude of his effect on others. He knows that his management—or mismanagement—of anxiety, for himself and others, has huge consequences for his ability to lead. It is critical to people's performance, health, happiness, and achievement.

Why? Because anxiety is contagious. Our brains are hardwired to pick up cues from our environment—including other people. We unconsciously monitor tone of voice, facial expressions, body language, eye contact, attentiveness, and other nonverbal cues. We interpret people's behavior. We sense their intentions. We feel their feelings. In fact, we are "inexorably drawn into an intimate brain-to-brain linkup whenever we engage with another person. That neural bridge lets us affect the brain and the body of everyone we interact with, just as they do us," says Daniel Goleman in *Social Intelligence*.

## We Are Hardwired to Connect with Each Other

- *We mirror what we see in others.* Swedish researchers found that merely seeing a picture of a happy face elicits fleeting activity in the muscles that pull the mouth into a smile. Indeed, whenever we gaze at a photograph of someone whose face displays a strong emotion—such as sadness, disgust, or joy—our facial muscles automatically start to mirror the other's facial expression.

- *Our cells help us connect with each other.* Neuroscientists have identified specific cells and neurons that make it easier for us to be social. *Mirror neurons* sense another's movements. *Spindle cells* process our social decisions. And *dopamine neurons* react to pleasure-inducing neurotransmitters that flow freely while we gaze into each other's eyes.

- *Your leadership style can affect your people's health.* Studies show that people's blood pressure goes up dramatically when they have to deal with a supervisor who is disrespectful, unfair, or insensitive. It remains normal when they work with a leader who is respectful, fair, and sensitive.

Have you ever walked away from a conversation feeling different from how you did before without understanding why? Perhaps you felt angry or sad for no apparent reason. Chances are you took on the feeling of the person with whom you were talking. Or you responded instinctively, without being aware of how you were affected by them.

Every encounter you have contains an underlying emotional component. It can be obvious or subtle. As you interact with a colleague or an employee, you experience his or her emotions, as well as your own. This can have positive or negative consequences. It means you have the ability to influence another's mood. You can make another person feel better or worse. But you are also susceptible to what someone else is feeling.

Your conversations are like an emotional dance. With each interaction, you exchange verbal and nonverbal cues with your partner. When your emotions are healthy and in sync, the dance goes smoothly. You glide from one topic to the next. You play off each other's ideas. It feels effortless. But when one or both of you experience unhealthy emotions, the dance feels more like a battle. You step on each other's toes. You fight for control, each determined to take the lead. Rather than dancing together, you are each dancing on your own.

Effective leaders are masters of the dance. They understand it's their job to know what people are thinking and feeling, and to respond accordingly. And they know that their ability to do this has huge business consequences.

Cadbury Schweppes CEO Todd Stitzer puts it this way: "If you think you can make it up the hill, and you're not aware that people are not following you, you're going to be a pretty lonely guy when you're near the top. So you have to know how people are feeling, and you have to monitor what comes out of your mouth. You're always self-correcting.

"I'm not perfect. I can be as grumpy as the next guy. I can get annoyed. But I have to be able to monitor that in a positive way."

Nobody is an island. We all influence and are influenced by others on an ongoing basis, and a lot of that influence occurs unconsciously. In the words of Jimmy DePriest: "As leaders, we tend to overestimate how much control we have *over* people, but underestimate how much influence we have *on* people."

Our workplaces are like large petri dishes, filled with nourishing and toxic people who are continually playing out their needs, conflicts, and aspirations. It's a jumbled mixture of personalities, opinions, and emotions, where people are motivated by different things and different kinds of leaders. We can find ourselves drawn to or repelled by what—and whom—we encounter.

### Good Organizations Make Good Leaders

We know it takes a good leader to create a successful organization. But it can also take a good organization to create a successful leader.

This lesson comes from the continent of Africa. The notion that "a person can only be a person through others" permeates African tribal communities. Leaders rarely have identities independent of their tribes.

The concept is called *Ubuntu*. It comprises many traditional African values and captures the significance of interdependence and group solidarity in African culture.

A growing number of African companies are bringing Ubuntu to the workplace—valuing transparency, collective decision making, community building, mutual respect, dignity, and compassion.

Emotions grow and multiply rapidly in this fertile environment. If the emotions are healthy, your organization can soar. But if they are unhealthy, your organization is headed for trouble. It's up to you, as the leader, to create an environment that fosters the growth of healthy emotions, including just enough anxiety.

How can you do this? First, you need a deep self-awareness and the ability to manage your own anxiety. You need to know where your healthy range of just enough anxiety sits on the anxiety continuum. What do you feel when you lean toward too much or too little anxiety? How do you know when you have just enough?

Next, you need to be able to gauge what others are feeling. You need to listen deeply and watch carefully. You also need to understand what motivates people. How hard can you push? When do you need to back off? What do they need from you?

Finally, you need to take the anxiety pulse of your organization on a regular basis. What is your organization's set point for anxiety? What does just enough anxiety feel and look like? What are the signs of too much anxiety and too little? Then, by making adjustments quickly, you can keep your balance. You can navigate change and uncertainty via the middle way. You can live and lead with just enough anxiety.

## How Anxious Is Your Organization?

*Instructions:* Place an "X" on each continuum below to indicate where you think your organization currently "sits" in each of the categories. Be honest and don't overthink your answers. To get a broader picture, ask people throughout your organization to complete this form.

**VISION AND GOALS**

_____Outdated          _____Inspiring          _____Grandiose

**CHANGE**

_____Distracting    _____Energizing         _____Threatening

**COMMUNICATION**

_____Vague             _____Open               _____Erratic

**TEAMWORK**

_____Aimless           _____High performing  _____Disempowering

**RELATIONSHIPS**

_____Neglected       _____Collaborative      _____Confrontational

**LEARNING**

_____Meaningless   _____Results driven     _____Haphazard

**ACCOUNTABILITY**

_____Unassigned    _____Empowering         _____Unrecognized

**DECISION MAKING**

_____Tentative        _____Effective           _____Arbitrary

**EXECUTION**

_____Careless          _____Results driven     _____Sporadic

**PERFORMANCE MANAGEMENT**

_____Ineffective     _____Well executed      _____Resisted

*Results:* Look at the overall pattern of your answers. "X"s on the left indicate too little anxiety. "X"s on the right indicate too much anxiety. "X"s in the center indicate just enough anxiety.

Let's not be naïve. Each of us experiences too little, too much, and just enough anxiety at some point. But leaders who live for long periods of time in too little or too much anxiety—who constantly hide their anxiety or wear it on their sleeves—are in danger of losing their ability to motivate the creative energy of their people. They are risking the health of their organizations.

Let's take a closer look at the three faces of anxiety: too little anxiety (TLA), too much anxiety (TMA), and just enough anxiety (JEA). What are the characteristics that distinguish them? And what impact do TLA, TMA, and JEA leaders have on their organizations?

Ask yourself . . .

- What effect do I usually have on the people around me?
- How well do I read and respond to other people's emotions?
- What is the underlying emotional tone in my organization?

## TOO LITTLE ANXIETY: THE FACE OF COMPLACENCY

I interviewed Vivendi CEO Jean-Marie Messier in Paris in 1995. He was a bright star at the time, France's CEO of the year. Intelligent, confident, personable, and assertive, Messier looked like the model JEA leader.

Messier's dream was to transform Vivendi—created by imperial decree in 1853 under Napoleon III—into a global champion of the digital age. To achieve this, he centralized capital allocation, divested operating subsidiaries, and reorganized the company into three groups: utilities, construction and property, and telecommunications and media.

Early results were encouraging. Under Messier's leadership, the company catapulted from a loss of 562 million euros in 1995 to a net income of 1.1 billion euros in 1998.

Acquisitions became the name of the game. In 2000, Messier's connection with Seagrams CEO Edgar Bronfman led to Vivendi's $34 billion acquisition of Seagrams, which owned Universal Studios. Messier then spent $20 billion picking up publishing companies, cable TV channels, TV production companies, and networks, as well as obtaining interests in various satellite and Internet companies.

Messier's dream became an obsession. He took one risk after another, overleveraging company assets to acquire new media targets. When AOL and Time Warner merged in 2000, Messier knew the Internet-based media "future" was imminent. He signed a huge deal with U.K.-based Vodafone to get Vivendi into the mobile Internet market.

Messier was seduced by the uncertainty—and the promise—of a rapidly changing marketplace. His only concern was that he would not act fast or boldly enough. Burning through billions of euros for numerous media ventures, Messier amassed enormous debt trying to get ahead of the turning tide. It was a losing battle. In 2001, Vivendi reported a loss of nearly 14 billion euros, the largest one-year loss in French corporate history.

In July 2002, Jean-Marie Messier resigned. He was only forty-four. Vivendi, one of France's twenty largest companies and the second-largest media conglomerate in the world, was only ten days from filing for bankruptcy. His replacement, Jean-René Fourtou, sold off most of the media properties Messier had acquired, many at steep discounts. Shareholders lost more than 100 billion euros in equity value.

Although I have not spoken with Messier since this catastrophe, it's not hard to speculate about what happened. Messier was a positive leader whose visions bordered on idealism. I suspect that he so wanted to be successful, to be right about his decisions, and to capitalize on digital opportunities that he became infatuated with the unrealistic belief that he could pull it off. Like many other digital entrepreneurs, he underestimated the magnitude of risk and his capability to navigate through a complex marketplace. He possessed an unwavering belief that things would work out favorably. Perhaps he saw himself as invincible and invulnerable. As a result, he created too little anxiety in himself, although he may have created too much anxiety in the people around him.

What you see is not always what you get. At first glance, Messier may look like a leader with too much anxiety. He was aggressive and driven. He took unnecessary risks and wanted to win at all costs. But I believe his grandiose dreams and his failure to see what might go wrong were his Achilles' heel. His is a story of too little anxiety.

How could anyone have too little anxiety in our crazy world? Believe me, it happens. In fact, cultivating too little anxiety is exactly the way some leaders attempt to handle the change and uncertainty in business today.

---

### Are You a TLA Leader?

*Instructions:* Check all that apply.

I USUALLY . . .
___feel uncomfortable with growth and change.
___focus on the positive while downplaying the negative.
___believe everything will turn out okay or will resolve itself.
___seek contentment, comfort, and security.
___find it hard to get in touch with my emotions.
___shy away from conflict.
___try to give everyone what they want.
___do whatever's necessary to avoid hurting people's feelings.
___have difficulty championing my own ideas.
___analyze everything to avoid making mistakes.

*Results:* Count your checkmarks.

- 0–3: You do not have too little anxiety.
- 4–6: You are leaning toward too little anxiety.
- 7+: You are solidly planted in too little anxiety.

---

Leaders with too little anxiety want to avoid discomfort. They are driven by one or more ingrained fears—the fear of their own emotions, of not being successful, or of being imperfect or disliked. Lacking emotional honesty with themselves, they shy away from emotional honesty with or from others. They prefer to sweep emotions under the rug or run away from them altogether.

Not surprisingly, TLA leaders tend to live in a bubble. They may have been spared from difficulty for most of their lives. Or they may have learned at an early age to protect themselves from the complexity and uncertainty that surrounds them. Some, like Messier, may actually seek out change and then run away from its potential dangers. In any case, TLA leaders are masters at denying or resisting their anxiety.

It's like they are wearing a self-imposed blindfold. It keeps them from having to face difficult problems and limits their ability to learn. It makes

them falter in the face of adversity. TLA leaders stay stuck in old ways of doing things or reach for quick fixes.

Over the years, I've identified four distinct sets of behaviors that typify TLA leaders. Not personality types per se, they describe four different ways that leaders express too little anxiety. You may know people who fit these descriptions. You may even exhibit some of these behaviors from time to time—we all do. TLA leaders, however, are quite at home in these behaviors.

### Idealistic Leaders

Idealistic leaders live in a fantasy world. They are driven by their need to have things work out favorably. So they tend to ignore reality and gloss over bad news. They focus on the bright side of things. Untroubled by unseen problems, they imagine themselves invincible or invulnerable. They can solve anything.

At least that's how it appears on the surface. Beneath their confident facade, however, idealistic leaders have fragile egos. I know a CEO who surrounds himself with "yes people" who won't criticize his ideas. While he may ask to be informed about what's happening, his people understand that he prefers rosy summaries to troublesome details. This is a leader who rarely asks, or tries to answer, the hard questions.

But his positive outlook makes this idealistic leader likable and easy to be around. He's good at spinning stories about desired futures and projected wins. His visionary rhetoric makes people feel good about how things are going and where the organization is headed.

## Idealistic Leaders

| How Others See Them | What They Say | How They Impact Their Organizations |
|---|---|---|
| • Arrogant<br>• Driven<br>• Egotistical<br>• Grandiose<br>• Unrealistic | • Imagine what we can create together.<br>• Don't think about the problem; focus on the solution.<br>• Everything will work out just fine. | • People waste energy trying to meet unrealistic goals.<br>• Difficult issues are ignored or minimized.<br>• Unexpected problems overwhelm people at all levels. |

Idealistic leaders get hijacked by their own rose-colored view of the world. They set themselves and their organizations up for disappointment. Their castles in the air are bound to fall apart sooner or later.

## Detached Leaders

Detached leaders isolate themselves from the world. Driven by the need to protect themselves, they operate best on their own or with minimal interaction. Many withdraw entirely from tense situations and relationships. Crises make them feel especially vulnerable. Their cold demeanor can be mistaken for arrogance.

The detached leaders I know are very capable, having developed the skills and knowledge they need to get things done with little reliance on others. They are often confident and self-assured. But their tendency to avoid confrontation means that difficulties can go unresolved.

## Detached Leaders

| How Others See Them | What They Say | How They Impact Their Organizations |
|---|---|---|
| • Clueless<br>• Ineffective<br>• Irrelevant<br>• Unapproachable<br>• Uncaring | • Don't worry. I'll take care of it.<br>• Let's think this through.<br>• There's no need for you to be involved. | • People feel abandoned and ignored.<br>• Key resources go unused or are misused.<br>• Unspoken responsibilities and unclear authority lead to poor decisions. |

One middle manager I know is so uncomfortable with emotional issues—especially at work—that he relies solely on analysis and rational thought. Figuring things out, he told me, is more important than schmoozing with others. Having the right answer is more important than forming strategic alliances. Unfortunately, this approach cuts him off from new ideas and critical information. It keeps him from understanding changes in the marketplace and leveraging opportunities for lucrative partnerships.

Detached leaders get hijacked by their inability to access their emotions. Unable to make meaningful connections, they avoid colleagues who bring too much emotion to their work. This creates a culture of aloofness, where people avoid the leader and the leader avoids the people.

## Overpleasing Leaders

Overpleasing leaders live in other people's worlds. They are driven by the need to make everyone happy. They are uncomfortable with conflict, their own power, and the power of others. This makes them consummate people pleasers.

Excellent team players, overpleasing leaders can be quite skillful at building consensus and bringing out the best in others. Like the executive I met recently. Her ability to summarize and synthesize diverse ideas enables her to craft plans that appeal to everyone. She is also good at recognizing others' achievements and giving credit where it's due. At the same time, she has trouble promoting her own ideas.

To avoid upsetting anyone, overpleasing leaders say what they think

### Overpleasing Leaders

| How Others See Them | What They Say | How They Impact Their Organizations |
|---|---|---|
| • Erratic<br>• Gullible<br>• Incompetent<br>• Timid<br>• Untrustworthy | • I'm sorry. I didn't mean to upset you.<br>• What does everyone else think?<br>• I'll go along with the majority. | • Critical tasks remain undone and problems unaddressed.<br>• Projects start and stop unpredictably, with little getting accomplished.<br>• Conflicts are avoided and stay unresolved. |

people want to hear. They often give in to the person with the strongest personality or the loudest voice. They do whatever it takes to avoid tension—internal and external—including not facing up to difficult people issues or performance problems. Political battles are definitely taboo.

Overpleasing leaders get hijacked by their anxiety about not being liked or accepted. Over time, they lose their identities and undermine their own authority. This keeps them from going out on a strategic limb, standing up for their people, or making the decisions necessary to keep their companies competitive.

### Cautious Leaders

Cautious leaders are frightened by the world they live in. Driven by their fear of change and uncertainty, they attempt to control everything by being totally certain before taking action. So they overanalyze data and plans, which leads to perpetual procrastination and indecision.

I know of one cautious leader who is so afraid of making mistakes that he continually vacillates between options. He asks for countless opinions. He gathers data. He holds meetings. And he focuses on all the things that might go wrong.

This leader's cautious focus and overly collaborative style have positive and negative effects. They make him transparent. They give everyone the chance to participate in key decisions. But they also make him frustratingly slow to act. He lacks the sense of urgency necessary to keep his company competitive. He's afraid of taking risks.

### Cautious Leaders

| How Others See Them | What They Say | How They Impact Their Organizations |
|---|---|---|
| • Timid<br>• Incompetent<br>• Insecure<br>• Preoccupied<br>• Unintelligent | • I'd rather err on the side of caution.<br>• Let's take our time with this.<br>• I need all the facts before I can decide. | • Work is continually delayed by unmade or poorly made decisions.<br>• People waste time in unnecessary or unproductive activities.<br>• The organization misses key opportunities for growth. |

Cautious leaders get hijacked by their fear of the unknown—and their fear of failure. They become adept at *not* making decisions. And they rarely take a firm stand. As a result, they miss opportunities or move too slowly to keep up with changing customer demands.

---

### Do You Work in a TLA Organization?

*Instructions:* Check all that apply.

MY ORGANIZATION . . .
\_\_\_lacks a sense of urgency.
\_\_\_fails to confront hard issues.
\_\_\_has little sense of direction.
\_\_\_holds an exceedingly optimistic vision of the future.
\_\_\_ignores information about small problems.
\_\_\_leaves talent untapped or underutilized.
\_\_\_misses out on opportunities.
\_\_\_pays little attention to what competitors are doing.
\_\_\_responds poorly to change.
\_\_\_tolerates mediocre performance.

*Results:* Count your checkmarks.

- 0–3: Your organization does not have too little anxiety.
- 4–6: Your organization is leaning toward too little anxiety.
- 7+: Your organization is solidly planted in too little anxiety.

---

Most of us gravitate toward one of these four leadership types when we're leaning toward too little anxiety. We might even exhibit symptoms of more than one type. There are some leaders, however, who demonstrate all four TLA types simultaneously. Take Lucent Technology CEO Richard McGinn, for example.

Expectations were high when McGinn took the helm of Lucent in 1996. After all, the company was newly spun off from the great AT&T, a combination of Western Electric and Bell Labs. The results should have been spectacular.

McGinn knew he had been handed an amazing opportunity. A highly personable guy, with an uncanny ability to paint a picture of dazzling success, he drew in initial investors like flies to honey.

But he couldn't get things done on the inside. Accustomed to the slow-moving Western Electric culture, McGinn was too bureaucratic in an industry driven by rapidly changing consumer demands and technologies. A cumbersome company structure and woefully inadequate financial controls only compounded the problem. Worst of all, McGinn relied too much on what had worked in the past, like voice equipment, and failed to take advantage of emerging trends, like Internet routers and high-speed optical equipment.

Under McGinn's leadership, Lucent stock tumbled 75 percent. He was fired in October 2000, on the heels of Lucent's fourth consecutive profit warning. His replacement, Henry Schacht, who came back from retirement to fill the void, commented: "We got ahead of our capacity to execute."

Richard McGinn was a TLA leader in many ways. He was *detached,* he failed to see or understand marketplace realities, and he refused to confront or replace nonperforming executives. When it came to developing new products, McGinn was *cautious,* continually ignoring the pleas of researchers eager to develop fiber optics. When things started to go south, McGinn did spin off several slow-growing businesses. Some analysts suspected, however, that he was trying to appease Wall Street, even though it might hurt Lucent's ability to compete in the long run—a sure sign of *overpleasing.* And through it all, McGinn was an *idealist,* certain that everything would work out in the end. It didn't.

McGinn's TLA leadership style set Lucent up for failure. He lacked the sense of urgency necessary to stay ahead of the competition. As a result, the company fell short of technical milestones for developing new products. It missed emerging opportunities. And it never developed the capability required to get new products to market in a timely manner.

## TOO MUCH ANXIETY: THE FACE OF FEAR

Joe Nacchio's cowboy mentality was just what Qwest needed at the start of the telecom revolution. His combative leadership style enabled the small company to compete among giants such as Bell, WorldCom, AT&T, and SBC. But as the playing field leveled out, Nacchio's bravado was misplaced. His obsession with winning created a too-much-anxiety (TMA) culture that took the company down a road of ruthlessness and ruin.

Nacchio was clear about what he wanted. "The most important thing we do is meet our numbers," he said in a 2001 employee meeting. "It's more important than any individual product, individual philosophy, or individual cultural change we're making. We stop everything else when we don't make the numbers." Nacchio showed no interest in how his demands might affect people. He was determined to have his way.

The pressure to achieve revenue targets at Qwest was phenomenal. As one former Qwest executive explained, "Joe, off the seat of his pants, could issue some very scathing diatribes about raising the bar. And you didn't want him zeroing in on you because he could rip you to smithereens." Everyone was expected to do whatever it took to meet or exceed stated targets.

People took Nacchio's not-so-veiled threats seriously. The pattern of inflating revenue by booking onetime sales as recurring sales became so commonplace that employees referred to the practice as a "drug" or an "addiction." Investigators eventually charged Qwest with fraudulently reporting $3 billion in revenue, in part to help facilitate Qwest's 2000 acquisition of U.S. West. The merger transformed Qwest from a fiber-optic data-service carrier to a full-service phone carrier, with the promise of greatly increased revenues.

In an environment of extreme anxiety, like the one Nacchio created at Qwest, employees tend to react in one of two ways. They follow the leader's example and become TMA leaders. Or they become paralyzed by their fears of retribution, unable to stand up for their values or challenge improper behavior. Either way, the organization is doomed to self-destruct.

Nacchio's self-serving behavior continued. He ignored warnings from the company's CFO and president that financial projections were vastly overhyped. His negative energy permeated the company. People were disempowered, afraid of losing their jobs, and caught in the cycle of destruction.

In 2002, Qwest's credit ratings were lowered due to its exorbitant debt. It was forced to write off $20 to $30 billion in goodwill associated with its acquisition of U.S. West, and its stock dropped 50 percent for the year. Analysts speculated that the company was worth more in parts than it was whole.

Nacchio's volatile behavior escalated as the company started to decline. He fought everyone who disagreed with him, launching a public campaign to deny suggestions by Morgan Stanley that he was using fuzzy accounting methods in reporting growth expectations. He also refused to consult with the Securities and Exchange Commission about possible improprieties. After five years of his confrontational leadership, perpetuated by sky-high levels of anxiety and fear, Nacchio was replaced as CEO of Qwest in June 2002. You could almost hear the collective sigh of relief.

Since Nacchio's departure, Qwest has had to restate $2.2 billion in revenue. In 2007, Joe Nacchio was convicted of nineteen counts of insider trading and sentenced to six years in federal prison. He was ordered to pay a $19 million fine and forfeit $52 million from stock sales. Nacchio plans to appeal.

One could reasonably assume that Nacchio is a guy with a big ego. He was impatient and demanding. Chances are good that he had trouble

---

### Are You a TMA Leader?

*Instructions:* Check all that apply.

I USUALLY . . .

___jump on any opportunity to grow and change.

___expect to be respected and admired.

___remind people often that their jobs are on the line.

___feel tense or frustrated.

___get overly impatient with others and do things myself.

___go out of my way to see that things are done right.

___wear my emotions on my sleeve.

___have a combative, argumentative disposition.

___question others' motives.

___worry about being taken advantage of.

*Results:* Count your checkmarks.

- 0–3: You do not have too much anxiety.
- 4–6: You are leaning toward too much anxiety.
- 7+: You are solidly planted in too much anxiety.

tolerating limitations in others because he couldn't accept limitations in himself. Either he was blind to the impact of his actions on others, or he didn't care. He was so driven by his desire for success—and probably his fear of failure—that he had to win at all costs. His impossible goals and explosive temperament created an environment of excessive stress and fear.

Most of us are all too familiar with too much anxiety (TMA). Today's complex world makes it difficult to avoid. But some leaders are vulnerable to making TMA a habit for themselves and their organizations.

Leaders with too much anxiety are compelled to take charge. Seduced by change, they will do just about anything to get what they want. Consummate fighters, they focus their personal power on making things turn out their way. But their take-charge demeanor masks deep-seated insecurities.

The problem is that TMA leaders are overly attached to success. Whether they think they have to be exact and right, powerful, or in control, their obsessions drive their behavior and create unhealthy energy around them. Behind their attachments is fear—the fear of inadequacy, failure, insignificance, or being taken advantage of.

TMA leaders often come from families that push hard for success. Their parents may have been successful themselves. Or they may have been hypercritical of their children's efforts as they were growing up. To TMA people, achievement is the name of the game. Life is about proving their capabilities to the world, as well as to themselves. Ironically, their drive for success blinds them to reality. It traps them in outdated mental models and blunts their learning and development. And it keeps them from attaining the acclaim they seek.

Emotionally, TMA leaders are out of touch with themselves. They often are deluded about their own capabilities and how others perceive them. Inside, they are frequently held hostage by their emotions—particularly anxiety, anger, sadness, and fear. Yet they wear their feelings on their sleeves. Their emotional transparency is the problem: They bring their inner chaotic energy to everyone around them. And their self-centeredness prohibits them from feeling empathy or compassion for others.

TMA leaders wage a constant battle against uncertainty. They attack change and push themselves and others through gap after gap to achieve

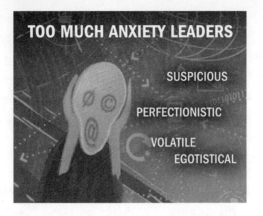

their goals. Their preoccupation with success keeps them focused on problems often to the point of exhaustion. There's no time for rest and relaxation. Forget learning. Living in the gap helps TMA leaders feel good about themselves. It proves they're on the road to success.

TMA leaders look like energetic Titans. But while they appear to be on top of things, they are unknowingly undermining their own success. Since much of their energy is negative, TMA leaders end up sabotaging their organization's achievements. They simply demand too much and give too little.

Let's look at four different ways that leaders exhibit too much anxiety. You may see yourself, your boss, or others in these sets of behaviors. We all act out our anxiety at some times and in some circumstances. But TMA leaders live here.

### Egotistical Leaders

Egotistical leaders want the world to revolve around them. They are driven by two needs: to be admired and to protect themselves from their feelings of inadequacy. Typically, they see themselves as the stars of the show. Dynamic and persuasive, they often are the stars. Their strong sense of self attracts many followers. And they're usually good at what they do.

But their inflated view of their talents and importance leads them astray. I know one egotistical leader whose opinion of himself grew distorted over time. He had a great vision for the company, but he imposed more and more unrealistic expectations on others, as well as on himself. Quick to point out others' errors, he refused to be accountable for his own mistakes. He belittled the ideas of others. And he never backed down in a fight. Eventually, he insulted or disempowered every person he needed to help him succeed.

Egotistical leaders like this feel they deserve special treatment. Unable to recognize their own weaknesses, they can't tolerate weakness in others. Or they surround themselves with ineffective people to reinforce their egos. Because they are so wrapped up in themselves, they are unconcerned about how their actions affect the people around them.

### Egotistical Leaders

| How Others See Them | What They Say | How They Impact Their Organizations |
|---|---|---|
| • Arrogant<br>• Dismissive<br>• Pretentious<br>• Self-absorbed<br>• Entitled | • We'll go with my idea.<br>• You should have done it this way.<br>• I'm responsible for making this happen. | • Top performers have no chance to shine.<br>• Creativity and participation are stifled.<br>• Resentment and frustration fill the organization and drown out productive energy. |

Egotistical leaders get hijacked by their desire for attention. The good news is that most people can see beyond their facade. The bad news is that these TMA leaders can do a lot of damage in a position of power—making people feel insignificant and zapping the productive energy of an entire organization.

## Perfectionistic Leaders

Perfectionistic leaders try to orchestrate the way the world works. Driven by the fear of failure, of making a mistake, or of not being good enough, they are accomplished micromanagers. Their attention to detail is a great asset. Indeed, it's often a sought-after quality—one to which some of us aspire. But it can become a debilitating obsession that sacrifices the big picture for irrelevant minutiae.

Perfectionistic leaders work long hours and expect others to do the same. There's always a right way to do things, and anything that deviates from what's expected produces a high level of anxiety. Consider the leader I know who nearly collapsed trying to keep up with the pace of change in her organization by taking care of everything herself. Her desire to be precise and make all the right decisions eventually drove her, and most of her people, over the edge.

Getting involved in every detail is how perfectionistic leaders manage their uncertainty. It helps to reduce their anxiety, or so they think. The downside—and it's a big one—is that micromanaging takes more time than leaders have. And since there's no such thing as perfect, it's both a losing battle and a surefire path to exhaustion.

### Perfectionistic Leaders

| How Others See Them | What They Say | How They Impact Their Organizations |
|---|---|---|
| • Obsessive<br>• Intrusive<br>• Mistrusting<br>• Overcontrolling<br>• Rigid | • I need a little more time.<br>• Let me take one more pass at this.<br>• Can we agree on how we're going to proceed? | • Creative, take-charge people feel suffocated.<br>• Too much time and resources are dedicated to unnecessary activities.<br>• Impeded work flows cause delays and missed deadlines. |

Perfectionistic leaders get hijacked by their fear of not living up to their own expectations. Their intense demands of themselves and others actually increase, rather than reduce, their anxiety. In turn, this demoralizes people, saps everyone's energy, and lowers productivity.

### Volatile Leaders

Volatile leaders believe it's just them against the world. They are driven by the desire to win, at any cost. Coming in second is unacceptable. So they wield their power like an emotional saber, cutting down whatever or whoever gets in their way. They make decisions solely to further their own interests, letting the consequences fall where they may.

It's likely that volatile leaders were once highly emotional children. They probably grew up in families where the loudest or most angry person ruled the day. Where kind words were rarely spoken and where gentleness was considered a weakness.

On an emotional level, volatile leaders are usually "all over the place." They may be angry one day and sullen the next. They may blow up in meetings. Or refuse to comment at all. Or they may use the threat of their anger to demean and manipulate people.

One leader I know sets impossible goals for people and then criticizes them when they fall short of reaching those goals. He is often disrespectful of other points of view and thinks nothing of ridiculing employees in front of their colleagues. People, he believes, are motivated by fear, and it's his job to push them. He likes catching people off guard. Surprisingly, this same leader can be charming and inspiring. An engaging presenter, he often speaks on various business topics. But his unpredictability makes him difficult to work with—people never know what to expect.

## Volatile Leaders

| How Others See Them | What They Say | How They Impact Their Organizations |
|---|---|---|
| • Abusive<br>• Dangerous<br>• High maintenance<br>• Manipulative<br>• Unpredictable | • That's the worst idea I have ever heard.<br>• You're wrong.<br>• Are you with me or against me? | • Constant tension causes mistakes and distracts people from doing a good job.<br>• Morale and productivity suffer.<br>• Loyalty becomes a thing of the past as people leave for more nurturing jobs. |

Volatile leaders get hijacked by their fear of looking weak or ineffective. Combined with their need to win, this makes them highly unpredictable and creates an unstable work environment. Often, the only way to be heard is to become volatile as well.

## Suspicious Leaders

Suspicious leaders are mistrustful of the world around them. Their own suspicious nature leads them to believe that people are inherently dishonest.

Given the chance, they think, people will take advantage of them. They must be ever vigilant. So they're always questioning others' intentions and motives.

Relationships are hotbeds of contention for suspicious leaders. Nobody can be trusted, even people they've known for a long time. I met an entrepreneur years ago whose suspicions kept him up at night. Struggling to survive in a highly competitive industry, he constantly worried about who was plotting what. How could he be sure his people would remain loyal? Were his suppliers being straight with him?

On the job, this leader provoked arguments with customers, partners, and suppliers by accusing them of wrongdoing. He also developed strict policies and procedures to protect the company and inspected people's work on a regular basis. Some of his systems were actually quite effective, while others just added unnecessary paperwork.

## Suspicious Leaders

| How Others See Them | What They Say | How They Impact Their Organizations |
|---|---|---|
| • Calculating<br>• Controlling<br>• Paranoid<br>• Sneaky<br>• Untrustworthy | • Why are you doing that?<br>• How can I be sure you're telling me the truth?<br>• I want you to sign this agreement. | • The work environment is one of mistrust and deception.<br>• Information is withheld or selectively shared.<br>• People's anger and insecurity distracts them from their work. |

Leaders like this assume that everyone thinks and behaves the way they do. They're comfortable blurring the truth, to themselves or anyone else, and routinely deny or cover up their own mistakes. Some even travel unethical roads to get where they want to go. After all, the end justifies the means, right?

Suspicious leaders are hijacked by their mistrust. They project it outward, and it comes back, full circle. Notoriously untrustworthy themselves, suspicious leaders create a culture where distrust, accusation, and deception are the norm.

---

## Do You Work in a TMA Organization?

*Instructions:* Check all that apply.

MY ORGANIZATION . . .

\_\_\_seems to be in the middle of a crisis all the time.

\_\_\_has a large gap between where it is and where it wants to be.

\_\_\_makes me feel incompetent.

\_\_\_has increasingly low levels of productivity.

\_\_\_turns everything into problems.

\_\_\_makes a lot of mistakes.

\_\_\_suffers from low morale.

\_\_\_uses fear to motivate people.

\_\_\_stretches people too far beyond their capabilities.

\_\_\_punishes people for errors and failures.

*Results:* Count your checkmarks.

- 0–3: Your organization does not have too much anxiety.
- 4–6: Your organization is leaning toward too much anxiety.
- 7+: Your organization is solidly planted in too much anxiety.

---

They called him "Chainsaw Al." Famous for turning around troubled companies—he had driven Scott Paper Company shares up 225 percent in eighteen months—Albert J. Dunlap was supposed to be Sunbeam's salvation when he took over as CEO in 1996. Instead, his TMA leadership style nearly upended the company.

Dunlap's volatile nature was evident from the beginning. At his first meeting with the board, the new CEO acted like a bull elephant trying to establish his position in the herd. He shouted. He threatened. He ranted and raged. Sunbeam had too many people, too many products, and too much overhead, screamed Dunlap. And he would change all that.

Dunlap made massive cuts. He eliminated half of Sunbeam's 6,000 employees and 87 percent of its products. He dropped essential functions and let skilled workers go. At the same time, he demanded impossible results. He gave generous stock options to entice people to stick it out, but, with insufficient resources to get the job done, things went from bad to worse.

At least that's what was happening on the inside. On the outside, Dunlap charmed analysts into believing in the impossible. Stock prices began to rise. It looked like Dunlap's egotism and abusive behavior were the price of success.

But success was short-lived. Software problems soon led to the company's inability to bill customers. Dunlap's outsourcing ended up costing more than the company had been paying for workers in-house. The company couldn't operate effectively. Shortfalls began to appear, as did the practice of booking future sales in the present—an apparent attempt to make things look better than they were. Key executives began leaving.

Dunlap reportedly ignored warnings that Sunbeam was facing a gap of nearly $81 million in the second quarter of 1998. Things were so bad that the company was meeting payroll with revolving credit. The board, worried that the company could default on its loans, met behind closed doors in June 1998. They discovered that the actual projected revenue gap could be a whopping $200 million.

Dunlap's turbulent reign ended in June 1998 when the board fired him—by telephone. Since then, Dunlap has paid $15 million to settle his portion of a class-action suit filed by Sunbeam shareholders. He is barred from ever serving as an officer or director of a public company. Sunbeam itself struggled for years to regain its market position, emerging from bankruptcy court in late 2006.

Although I've never spoken to Al Dunlap, I believe his behavior speaks for itself. He's a great example of a TMA leader. Sunbeam employees say he was *volatile* to the point of near-violence and *egotistical* to the end. He used his temper to get what he wanted, with no concern for the people he verbally abused. In fact, he reportedly told people to be grateful for what they had at Sunbeam—what *he* had given them. Dunlap created an atmosphere of mistrust, fear, and negative energy.

Ask yourself . . .

- Do I lean toward TLA or TMA under stress?
- Which type(s) of TLA or TMA leaders am I most like at my worst?
- What kinds of situations bring out the worst in me?

# JUST ENOUGH ANXIETY: THE FACE OF SUCCESS

*A loving person lives in a loving world. A hostile person lives in a hostile world. Everyone you meet is your mirror.*

—KEN KEYES JR., *Handbook to Higher Consciousness*

What do you see when you look in the mirror? Do you see the face of complacency? The face of fear? Or do you see the face of success? You've probably seen all three at different times in your life.

We all lean toward too little or too much anxiety under stress. Our genetic makeup, personal development, life experiences, and beliefs and expectations combine to define how we handle change and uncertainty. Some of us are drawn repeatedly into too much anxiety. Others of us gravitate toward too little. Nobody remains in the middle all the time.

Your goal as a leader is to maintain your balance. Getting diverted from the middle way for too long has dramatic consequences for your organization. Too little anxiety produces ineffective energy, which leads to gradual decline. Too much anxiety generates chaotic energy, which leads to sporadic decline. Only just enough anxiety creates the productive energy you need to achieve sustainable growth.

To be a JEA leader, you need to know when you're moving toward too little or too much anxiety and make a quick course correction back to the center. To do this, you need to be self-aware and to understand how you are affecting others. And you need to know what attitudes and behaviors you can strengthen to get back to JEA. The table below outlines what you need to focus on to bring yourself back into balance the next time you find yourself leaning too far into too little or too much anxiety.

Finding your way back from too little or too much anxiety is a task done repeatedly—not a once-and-done deal. Yet each rebound gets a little easier, because you begin to understand what works. You know what you need to do. Doing it, however, takes patience, persistence, and a good sense of humor.

Rand Construction Corporation founder Linda Rabbitt is a real JEA leader. Her deep awareness of herself and other people enables Linda to see things for what they are, while envisioning what they can be. She has both an open mind and an open heart. She understands the role anxiety

| If you are being . . . | You need to find the balance between . . . |
|---|---|
| IDEALISTIC | remaining positive and optimistic *and* looking reality straight in the eye |
| DETACHED | being logical and objective about the business *and* making deep emotional connections with your employees and customers |
| OVERPLEASING | participating as a team player *and* standing up for yourself and your beliefs |
| CAUTIOUS | maintaining stability and making prudent decisions *and* taking risks and being innovative |
| EGOTISTICAL | acting with pride and confidence, *and* being humble enough to listen and learn from others |
| PERFECTIONISTIC | striving for excellence *and* accepting imperfection in yourself and the people around you |
| VOLATILE | remaining competitive and achievement-oriented *and* respecting the needs and concerns of others |
| SUSPICIOUS | protecting yourself and your organization's assets *and* demonstrating trust and trustworthiness |

plays in her life and the power of just enough anxiety to maximize growth and performance—in herself and others.

"I'm willing to live with a lot of uncertainty in the quest for being better tomorrow than I was yesterday," Linda admits. She learned this from her parents, who believed in constantly raising the bar in order to accomplish something and make a difference. "Yesterday, my eighty-one-year-old mother said to me, 'I just didn't accomplish anything today.' I said, 'Mother, you're eighty-one. What are you trying to accomplish?'" It's easy to see that the apple doesn't fall too far from the tree.

Yet aware that her high expectations can create anxiety for others, Linda constantly monitors the anxiety in her organization. "If I see certain behaviors happening around here, I can pretty much predict what's going on and what I need to fix." She then helps people manage their anxiety by listening to them, openly acknowledging their accomplishments, and letting them know about her own frailties. "If I set the bar really high, and I look and act like I'm perfect, it doesn't do anyone any good. I have to be human. So I tell stories about ways that I've failed. When you have high expectations, you're not going to always achieve them. Sometimes you're going to fall on your face."

This kind of honesty, combined with her public praise of people's best efforts, buys Linda the freedom to raise the bar whenever she needs to. "It gives me the moral authority to privately stick my foot up somebody's rear end when I have to. That's really how we achieve the balance and create just enough anxiety."

Being a JEA leader is all about balance. It's about balancing between too much and too little anxiety. It's about balancing between being nice and being tough. And it's about balancing two opposing views at the same time, taking the middle way—what I call living in paradox.

JEA leaders are masters at living in paradox. In fact, their ability to master three key paradoxes helps them become JEA leaders and create just enough anxiety throughout their organizations. In the next three chapters, we will look closely at each of these paradoxes, and I will introduce you to extraordinary leaders who are bringing them to life.

# 5

# REALISTIC OPTIMISM

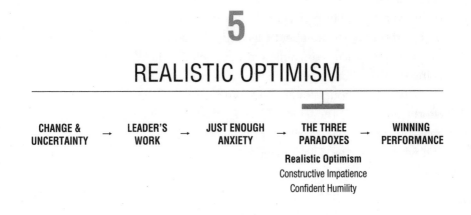

| CHANGE & UNCERTAINTY | → | LEADER'S WORK | → | JUST ENOUGH ANXIETY | → | THE THREE PARADOXES | → | WINNING PERFORMANCE |

**Realistic Optimism**
Constructive Impatience
Confident Humility

An expectant silence fills the room as the maestro steps up to the podium. It's as if everyone is holding their breath. He raises both arms. Every orchestra member sits at attention, instrument ready, eyes fixed on the man holding the baton. With a single downstroke, the concert hall erupts into the unmistakable opening refrain of Beethoven's Fifth Symphony.

When Jimmy DePriest conducts the Oregon Symphony, he is actually standing in two places at the same time. He is the imposing figure at the podium, paying attention to every instrument and directing every note. And he is also the observer in his own mind, imagining the music as Beethoven meant it to be played.

"This goes on simultaneously," Jimmy says, "and I'm changing the performance based upon the feedback I'm getting from the orchestra. Where is it falling short? Where is it exceeding expectations?" By constantly comparing the actual with the ideal, he creates an exceptional performance.

The six-foot-three conductor accomplishes this task over and over again by balancing contradictions. He hears the "future" performance in his mind, while attending to the reality of the moment. He pushes orchestra members to perform at the top of their game while making it safe for them to stretch and grow. And, baton in hand, he leads with confidence and power while humbly listening to and learning from his musicians.

Jimmy DePriest exemplifies what it means to live in paradox. By standing in two places at the same time, he transforms the notes from more than one hundred instruments into an enchanting musical experience for every member of the audience. It's enough to make you believe in magic.

## THE POWER OF PARADOX

*The most fruitful developments frequently take place at those points where two different lines of thought meet.*

—WERNER HEISENBERG, twentieth-century German physicist
and Nobel Laureate

A paradox exists when two opposing ideas contain equal power or truth. Both are real and have merit. And yet they contradict each other—like good and evil or right and wrong.

The notion of paradox dates back thousands of years. Ancient Chinese philosophy talks about yin and yang—two opposing but complementary principles found in all elements in the universe. All the opposites we experience—health and sickness, wealth and poverty, power and submission—are due to the temporary dominance of one principle, as they toggle back and forth.

In fact, the very existence of its opposite validates each side of a paradox. You can't have winning without losing or pleasure without pain. The two are interdependent and their relative strength is always changing. Night turns into day. Happiness is replaced by sadness. Success is stalked by failure.

What does this have to do with leadership? How can knowing about paradoxes help you create just enough anxiety for yourself and your organization?

Think about it. Businesses are constantly moving back and forth between opposing conditions. We strive to cut costs *and* increase revenues, improve quality *and* efficiency, and challenge *and* inspire people—all at the same time. Plus, we watch the pendulum swing between growth and decline. We're on top for a while and then find ourselves struggling to keep up with the competition.

If the world were static, we could effectively live and lead from a single point of view. But in an uncertain world, life and business are more complicated, and conditions are constantly changing. As leaders, we need to develop attitudes and actions that reflect multiple, even contradictory, points of view. We need to develop a "both/and" instead of an "either/or" mind-set.

Your success as a leader depends on your ability to assess where you are *and* envision where you're going. You need to act with certainty on what you know *and* be open to new learning and course corrections. You need to be authoritative *and* collaborative.

But living in paradox is tough. It requires that we live in the gap where anxiety resides. So to ease our anxiety, we tend to gravitate to one side of the paradoxes in our lives.

Take me for example. I'm an ambitious guy, some would say driven. I like to control my own destiny. People describe me as strong, confident, and self-sufficient. But I'm also sensitive and emotional. I have a strong desire for making deep, intimate connections. I'm compassionate and generous. And I'm no stranger to feeling humble, confused, and vulnerable.

I kept these "hard" and "soft" sides of myself separate for years. Like most men, I showed only half of who I am to the world. The rest I kept hidden or shared only with close friends and family. Still, I often felt like one person on the inside and another on the outside.

The truth is that for a long time I didn't even let myself experience the real, whole me. But I came to realize the importance of embracing— and expressing—all of myself, in my personal life and my business. This created just enough anxiety in me, and that's a good thing. I am a strong, intense, ambitious, and successful man who is also warm, compassionate, loving, and vulnerable. Like everyone else on the planet, I am a paradox.

Hanging out on only one side of a paradox is self-defeating. You limit your possibilities just like I did when I hid half of my true self. You undermine your leadership capabilities, as well as your performance, and hamper your ability to deal with the complexity of human behavior and business problems. You think too narrowly and deplete your energy as you work hard to defend yourself from people sitting on the other side.

Do you ever try to justify an either/or point of view? For example, do you think like a Republican or a Democrat? Do you promote economic growth or environmental responsibility? Are you for or against gay marriage? Whatever viewpoint you may argue, you probably feel a degree of tension between yourself and your opponent. When these conflicting points of view are in your own mind, which they often are, you feel a similar tension—what psychologists call *cognitive dissonance*. Whether it's external or internal, this tension is uncomfortable.

JEA leaders are comfortable living with this tension. In fact, it gives them a definite competitive advantage. They expand their options and gain power from entertaining two opposing views at the same time. In their minds, one plus one equals three.

As I've traveled around the world, I've observed that JEA leaders see, think, and act in very specific ways. They lead from the center of three key paradoxes: *realistic optimism, constructive impatience,* and *confident humility.*

Each of these leadership paradoxes exists on a continuum, as shown below. At one extreme are leaders who are idealistic, complacent, or self-doubting. They possess too little anxiety and create ineffective energy in their organizations. At the other extreme are leaders who are cynical, careless, or arrogant. They take on too much anxiety and create a chaotic environment in their organizations.

JEA leaders find their power in the center. Because they live with just enough anxiety, they are able to be optimistic *and* realistic, constructive *and* impatient, and humble *and* confident. As a result, they spur innovation, build winning companies, and consistently outperform their competitors.

In these next three chapters we will look closely at these three leadership paradoxes. You will see how your ability to master each paradox enables you to unleash productive energy inside your organization for

## THREE LEADERSHIP PARADOXES

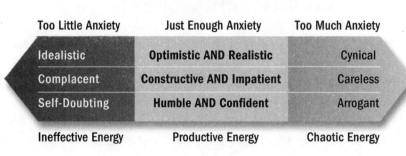

| Too Little Anxiety | Just Enough Anxiety | Too Much Anxiety |
|---|---|---|
| Idealistic | Optimistic AND Realistic | Cynical |
| Complacent | Constructive AND Impatient | Careless |
| Self-Doubting | Humble AND Confident | Arrogant |
| Ineffective Energy | Productive Energy | Chaotic Energy |

sustainable, profitable growth. You will gain insight into your own abilities and you will find ways to strengthen your skills.

Here's how it works. You start by developing an open mind and an open heart. This enables you to experience just enough anxiety within yourself. Your capacity to harness your anxiety enables you to live in a world of paradox. By mastering the three leadership paradoxes, you create just enough anxiety for others. This energizes people to perform at their best. And it all starts with you.

Let's dive right into the first paradox: *realistic optimism*. Living and leading in this paradox involves telling the truth about the present while dreaming the future. It is how JEA leaders keep moving forward in a world that keeps changing. Let's take a closer look at each part of this paradox.

## TELLING THE TRUTH

*Most companies don't face reality very well. That's the basic reason they can't execute.*

—LARRY BOSSIDY AND RAM CHARAN, *Execution*

| Too Little Anxiety | Just Enough Anxiety | Too Much Anxiety |
|:---:|:---:|:---:|
| Idealistic | Optimistic AND Realistic | Cynical |
| Ineffective Energy | Productive Energy | Chaotic Energy |

Being realistic is all about seeking and speaking the truth—for yourself and others. It starts with being honest about who you are: your strengths and shortcomings, hopes and fears, triumphs and failures. It involves knowing how people see you, and how you affect them. In fact, truth telling encompasses everything you say and do.

JEA leaders take time to look into their own motives and beliefs. They ask for feedback and are not afraid of what they will hear. They listen deeply to what people say, while observing their behavior, picking up on their feelings, and assessing their intentions.

JEA leaders are transparent. Their honesty makes them credible, dependable, and predictable. They build trust. People know they can count on these leaders to tell it like it is and to follow through on their commitments. To JEA leaders, their word is their bond.

---

### How to Build Trust in Your Organization

- Tell the truth.
- Keep your promises.
- Avoid surprising people with bad news.
- Work for the common good.
- Honor people's values and feelings.
- Express confidence in people's abilities.
- Be your true, whole self at work.
- Gather data about what's really going on.

---

People differ in their ability to be truthful. Some speak bluntly and expect the same in return. Some are open and honest, but want others to be more indirect. Some are indirect in their communication, but like others to give it to them straight. A few verge on cruelty in the name of honesty.

Some people are simply afraid of the truth. They're concerned that confronting reality will mean admitting mistakes. It will involve facing limitations or not having answers. It will lead to disappointment. Most of all, they worry, reality will interfere with their self-image or wreak havoc with the image they want the world to see.

Leaders who fear the truth frequently fail to look long or hard enough at their businesses, and they pay a high price. Without a clear, honest understanding of what's real, they miss critical information, misjudge trends, or overlook changing customer demands. They underestimate the competition. They gloss over their moneymaking process and miscalculate their financial targets against the environments in which they operate. They overlook problems. Or they delude themselves into thinking they are in better shape than they are. Their ignorance-is-bliss attitude, combined with the high level of anxiety that drives it, can have catastrophic consequences.

At the other end of the realistic spectrum is cynicism. Cynical leaders get swallowed up by the reality of the moment. They are crisis-driven and short-sighted problem solvers. Stuck in a cave of their own making, they can't see the world around them. Instead, they see *only* problems and overreact to negatives in their organizations. Overwhelmed by too much anxiety, they live in fear of risk and failure.

Many cynical leaders see the cup as half empty and are unable to imagine possibilities or inspire others. They micromanage almost everything and frequently engage in reckless cost cutting to manage their own anxiety. These actions create too much anxiety in others. People around them are in constant fear, never knowing where they're headed or whether everything will fall apart tomorrow.

JEA leaders are neither afraid of the truth nor cynical about it. They continually assess their strategy, financial targets, and customer base, as well as their operating margins, cash flow, and talent. They face problems and opportunities head-on and look at all sides of an issue—seeing things as they are, not as they want them to be. They know that being honest with themselves and others is an act of courage. And it's the only way to run a business in a world of uncertainty.

Two billion times a day, Procter & Gamble brands like Crest, Charmin, Folgers, and Pringles touch the lives of people around the world. Nearly 140,000 employees make the company's 300 brands live up to their promise to make everyday life just a little better, for people in more than 180 countries.

How does CEO Alan Lafley make sure this happens? He digs for the truth. "At the company level, we have a very simple strategy that has the whole company's goals, objectives, strategies, and measures all on one page. Every quarter, my leadership group goes through and asks how we're doing. We track item by item, year by year, business by business. And we track by color: red is off track, yellow is heading to track but not yet on track, and green is on track. Then we go through and discuss them," he explains. "We spend thirty seconds on the greens; we spend a lot of time on the reds."

If there's a gap in any unit, Alan and his team confront it head-on. "So let's say we have a red one, say our Philippines business is off track. The guy who is the responsible leader for that business says, 'I've got a problem, here's how big it is, this is why we think we have it, here are the resources that I need to resolve it, and this is why I need help.' We try to get all the connections going to mobilize resources so we can work on it."

Simple, but not so easy. Especially with twenty business units—from household and beauty products to pet food and diapers—in eighty countries. "Each team has an action plan, including when the action will be completed and what the measurable result will be. Same system all the way down through the company."

The way Alan sees it, the truth sets people free. "People will perform better if they know what the mission is, what their role is, and how they'll know when they've completed it. It's not rocket science. Some say, 'Well, gee, that's awfully controlling.' And I say it isn't controlling at all, it's liberating. We don't tell them how to do it. We just agree on what to do. And if all those 'whats' are achieved, they add up to good business units running successfully. Then they add up to good sectors running successfully. And they add up to our company's success."

Here's a guy whose commitment to simplicity and execution makes it next to impossible to hide the truth—what's really going on inside the business. By monitoring closely where the business is at any point in time, and tackling the tough issues head-on, P&G consistently outexecutes the competition.

Ask yourself . . .

- Am I inherently realistic or cynical?
- What more can I do to communicate openly and honestly?
- How committed am I to seeking and speaking the truth?

## DREAMING THE FUTURE

*I could not accomplish anything if I did not have hope within me; for the gift of hope is as big a gift as the gift of life itself.*

—VÁCLAV HAVEL, first president of the Czech Republic

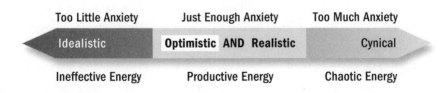

| Too Little Anxiety | Just Enough Anxiety | Too Much Anxiety |
|---|---|---|
| Idealistic | Optimistic AND Realistic | Cynical |
| Ineffective Energy | Productive Energy | Chaotic Energy |

Being optimistic is all about dreaming the future. It's about believing that tomorrow will be better than today. If you're optimistic, you see the glass half full. And you know you can refill it, even if it appears to be leaking.

Optimism starts with your belief in yourself and your ability to change for the better. It means believing that people have control over their fate and can master their environment. According to studies in science and medicine, these beliefs are contributing factors in our success, and even our health.

It's all about hope. Hope engages and excites people about what's possible. It motivates and mobilizes human energy. It enables people to believe in themselves and gives them a reason to perform their best, day after day, month after month, and year after year.

Without hope, we drown in everyday problems. We live in darkness, unable to see the light ahead. Eventually, we succumb to doubt and fear. In contrast, our hope allows us to rebound after difficulties. Hope puts smiles on our faces, even in the midst of a major crisis.

JEA leaders articulate hope. They exude optimism. And they possess an extraordinary capacity for dreaming—and creating—the future. To JEA leaders, problems are temporary and fixable. They envision positive results, essentially seeing the end from the beginning. Plus, they see and bring out the best in people. They build collective visions that inspire people to do their best to turn those visions into reality.

Some leaders are unable or unwilling to dream the future. They may have encountered too many insurmountable difficulties in their lives. They may have learned early on to avoid disappointment by striving for too little. Or they may just believe that there's no need to change anything—that what worked in the past will continue to work in the future. In each case, their fear of failure drives them to keep their expectations low. They set easy-to-reach goals. They tolerate mediocre performance. To them, success is about averting catastrophe.

On the other hand, it's possible to aim too high. Optimism, without a dose of realism, leads to idealistic thinking. Leaders who operate at this level boast of grandiose dreams that have little basis in objective reality. They underestimate problems. They overestimate their abilities.

Often quite charming, even charismatic, idealistic leaders strive to get others to join them in their fantasy worlds. They readily dismiss anything or anyone contradicting their ideals. By setting goals that don't make sense—or by reaching well beyond their organization's capabilities and resources—these leaders lose their credibility and the loyalty of their people. Their ideal visions become grand delusions.

Whether they believe that all is well or dream of a grand future, these leaders live and lead with too little anxiety. They also create too little anxiety for anyone who buys what they're selling. Those who follow them are implicitly agreeing to close their eyes to trouble, to see only the positive side of things. However, those who don't buy in, who see the reality of the world around them, may experience too much anxiety in their presence.

The optimism of JEA leaders illuminates possibilities, generates positive emotions, and creates just enough anxiety. Because they live in a world full of options, JEA leaders are comfortable with ambiguity, uncertainty, and unpredictability. They envision success. They are confident and courageous, willing to feel vulnerable as they navigate through the unknown.

In a small village in Bangladesh, a young woman who has next to nothing uses a small loan to buy a cow. She repays the loan by selling the cow's milk and then buys a small calf. Then, she dares the impossible. She takes out a second loan to build a house with a tin roof. Her next goal: a cell phone.

Who is making this possible? Muhammad Yunus, father of the microcredit movement, founder of Grameen Bank, and breaker of all the rules of traditional finance. I met with Muhammad several years ago in New York City, before he and Grameen won the Nobel Peace Prize "for their efforts to create economic and social development from below."

Muhammad is a man with a compelling vision. He is driving social change one rupee at a time. Through Grameen Bank, he is unleashing possibilities by enhancing people's self-esteem and putting systems in place that allow them to succeed. The result: a 98 percent loan repayment rate in the poorest nations in the world.

"All human beings are basically entrepreneurs," notes Muhammad. "People want to solve problems, take on challenges, and discover their talents. It's just a matter of opening up the environment and giving them opportunity.

"We're all capable of doing much more. It's institutions and concepts that limit us and keep us down. We're almost like a bonsai tree, a tiny plant kept tiny because of the way we're planted. If we had a better place, we would be tall and reaching for the sky."

Muhammad Yunus has proven his theory in the most difficult of environments, where paying back loans is countercultural and lending money to women is unheard of. "We wanted to lend to the poorest first; that's why our borrowers are 97 percent women. When they succeed, their families benefit. The wealth trickles down."

Grameen Bank requires borrowers to organize into groups of five. Instead of providing collateral, the borrowers guarantee one another's loans. They become human collateral—if one defaults, they all lose. If one wins, they all win. As a result, the bank has no need to pressure borrowers. Accountability lives inside people's heads and in the spaces between them. Borrowers motivate themselves and each other—the epitome of high-performance teams.

Today, with a staff of just over 22,000, Grameen operates more than 2,400 branches in more than 78,000 villages—more than 93 percent of all Bangladesh villages. Its success is being replicated by more than 250 institutions in nearly a hundred countries. Since its beginning, the bank has given out more than $6 billion to more than 7 million people. "These millions of small people," says Muhammad, "with their millions of small pursuits, add up to the biggest development wonder in the world.

"We have started believing the unbelievable. There is no reason anyone should remain poor on this planet. Success breeds success."

There's a profound lesson in the work of Muhammad Yunus and Grameen Bank. If people in Bangladesh and other impoverished countries can rise above their so-called limitations, people everywhere can do the same. No leader, company, or nation can say it's impossible to unleash the human potential with which they've been entrusted. Every individual in every factory, office, and city can be a leader on his or her own stage.

Ask yourself . . .

- Am I inherently optimistic or fearful?
- How much control do I believe people have over their lives?
- What more can I do to empower the people around me?

## REALISTIC OPTIMISM IN ACTION

*The foremost challenge for leaders today is to maintain the clarity to stand confidently in the abundant universe of possibility.*
—ROSAMUND STONE ZANDER AND BENJAMIN ZANDER, *The Art of Possibility*

Realism and optimism are each powerful qualities in their own right. Combining them, however, creates something very special. It enhances your power exponentially. It's like a chemical reaction in which two elements produce a potent third result. When you master realistic optimism, you create just enough anxiety to generate productive energy and drive your organization forward.

Let's see what lessons we can learn about this catalytic process from three JEA leaders. What effect does their realistic optimism have on oil, yogurt, and accounting?

### Think in the Present and Future Simultaneously

"In order to survive in this business, you have to be an optimist. If you can't demonstrate there's a positive future, you can't be effective." So says Dave O'Reilly, chairman and CEO of Chevron Corporation.

"It's important for the organization to know that we're working on the future: getting the right access to future energy supplies, and developing the technology to find sources of energy we couldn't find before. For example, we're working on a big gas project in Australia now. It started in the late 1980s. We haven't started production there yet. We'll probably start in 2010 or 2011. But once it starts, the project will be producing gas for a long time—maybe until the end of this century."

But optimism alone isn't enough. "At the same time, you need to demonstrate urgency. The majority of our people are working on delivering what people want today. They're the ones actually extracting the oil, transporting it, converting it, and shipping it to the customer.

"I like to set deadlines for them and be clear about when we expect to get things done. We never leave a meeting of the management team without agreeing to our goals and deadlines for achieving them.

"I don't think there's a conflict between being optimistic and realistic. But there's a big difference between the two," says Dave.

---

### Tips for Being Realistic and Optimistic

- Be flexible yet focused about what you want.
- Balance achieving goals with discovering them.
- Be aware and wary about what you know.
- Balance facts and figures with imagination.
- Be objective and optimistic about what you believe.
- Balance reality testing with wishful thinking.
- Be practical and magical in what you do.

---

### Have the Courage to Dream and Deliver

"Don't let folks tell you it can't be done. There's always a way if you believe in it enough." These are the words of Gary Hirschberg, the founder and CEO of Stonyfield Farm, an organic yogurt company based in rural New Hampshire. Over the course of twenty years, Gary turned $500 and seven Jersey cows into a $250 million organic yogurt business with a compounded annual growth rate of nearly 27 percent.

A passionate dreamer, Hirschberg also understands that the day-to-day realities of business have to be faced head-on. And he knows that reality can be harsh. Quoting Lily Tomlin, he quips, "'Reality is the leading cause of stress for those who are in touch with it.' There's nothing easy about business, and I struggle every single day. One principle that works for me is to be brutally honest about what's going on—what we do well and what we don't do well, and where our work is still unfinished."

This ability to balance optimism and realism is at the heart of Gary's success. And he does more than just talk about his ideals. He demonstrates his desire to make the world a better place in the way he does business on a daily basis. As he puts it, "When we talk about reducing carbon emissions, we're actually doing it. When we talk about organics and saving family farmers, we're actually doing it. When we talk about donating to environmental causes, we're actually doing it."

Gary's commitment to his mission, and his courage to play by different rules, have resulted in remarkable customer loyalty and a growing market share. Stonyfield is now the third-largest-selling yogurt brand in the United States, and the largest organic yogurt producer in the world. In 2001, the company formed a strategic partnership with the French-based company Groupe Danone, which opened a global door for the yogurt maker. The deal demonstrates realistic optimism at its best. Gary held out for a controlling partner that would allow him autonomous leadership of Stonyfield, while providing the global distribution capabilities the company needed. Not bad for a company built on a dream, a handful of cash, and a few cows.

## Trust Yourself to Create Your Own Destiny

Just ask Dennis Nally at PricewaterhouseCoopers about the power of realistic optimism. When the well-established audit and consulting firm was upended by changes in accounting standards, the anxiety throughout the organization was palpable. It was Dennis's job to help people face the reality of the situation, while painting a picture of the future that would inspire them to even greater heights. By doing both, Dennis laid a foundation of trust on which a new PwC could be built.

In a profession marked by predictability, uniformity, and control, change can be threatening. To turn people's anxiety into productive energy, Dennis had to understand where people were. Then he had to help them reframe how they looked at change. He did both.

"Change creates anxiety. It creates uncertainty," he told me. "And those are not good, natural feelings for most people. I'd say most people long for stability, predictability. They think, 'Boy, wouldn't it be great to be back in those good old days, the way things were always done.' People really like calm water. So how you turn those tendencies toward the positive is the real key.

"The only way you can effectively deal with anxiety is to trust yourself and have the trust of the organization. If you're trying to lead an organization down a path where you've never been before, and there isn't trust and leadership, I don't know how you'd ever pull that off," says Dennis. "And trust takes constant communication. Communication that's open so people feel they can raise any issue and get a response, whether they like it or not.

"It's important to be realistic in your communications, but at the same time to create a positive view as to where you're trying to go and what the possibilities are. And you have to believe in what you're saying. If people hear a bunch of words and see only shallow attempts to deal with the problem, you're not going to get buy-in."

Dennis's authenticity and credibility enable him to cultivate trust throughout PwC. After all, people will follow you only if they believe you are being honest with yourself and others, if you're walking your talk. "If I see a leader prepared to stretch himself or herself, and go in a new direction, I'm more willing to go in that direction and follow that individual. So you've got to be prepared to expose yourself. If people don't see you willing to embrace change, to raise the bar for yourself, how could you ever ask 25,000 people to do that? People who know me know that we're going places where I've never been before.

"To me, change means opportunity. For PwC, it's an opportunity to demonstrate to our clients and our people that, if we're not relevant in everything we do, our business will be obsolete. I really believe that if we seize opportunities, great things can come out of it."

Dennis Nally is mobilizing the people of PwC. He is stewarding the firm and its 2,200 American partners through change. His ability to see change as opportunity, to acknowledge reality and tell the truth, while imagining the future, is enabling the firm to advance.

"If you become too comfortable, you lose competitive advantage. A leader's role is to make sure that the organization is constantly challenging itself, constantly trying to look down the road, constantly trying to move forward. You want to be positive; you want to see change as an opportunity. But at the same time, people need to know that you're being realistic in how you assess things. If you're not realistic, you're not going to have the trust you need to move forward." It's unlikely that PwC will become obsolete on Dennis's watch.

## WHAT'S YOUR REALISTIC OPTIMISM POTENTIAL?

How realistic and optimistic are you? If you're like most of us, you lean more toward one than the other, depending on how you've learned to see the world and manage your own anxiety.

If you're primarily realistic, you're good at assessing the current situation and are problem-oriented, fact-based, and a great short-term thinker. You are direct and honest about what is. At the same time, you may see life's cup as half empty, and focus on near horizons to manage your anxiety about the unexpected.

If you're primarily optimistic, you're imaginative, solution-oriented, and a great long-term thinker—hopeful about what *might be*. The danger for you is in failing to see what's right in front of you. You may concentrate on tomorrow to manage your anxiety about setbacks and disappointments today.

If you're a JEA leader, you're able to live in the present *and* the future simultaneously. You thrive in uncertainty while closing the gap between your current reality and desired future. You're open and honest about what exists while envisioning and articulating what's possible.

The quiz and table on the next pages will help you find where you sit on the continuum of realism and optimism. Once you know where you are, you can move toward the center. You can learn to live in paradox, both inside yourself and in your relationships with others. Remember: It takes vigilance to keep your balance.

---

### How Realistic and Optimistic Are You?

*Instructions:* Place an "X" next to the *one characteristic in each pair* that best describes you. Consider asking your colleagues or direct reports to complete the checklist to learn how other people see you.

I AM . . .
1. ___fact-based.
2. ___imaginative.

3. ___able to see others' faults.
4. ___able to see others' potential.

5. ___direct and honest about what *is*.
6. ___idealistic about what *might be*.

7. ___able to assess situations from all angles.
8. ___able to look beyond what's right in front of me.

9. ___prone to set readily attainable goals to ensure success.
10. ___prone to set very high goals to stretch people.

11. ___someone who sees more problems than opportunities.
12. ___someone who sees more opportunities than problems.

13. ___good at assessing the current situation.
14. ___good at finding solutions.

15. ___likely to concentrate on today to avoid worrying about the future.
16. ___likely to concentrate on tomorrow to avoid being disappointed today.

17. ___sometimes perceived as negative.
18. ___sometimes known to avoid big challenges.

19. ___always aware of my own strengths and shortcomings.
20. ___always striving to be my ideal self.

*Results:* Count how many "X"s you have for odd-numbered items and how many "X"s you have for even-numbered items. Having more odd-numbered "X"s means you are more realistic. Having more even-numbered "X"s means you are more optimistic. If your answers are equally distributed, you are able to balance being both realistic and optimistic. You are a JEA leader.

Learning to live and lead with realistic optimism enables you to create just enough anxiety throughout your organization. It unleashes people's productive energy. And it gives you—and everyone around you—the focus and momentum you need to navigate through the seas of uncertainty and change.

If you find yourself becoming too idealistic, take these steps to move back into optimism:

- Take time to consider possible setbacks or problems.
- Periodically assess your desired outcome to make sure it addresses current problems or opportunities.
- Check in with people you trust to test your perceptions.

If you start becoming cynical, you can move back to being realistic by taking these actions:

|  | Too Little Anxiety | Just Enough Anxiety |  | Too Much Anxiety |
| --- | --- | --- | --- | --- |
| If you are . . . | Idealistic | Optimistic | Realistic | Cynical |
| On the inside you . . . | are a grandiose dreamer<br><br>are blind to the consequences of your behavior<br><br>ignore problems | have a strong desire to improve yourself<br><br>have positive outlook about your own potential<br><br>view problems as opportunities | are self-aware<br><br>understand your strengths and shortcomings<br><br>have a realistic sense of self | focus on the negative<br><br>set unrealistic goals for yourself<br><br>resist or attack change and uncertainty |
| On the outside you . . . | create an impossible vision for the organization<br><br>expect more from people than they can deliver<br><br>avoid difficult business challenges | envision excellence and great performance<br><br>inspire others to reach for possibilities<br><br>create long-term solutions | are open with others about what is and isn't working<br><br>face problems head-on<br><br>are honest about marketplace realities | focus on the worst in others<br><br>expect resistance to change<br><br>set fires and live in crises |
|  | Ineffective Energy | Productive Energy |  | Chaotic Energy |

- Focus on your desired outcome (instead of the problem).
- Look for something positive in every action and individual.
- Regularly review your assumptions to test their validity.

The JEA leaders I've talked about in this chapter are all dreamers and pragmatic problem solvers. Comfortable with ambiguity, risk, and failure, they address day-to-day issues in the context of current tactics and future plans. They motivate others through inspiration and challenging assignments. These realistic and optimistic leaders communicate openly and honestly about their vision and provide road maps to achieve that vision. They challenge people with aggressive goals, provide the support and resources needed to achieve them, and constantly ask questions to ensure that people personalize the direction as their own. Through their actions, they generate just enough anxiety in their organizations. People know where they're headed and feel hopeful, engaged, and energized about the contribution they are making.

Now, let's move on to the next paradox: *constructive impatience*. What do these two qualities bring to the table? And how do JEA leaders bring them to life?

# 6

# CONSTRUCTIVE IMPATIENCE

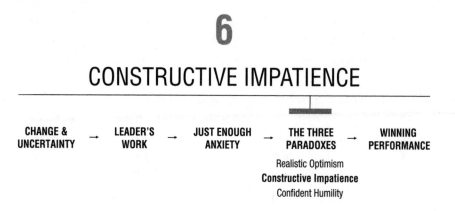

| CHANGE & UNCERTAINTY | → | LEADER'S WORK | → | JUST ENOUGH ANXIETY | → | THE THREE PARADOXES | → | WINNING PERFORMANCE |
|---|---|---|---|---|---|---|---|---|

Realistic Optimism
**Constructive Impatience**
Confident Humility

*Chaos is actually a fertile state, a creative state, a state of pure energy and great potential.*

—WILLIAM BRIDGES, *The Way of Transition*

"I'm an accomplishment junkie," admits Cadbury Schweppes CEO Todd Stitzer. "I love to challenge myself beyond my comfort level."

And so he has. Since taking the helm in 2003, Todd has led the 183-year-old confectionery maker—with brands like Dairy Milk and Trident—on an unprecedented growth drive. Under his leadership, Cadbury has undergone a $10 billion acquisition spree, ramped up profits, and outpaced Coca-Cola and Pepsi in market-share growth in the U.S. soft drink market. It's now number one or two in twenty-three of the world's top fifty confection markets. The company's 2006 annual report, titled "A Passion for Winning," reflects Todd's think-and-act-big leadership style.

When I spoke to Todd in London, he told me the story. "When I became CEO, I challenged people to make the company and themselves the very best they could be. Cadbury Schweppes competes with giants—like Nestlé, with nearly $69 billion in sales, and Coke, with $24 billion. Being among the best, feeling that you've danced with elephants and avoided being stomped on, appeals to a lot of people. So I set a goal to be a top-quartile performer in our industry."

But that's just for starters. Todd's ultimate goal is to make Cadbury Schweppes the number one confectionery in the world. And he knows that his ability to stretch people beyond their limits in a constructive way is the key to achieving his goal. By asking for the slightly impossible, he creates just enough anxiety to get people on board and move them forward.

Having engaged and capable employees creates enormous value. It means people are willing and able to do whatever it takes to get something done. "It's not about exploiting people's goodwill," says Todd. "It's about having motivated teams of people who can collaborate to be bigger, better, and more than ever before.

"In my time here, we've done more than forty acquisitions. We've learned, as a team, how to bring people on board in a productive way. We've assembled people from different companies and made them integral members of our winning team. As a result, we've fashioned an unbelievable portfolio of brands, both in confectionery and beverages."

What enables this "accomplishment junkie" to succeed is his ability to live with and create discomfort and excitement inside himself and for the people around him. This, combined with his knack for speaking directly to people's inherent desires to win, is Todd Stitzer's secret to winning performance.

## GETTING COMFORTABLE WITH DISCOMFORT

*The ultimate measure of a man is not where he stands in moments of comfort, but where he stands at times of challenge and controversy.*
—MARTIN LUTHER KING JR., American civil rights leader and Nobel Laureate

Many of us prefer the easy road. We possess a natural inclination to stick with the status quo, to resist the unknown, to stay comfortable. It's tied to our ancestral drive to survive. We're afraid of trying something new. We want to avoid change, so we don't push ourselves to our next level of performance.

We think life is *only* about creating safety and pursuing contentment. But it isn't. Life is filled with pleasure and pain, satisfaction and suffering, delight and difficulty. By focusing on only the comfort side of the picture, we cut ourselves off from the full range of human experience—and the knowledge and skills that come with the other side. We inhibit our performance.

If you're uncomfortable with discomfort, you probably run away from uncertainty and change. You hide from the tough issues. You may play it safe and refuse to take risks. You may try to steer clear of difficult conversations and conflict. Or you may fail to challenge others—or yourself—to greater performance. In any case, your motivation in life is to avoid tension, distress, and uneasiness. You're afraid you'll open up Pandora's box. And who knows what's inside?

To live and perform fully, you have to step into the unknown. You have to challenge yourself to grow, to change. And change is uncomfortable. Your fear and anxiety—and your discomfort—are natural, human reactions to life.

Arbitron chief administrative officer Kathie Ross explains it this way: "In Western society, there's a natural inclination to move toward comfort, because we can. It takes enormous discipline to say that's not what's best for me in the long run. You have to stretch yourself and do things that are not comfortable to become the person you want to be. Unless you embody this kind of behavior as a leader, it's hard to bring it out in other people."

Kathie learned at an early age how to live with discomfort. "One of the most important lessons in my life came from losing my mother when I was young. Encountering the ultimate anxiety—the loss of someone I loved—so early taught me that I could weather my greatest fear.

"When things get out of control, you just have to let go and trust the universe to provide the comfort and love you need. Then it's up to you to provide support to others when they're going through something tough.

"This give-and-take is what allows you to live with anxiety. The art of leadership is in knowing how much discomfort and anxiety individuals and organizations can handle." This leadership philosophy comes in handy as Kathie tackles issues in human resources, organizational effectiveness, program management, real estate, marketing communications, and investor relations.

Kathie Ross and other JEA leaders are at ease with uneasiness. They understand that some discomfort is essential for learning and change.

They stretch themselves by continually raising the bar. They seek to increase the amount of discomfort they can live with.

JEA leaders are not afraid of healthy conflict. They nurture it, in fact, knowing it will lead to bigger and better solutions. And they understand that being comfortable with conflict is necessary for deepening relationships, challenging people, and motivating high performance.

We all need to develop a healthy relationship with discomfort and conflict. Life and business today are fraught with contradictions, disruptions, and chaos. Their dramatic ups and downs and unexpected twists and turns can make anyone feel uncomfortable. And our workplaces, filled with strong egos bumping up against one another, make conflict inevitable. With everyone striving to get their needs met, miscommunications, mistakes, and mix-ups are bound to occur.

To be a JEA leader in today's topsy-turvy world, you must allow yourself to feel vulnerable, to sit with pain, and to be a little scared. You must experience the full range of emotions—including anger, sadness, and fear—and channel these feelings in healthy ways. You must question your own ideas and be okay when answers are not immediately forthcoming. And you must be open to having others push back and disagree with you.

Your ability to live with discomfort on the inside impacts your ability to handle discomfort on the outside. If you have trouble dealing with your inner turmoil, you will find it hard to understand or address the turmoil around you. If you're able to manage your own discomfort, you will be able to nurture and support others when they're feeling uncomfortable.

It's a lot like coaching kids in soccer, softball, or lacrosse. You engage them first to make it fun and safe. You create an environment in which they can practice and develop their skills. And then you stretch them by introducing new plays, new fundamentals, and new tactics that deepen their knowledge of the game and expand their skills. By helping them gradually step outside their comfort zones, you enable them to grow into their potential. And it's more fun.

When you get this right, you create just enough anxiety for yourself and others. You unleash vast amounts of human energy. And you lead people to levels of success they've never reached before.

You can accomplish this by learning to live in the second JEA paradox: *constructive impatience*. This involves engaging people and making it safe for them to take risks, while challenging them to higher and higher levels of performance. Let's take a close look at each side of this paradox.

## MAKING IT SAFE

*If you find it in your heart to care for somebody else, you will have succeeded.*

—MAYA ANGELOU, poet, educator, and civil rights activist

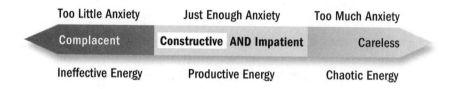

Being constructive is about creating a psychologically safe environment. It involves building trust by demonstrating respect and appreciation. When you are constructive, you are predictable and credible, honest and open. You foster participation and learning.

In a safe, constructive environment people feel good about themselves, their work, and their organization. Their job has meaning. They're valued. This enables them to take risks, to stretch beyond their current images of themselves. They are more flexible and adaptive and more willing to change.

People who feel safe are also better team players. They are more responsible, accountable, and committed. They have just enough anxiety to enter their discomfort zones freely, which uncaps the energy within them.

JEA leaders are masters at creating safe environments. They understand themselves and what they need to feel safe. So it's easy for them to build deep, safe connections with others. Instead of creating islands of self-interest, they emphasize collaboration and community. Win-win solutions are the name of the game.

Some leaders have trouble being constructive. It goes against their nature. They live a life of disrespect, mistrust, and arrogance. They may have been taught early on that being too nice is a sign of weakness. They may see collaboration as a waste of time. Or they may just think that safety buys mediocrity. People need fear to be motivated. There's simply too much to do to worry about how people feel.

These leaders don't quite understand that too much fear is poison to an organization. They fail to see that fear often breeds hostility or passivity. People are more likely to complain, blame, or be deceitful. Often convinced they're being taken advantage of, they become mistrustful, indecisive, or vindictive. Or they become disengaged—conservative, apathetic, and conforming.

At the other extreme are leaders who go overboard to be constructive. They become overprotective, smothering people's creative spirit and enthusiasm. These leaders are afraid of their own feelings and the feelings of others. They may be motivated by a strong need to be liked, or by the fear of making a mistake. Under the guise of protecting others from dangers or uncertainty, they are really trying to protect themselves.

Complacent leaders will do just about anything to avoid confrontation. They rely on consensus and group process to move things forward. Their lack of courage typically results in analysis paralysis, with no decision ever being considered final. Reluctant to change people, products, or processes, complacent leaders generate too little anxiety. They underestimate the untapped human potential available to them. People in their organizations end up losing interest in their jobs and confidence in their leaders.

---

### How to Be Constructive

- Focus on the best in people.
- Be willing to compromise.
- Model collaboration.
- Honor people for who they are.
- Involve people in decision making.
- Help people find meaning in their work.
- Turn mistakes into lessons.
- Share yourself—be authentic.

---

JEA leaders balance their sense of urgency and drive for results with their understanding of people's need to feel safe. They know that people do their best work when they feel valued and respected. By creating a positive environment, they are able to challenge people into their discomfort zones and generate real buy-in. It's this extra push that enables JEA leaders to tap into people's discretionary effort and unleash their productive energy—the key to winning performance.

People drive results. And people are most productive when they feel safe. When they know they can step into the unknown, risk failure, and still feel good about themselves.

Just ask Kathie Ross. "Creating a fun, engaging, collegial culture is critical to success. But you have to understand your own emotions and deal with your own shit," she says. "You need to express the whole range of emotions authentically and appropriately, including humor, which is enormously helpful in managing anxiety and helping people feel comfortable.

"I don't think most executives come with the skill set to do this. It's not that they don't have open hearts. They just don't understand the importance of a safe environment. It's not something they pay attention to."

So what does it take to create such an environment? "To me trust is key," says Kathie, "even if you don't like somebody. You need to know that people are telling it like it is, and that if they make a promise, they'll follow through. You have to believe what they're telling you, or you can't function effectively.

"But you don't have to be married to everybody you're working with. It's possible to have different styles, even different values, to a point, and still have trust."

On top of trust you need a passion for results. But "having passion doesn't give you license to be out of control. Some of the most difficult people I've ever worked with would claim to be passionate. But they were really just emotionally unstable. They thought it was okay to vent whatever emotion was wandering through their psyche at the time." They created too much anxiety.

"One of the things that shuts down creativity faster than anything else is fear. People have to be in a place that allows them to try things out, to be okay no matter how it works out, and, if they fail, to learn from it and move on quickly. They need to feel safe enough to use their anxiety instead of running away from it."

It all starts with you. The way you handle uncertainty impacts how safe people will feel around you. It determines how much they will trust you to lead them through change. "If you focus your energy on the problems and risks, they become larger—for you and your people. If you focus on solutions, on small wins that you feel confident you can make, it energizes people. They see how they can make steady progress despite looming uncertainties.

"Leaders have to center themselves between too much and too little anxiety. They have to be a buffer for their people while pushing them to achieve. They have to balance safety and growth."

Kathie creates safety at Arbitron by hiring people who have this capacity for just enough anxiety. She also makes sure the right people are in the right jobs. "If you don't do this, it takes a lot of energy to manage. But if you do, you unleash energy. Eighty percent of your task is done.

"Still, even with the right people in the right jobs, it's up to you as a leader to help people manage change. You've got to help them set their worries aside and focus on what they can control, on the progress they can make. And that's a real challenge because there are times when the uncertainty is overwhelming.

"The things that have caused me the most anxiety in my career have always been the people decisions. Those changes are enormously painful. I always lose sleep. I always feel the physical manifestations of the burden of making those decisions."

Through it all, however, Kathie keeps her balance. In fact, her centeredness is the key to her success. "You have to be in a healthy place. For me, it's about being centered spiritually, emotionally, and physically. That's what helps me be strong."

Kathie is a person who leads from the inside out. With an open mind and an open heart, she knows the effects of safety and fear on the people around her. She understands the power of creating a safe environment—one that allows people to be their full selves at work.

Ask yourself . . .

○ How comfortable am I with feeling discomfort inside myself?
○ Do I generally seek out or shy away from conflict?
○ What kind of environment am I creating at work? Is it safe? Fun? Creative?

## CHALLENGING THE LIMITS

*Only those who dare to fail greatly can ever achieve greatly.*
—ROBERT F. KENNEDY JR., U.S. attorney general

| Too Little Anxiety | Just Enough Anxiety | Too Much Anxiety |
|---|---|---|
| Complacent | Constructive AND Impatient | Careless |
| Ineffective Energy | Productive Energy | Chaotic Energy |

Being impatient is about challenging the limits—pushing yourself and others to expand your capabilities beyond what you thought possible. It's about setting bold goals and unleashing your organization's hidden potential.

No matter how motivated we are to achieve something or make a difference, stretching ourselves takes courage. It requires maturity and a clear vision of who we want to be. And it helps to have someone who challenges us. Someone who pushes us out of our comfort zones.

At the same time, we all have an inborn desire to win. It's this desire that JEA leaders tap into to unleash productive energy. They know what people are capable of and they know that the best time to push people is right before people think they're ready. Sure, it's uncomfortable. It's scary. But the very anxiety people feel at the prospect of stretching beyond their current limits is what enables them to accomplish the task.

JEA leaders are impatient by nature. They're driven by their desire to be the best. They seek out challenge and thrive on change. Always in motion and committed to winning, they tenaciously pursue success. And they believe wholeheartedly that success is within their reach. They see, touch, taste, and feel it. And they are willing to do what it takes to turn their visions into reality.

Too much impatience can push you over the edge, however. Not long ago I was working hard to keep up with a growth spurt in our company. I was being pulled in many directions, traveling a lot, and I was tired and overly impatient. Yes, I'm committed to healthy leadership, but I was unknowingly taking my anxiety out on my team. Fortunately, we were testing a new 360-degree performance evaluation at the time. People described me as bold, honest, and a strong leader. But they also told me I was being unpredictable and moody at times. I wasn't listening to them very well and was jumping to conclusions. To be honest, I was surprised and embarrassed by the feedback, but grateful for the chance to examine my actions. After a long, candid conversation, we were able to get our team back on track.

I see now that it was my *resistance* to my discomfort with the stresses of the business that created too much anxiety in me. This led to increasing levels of tension and conflict between my team and me. At the same time, it was my *acceptance* of my discomfort in hearing people's feedback that allowed me to have an honest conversation with them about my performance. The experience has helped me make positive changes in how I look at and handle the pressures of a growing business.

Not all leaders are impatient. They want to succeed but are unwilling or unable to push themselves or others to get there. They may never have learned how. They may have an ingrained fear of failure and figure that the less they risk, the less they'll lose. Or they may have an underlying fear of success and hold themselves back by setting low goals or finding obstacles at every step.

Some leaders are too impatient all the time. They push too hard, often becoming overly aggressive, impulsive, or reckless. Their fear of failing or missing out on something drives these careless leaders to set impossible targets and unattainable performance objectives. Determined to win at all costs, they motivate through criticism and blame. They shut people out and override objections or anything that slows things down.

Careless leaders are obsessed with ferreting out underperformance. They can even become abusive. Everything is urgent. Their inconsistency, instability, and impossible demands create too much anxiety for those around them. People feel stressed, afraid of what's coming next. It's under circumstances like these that unethical behavior is most likely to surface, as employees give up their values to meet performance targets. The end becomes more important than the means.

The behavior of careless leaders looks like impatience on steroids. They are rude and insensitive. They are judgmental and dismissive. They tear people down. Hijacked by ambition, these leaders live in a constant state of turmoil. Often poor communicators, they like to prolong and inflame conflicts, keep score, play politics, and exact revenge. They build their success at the expense of others.

---

### How to Use Impatience

- Always look for opportunities to improve.
- Set sky-high goals.
- Push people to do their best.
- Keep your eyes on the road ahead.
- Tie your success to the success of others.
- Give people what they need to succeed.

---

JEA leaders are different. Driven by their passion for results and a strong sense of urgency, they're constantly raising the bar. By challenging people to improve their skills, JEA leaders help individuals and teams achieve success. When this happens, everybody wins.

The top 125 executives walked into the room to the tune of "We Will Rock You" by the British rock group Queen. CEO Todd Stitzer had brought them together to debate and challenge what the executive committee wanted to do to make Cadbury Schweppes number one. "The idea was to challenge us to rock our competitors, rock the financial markets, and rock ourselves out of any complacency. You have to transmit that sort of passion and urgency. And you've got to be completely focused.

"Once we had agreed on the goal of becoming a top-quartile performer, I asked people, 'What would it take for you to get there?' Using an iterative process, we figured out how to turn our vision into reality."

Todd captured the company's direction with the phrase "Invest, Innovate, and Execute." It grabbed people's attention and provided a road map for moving forward. He also galvanized people to make sure they were on board. And he put people on notice that he was expecting them to perform at their best. It was an uphill struggle at first.

"Initially, Cadbury Schweppes felt like a bunch of refugees from a million consumer-products companies. Everybody had their own way of doing things. It was like the Tower of Babel. Everybody had different metrics. It was ridiculous.

"As soon as we completed our goals, we increased the frequency and clarity of communication. We made sure we had monthly voice mails from me to the top 125 people. We published a newsletter every three months. And every year we have a global leadership conference."

Todd continually reset the rules of the game. "In 2003, we made our biggest acquisition of all: Adams. We had an intense internal discussion about what targets we were going to commit to publicly. We finally agreed to 3 to 5 percent revenue growth, 50 to 70 basis points margin growth, and a billion and a half pounds of cash flow over a four-year period.

"Adams's incubation period for innovation was twenty-four to thirty-six months. I said, 'Team, we have an acquisition case that requires 7 percent revenue growth in three years. So could you please reduce your incubation period to nine to eighteen months?' Ultimately, when they came back, I asked them to reduce it further to six to fourteen months. And they did. We outinnovated Wrigley in 2004, less than two years after buying Adams.

"Getting people on board is not about my telling people what to do. It's a challenge and questioning process. 'Why can't you do that? Here are some examples. Now go away and see if you can get some more.'" It's about using constructive impatience to increase buy-in and commitment.

Like all JEA leaders, Todd knows he needs to channel his impatience to bring out the best in people. He needs to promote collaboration. Only then will people truly get on board and attain performance levels above and beyond themselves.

"I always look for people with what I call a high heart rate—people who've got high levels of energy, but are also driven collaborators. They have to know where they're going and want to bring people along with them. They have to get multiple inputs quickly and make decisions based on facts and logic. And they have to possess enough emotional intelligence to deal with high stress and a fair degree of anxiety. They've got to have that desire to win and the ability to live with the uncertainty of knowing that life's not perfect.

"But working in England, I've had to be a little less American in order to drive collaboration. Americans tend to go to a meeting and want to make a decision. In Europe, that's not the case. You go to a meeting to bless a decision that you've talked about with all the participants ahead of time. Surprising people in a meeting may be viewed by Europeans as threatening or confrontational. It's not a good way to come to a positive decision."

As driven as he is, Todd understands that the right amount of impatience mixed with a constructive push for excellence is the formula for creating the right amount of anxiety. Leaders can't expect people to give their best and follow blindly, or to be intimidated into driving growth without a sense of balance and fairness. "I often describe my job as balancing the financial desires of shareholders and the personal desires of employees. If you can marry up employees' desires for personal satisfaction, professional growth, and financial success to your shareholders' need for perpetual growth, you can maintain high performance over time." Demanding too much creates paralysis. Demanding too little is debilitating.

Todd Stitzer is a highly confident CEO who has found ways to translate his passion for winning in healthy, productive ways. He's integrated his inner drive for accomplishment with his desire to make Cadbury Schweppes one of the best companies in the United Kingdom. A place where people feel proud to work. And by all measures, Todd has succeeded beyond anyone's expectations—except perhaps his own.

Ask yourself . . .

- ° What does it mean to be among the best in my industry?
- ° Am I comfortable setting ambitious goals for myself?
- ° Do I challenge my direct reports into their discomfort zones?

## CONSTRUCTIVE IMPATIENCE IN ACTION

*Leaders probe and push with a curiosity that borders on skepticism, making sure their questions are answered with action.*

—JACK WELCH, *Winning*

Leading with constructive impatience is a lot like pulling a rubber band. If you pull too hard, you break people's spirits. If you don't pull hard enough, you fail to maximize their potential. But if you find the right tension, amazing things happen. You engage people's hearts and minds and create just enough anxiety to stretch them to their limits—and beyond.

But how do you master this powerful paradox? Let's see how two JEA leaders use constructive impatience—one in a not-for-profit association and the other in a county government.

## Speak to People's Desire to Win

"I love change. I love accomplishing things." So says Anne Bryant, executive director of the National School Boards Association.

"I was getting too comfortable in my previous job. I'd been there for ten years and we kept reinventing things. The organization was on edge. We were accomplishing goals. The staff was energized. But I wasn't on edge. I wasn't at my best personally."

Anne jumped at the opportunity to lead NSBA. She knew she could help the association, public school boards, and students across the country raise the bar. But first, she had to raise the bar for herself.

"I had never been a school board member. I was passionate about public education, yet didn't know anything about this organization. But one of my strengths is listening. So I started going out and talking to people in the field, to the heads of the unions, administrators, and state boards. I had thirty-five lunches with all the heads of the organizations and asked, 'What is NSBA now? What should it be? How could it be a better leader? A better partner?'

"I got an earful. Armed with their feedback, the board and I, through a strategic-planning process, came up with the idea of raising student achievement. That sounds like a no-brainer today, but the words 'student achievement' were not in the lexicon ten years ago."

Anne engaged a lot of people in the planning process. She understood that giving them a voice would generate energy and ensure buy-in. And she trusted them to steer the organization in the right direction.

"People are scared of change because they don't know what the end result is. So I involved the staff, along with the board and elected school board members, in the process of developing our strategic plan. Hal Seaman, who had been a candidate for the job, was my deputy at the time. Now I had never worked with a deputy, and he had never worked with a woman boss, so we thought we'd try it for a while. We gave ourselves six months. He's a great guy, and it worked wonderfully.

"About three months into the process Hal came to me. There were small groups all over the building with flipchart papers, answering questions. He asked, 'Do you have any idea what you're doing?' And I said, 'What do you mean?' And he said, 'Do you know what the outcome is? Do you know what strategic plan we're going to come up with?' And I said, 'I

don't have any idea.' And he said, 'So why are we doing all this?' And I said, 'Because the process we're going through will get us there.' And he said, 'Oh.' I said, 'Trust me. We will come out of this chaos with a direction for this organization. I just know it.'

"When you ask good people, they'll come up with the right answer. We don't hire stupid people, and school board members are very dedicated, smart people working their buns off in their communities for the right endgame, which is kids. They'll all tell you they're working for kids."

The strategic-planning process produced four big, hairy goals that operationalize NSBA's vision of the future. It led to performance objectives and benchmarks designed to move the association forward.

Anne is now using constructive impatience—and just enough anxiety—to help people close the gap between where they are and where they're going. "People underestimate the creativity that happens when you get out of your comfort zone," says Anne. "When I came here, there was no Web page. So I said—and this was creating anxiety on purpose—'By the next meeting we will have a Web page.' People said it wasn't in the budget. So I asked, 'How much do you think it costs?' And they said, 'We've been to consultants who told us they'd charge us up to $60,000.' I said, 'Do you want my former office staff to come over here and tell you how to set up a Web page?' Embarrassed, they said, 'Of course not. We can do it.' And we had a Web page within about a month and a half.

"I'm good with people who have confidence and energy. They're willing to make mistakes and are not intimidated by authority. They want to take risks. People who are not living up to their full potential make me anxious. And if someone is negative or unwilling to jump on the bandwagon and go forward with us, then I'll just say, 'Okay, get off.'"

Anne pushes herself harder than anyone. Helping her stay balanced are her "wonderful team" and a husband who is quick to tell her, "Anne, you're over the edge."

Achieving success is not all about performance, however. It's also about people. Anne holds Bagels with Bryant meetings to welcome new people into the fold. She celebrates people's tenure at Anniversaries with Anne every month. "We talk about NSBA. I love asking them what their first day was like. And then I always ask, 'What would you like to change?' Then we just talk."

Anne Bryant believes in performance and people. "All you have to do is look at children to know we're genetically wired to be creative learners. When a child runs to the edge of the ocean to watch a wave come in, he wants to be able to run back to Granny or Mom. He runs to the water and sees this big wave coming. Then he squeals and runs back, because he knows he's safe. So you take the child's hand and you go to the wave and say, 'The rule is, when you're near the ocean, you have to be holding somebody's hand.' You teach him that taking risks is okay when he has the right support."

Anne Bryant is a true change leader. She has performance in her genes. She's willing to travel down blind alleys and is comfortable with discomfort inside herself and others. She trusts people and the process. Anne has that special touch—she can push you and kiss you at the same time.

---

### Tips for Being Constructive and Impatient

- Challenge and support people to do their best.
- Balance setting stretch goals with getting buy-in.
- Enter conflict with purpose and curiosity.
- Balance winning with win-win.
- Know when to move forward and when to stay where you are.
- Balance urgency and right timing.
- Find the stretch point for each person.
- Balance growth and stability.

---

## Challenge People with the Power of Purpose

You might be surprised to find a county government as a great example of constructive impatience. But one award-winning community with a triple-A bond rating is exactly that. It's my home base: Arlington County, Virginia—a place where the government provides value, local politicians have earned respect, and people want to live.

Arlington County has an annual budget of $1 billion and more private office space than downtown Boston, Dallas, Denver, or Los Angeles. Its 200,000 highly educated and demanding residents speak 105 languages. County Manager Ron Carlee tells how he's leading this complex, high-performance organization.

"We're in 200 dramatically different lines of business," Ron told me. "Picking up trash is different from preparing the football field. They're both different from going into a manhole in freezing weather to replace a broken water pipe, which differs from running into a burning building. Or responding to a 911 call. Or counseling someone with substance abuse or HIV. Or inspecting a high-rise building. And that just scratches the surface."

What connects all these businesses is the desire to create a really great community. It provides a context and common thread for hundreds of seemingly disparate projects. But it's a tough mission to measure progress against.

"I have no idea how to achieve what I'm trying to achieve or when I've achieved it," says Ron. "There is no bottom-line metric. And that uncertainty creates anxiety. We're always questioning ourselves. Are we doing the right thing? Are we doing it in the right amount? Have we created the right environment? Is this the right building mix? Are these the right kind of streets? Is this transportation system working?"

The constant questioning is how Ron stretches himself and his team. He's always looking for ways to improve, even when the county gets good marks, as it did during and after 9/11. The Pentagon, after all, is protected by Arlington County firefighters.

"As we were responding to the 9/11 attack, I initiated an After Action Report. I wanted an independent team to gather and evaluate data from throughout the organization to help us learn. And what that evaluation and other independent evaluations, including ones by Harvard and Congress, have shown is that we did an exceptional job. We were cited as a model of teamwork, internally and externally."

But Ron pushed for improvements. "We couldn't afford to do less than we did before," he admitted. "We couldn't afford to drop below that bar. We've done more to enhance our capacity to respond to an emergency in the first five years after 9/11 than we did in the twenty-five years before.

"If you're not moving forward you're sliding backward. There's no such thing as a stationary position in life or in the world. The problem with a good organization is the danger of complacency. People ask, 'Why do we need to do anything different?' That's when the leader has to come in and push. He or she has to create the right amount of anxiety to get people to understand that they can't rest on their laurels.

"What I have to do is get people to stretch themselves beyond their individual discipline, to work with others. It's the collaboration that creates anxiety. Once you expand beyond your own sphere, you begin to lose control. You're in a more ambiguous environment.

"Most of what I do is conversation. It's an ongoing, collective conversation about how we can best deal with what's going on. There's a lot of back and forth and pressing and pushing one another.

"The impatience, the pushing, has to be balanced with a genuine concern for the people. And I use the word *genuine* intentionally, because anybody can say they care. You have to mean it. And you have to say it often. It took me a while to learn this. You have to do the right things and say the right things. Sometimes you have to tell people you're doing the right things for them to recognize that you are.

"The only way to accomplish anything is through your employees. You have to advocate for them because they're the ones delivering for you. You have to ask, 'Am I showing people the concern and empathy and caring they need to remain connected and feel valued in what they're doing?'

"Yet the greatest challenge is creating space for risk. The creativity is there; you just need to give people permission to use it. You need to get out of the way and let people go.

"Fortunately, people come here looking for meaning. So it's not a hard sell for most of them. But I've got to provide the context. It's up to me to let them know how their job fits into the bigger picture—that it does, in fact, have meaning."

Ron's efforts are paying off. A comprehensive Citizen Survey, conducted in 2004 by an independent third party, shows that Arlington County rates significantly above average when compared to other communities its size—in *all* service categories. In fact, the Arlington survey results were so high that the survey company had to recalibrate its national "best in class" benchmarks.

For Ron Carlee, constructive impatience is about creating an environment where people feel free to stretch themselves in service to a larger mission. His secret: lots of communication and context setting, both inside and outside of county offices.

"I bring people in from all levels of the organization to talk with me and each other. We sit around a conference table and engage in mission-driven, problem-solving discussions. My role is to help people understand why each person needs to be in the room. It creates connectivity and sets up communication channels throughout the organization. They go back and talk about what they heard, what they understood, and why we're doing something.

"The more this goes on, the more it becomes the way our people do business. Open discussions are also a big part of how we connect with Arlington County citizens—our customers. They give us a sense of connectedness with the community and help our citizens know that this is an organization that's really working for them. Their feedback is one of the best tests we have for measuring our success. We can think we're creating a great community, but if people don't like living here, what have we accomplished?"

There's no question that Ron Carlee is running a big business with demanding customers. In fact, I'm one of them. Here's a man who has the courage to stretch himself, challenge others, and define new levels of excellence. He is charting a new course for county government. Ron is modeling constructive impatience for leaders in organizations of all shapes and sizes.

## WHAT'S YOUR CONSTRUCTIVE IMPATIENCE POTENTIAL?

Do you tend to be more constructive or more impatient? Chances are you lean toward one side of this paradox most of the time, and especially under pressure.

If you're mostly constructive, you focus on people and the work environment. You are adept at creating meaning, fulfillment, and collaboration. Your desire to minimize conflict, however, may make you too conciliatory at times.

If you're mostly impatient, you focus on performance and results. You set audacious goals to stretch people beyond their comfort zones. But your need to succeed may cause you to take unnecessary risks, including the risk of alienating the people around you.

If you're a JEA leader, you exemplify grace under pressure. You balance urgency with patience and your passion for results with your compassion for people. You're able to foster people's hunger to get ahead, while providing them with needed support. You stretch their capabilities in a setting that is creative and fun. Whether you are raising the bar, doing more with less, increasing sales, or improving performance, you know how to get more out of your organization—day by day and year by year.

Use the quiz and table on the next pages to figure out where you sit on the continuum of constructive impatience. Once you know where you are, you can begin to move toward the center. By learning to embrace both sides of this paradox, you can stretch your organization while remaining sensitive to the needs and emotions of its people.

---

### How Constructive and Impatient Are You?

*Instructions:* Place an "X" next to the *one characteristic in each pair* that best describes you. Consider asking your colleagues or direct reports to complete the checklist to learn how other people see you.

I AM . . .
1. ___ambitious.
2. ___compassionate.

3. ___able to see people bigger than they see themselves.
4. ___able to see accept people for who they are.

5. ___comfortable with conflict.
6. ___uncomfortable with conflict.

7. ___concerned primarily with progress.
8. ___concerned primarily with people.

9. ___prone to move too fast.
10. ___prone to move too slow.

11. ___someone who sets very high goals.
12. ___someone who makes sure goals can be met.

13. ___good at tapping into people's potential.
14. ___good at supporting people through change.

15. ___likely to make decisions on my own or with little input.
16. ___likely to involve a lot of people in decision making.

17. ___inclined to change things.
18. ___inclined to keep things as they are.

19. ___usually on a fast track and enjoying the ride.
20. ___usually collaborating with others and enjoying the relationships.

*Results:* Count how many "X"s you have for odd-numbered items and how many "X"s you have for even-numbered items. Having more odd-numbered "X"s means you are more impatient. Having more even-numbered "X"s means you are more constructive. If your answers are equally distributed, you are able to balance being both constructive and impatient. You are a JEA leader.

Learning to be both constructive and impatient will enable you to stretch people without disempowering or overwhelming them. It will ignite their desires to outperform themselves. And it will give you—and your organization—the energy you need to move forward with confidence in an uncertain world.

JEA leaders, like the ones in this chapter, shed light on the people around them. They combine respect and collaboration with a sense of urgency and action. By involving the right people in the right way at the right time, they are able to think deeply about problems and then come to quick decisions. They inspire people's best work by being both trusting and challenging at the same time. Because they know when to think and when to act, they create just enough anxiety in others. People around them feel safe to take risks and make mistakes. They are comfortable being challenged to stretch into their next level of performance.

If you start sliding into complacency, you can move back to constructive leadership by taking these actions:

• Break big goals into small steps.
• Learn to live with discomfort by stretching yourself a little more every day.
• Take a course in having difficult conversations.

On the other hand, if you find yourself becoming careless, you can follow the steps below to restore a productive level of impatience:

|  | Too Little Anxiety | Just Enough Anxiety | | Too Much Anxiety |
| --- | --- | --- | --- | --- |
| If you are . . . | Complacent | Constructive | Impatient | Careless |
| On the inside you . . . | protect yourself from having to change<br><br>ignore feedback from others<br><br>avoid learning and growth | lean into life's challenges and opportunities<br><br>are comfortable with yourself<br><br>learn from mistakes and imperfections | seek out challenging experiences<br><br>feel passion for winning<br><br>set high goals | need constant change<br><br>want to win at any cost<br><br>have little regard for how your actions impact others |
| On the outside you . . . | avoid confrontation with others<br><br>promote the status quo<br><br>rely on consensus | create a healthy, safe, respectful workplace<br><br>involve people in decisions that affect them<br><br>help people find meaning in their work | focus on results more than people<br><br>push/pull people out of their comfort zones<br><br>set increasingly higher standards and goals | set impossible targets<br><br>motivate through criticism and blame<br><br>take unnecessary risks |
|  | Ineffective Energy | Productive Energy | | Chaotic Energy |

- Learn to recognize when you're about to put your foot in your mouth.
- Slow down by giving things more time to develop.
- Seek out other opinions instead of acting boldly on your own.

The third and final JEA paradox is *confident humility*. Perhaps the most counterintuitive of the three, it offers significant promise for our world today. Let's see how JEA leaders are blending the two sides of this paradox.

# 7

# CONFIDENT HUMILITY

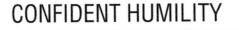

CHANGE & → LEADER'S → JUST ENOUGH → THE THREE → WINNING
UNCERTAINTY     WORK     ANXIETY     PARADOXES     PERFORMANCE

Realistic Optimism
Constructive Impatience
**Confident Humility**

*Every social trait labeled masculine or feminine is in truth, a human trait.*

—WILMA SCOTT HEIDE, American author

No man is totally masculine, no woman purely feminine. The terms *man* and *woman*—as well as *male* and *female*—reflect our biology. They define our gender. But they do not explain who we are.

We are composites. We have *both* masculine *and* feminine traits within us. How much we develop and display these traits depends on our social conditioning, life experiences, and deeply held beliefs and assumptions. Healthy, mature individuals are comfortable with both sides of their character.

The Western notion that we possess both masculine and feminine characteristics was developed in depth by psychologist Carl Jung in the first half of the twentieth century. He referred to the feminine component in males as the *anima* and the male component in females as the *animus*. Part of our psychological development, according to Jung, involves the integration of these two components. Since then, many decades of research have reinforced and enhanced Jung's identification of masculine and feminine characteristics.

But the idea of balancing feminine (yin) and masculine (yang) energies goes back much further in the East. The yin-yang symbol shown here represents the ancient Chinese understanding of how the world works. The outer circle represents the world, while the black and white shapes within the circle represent the interaction of the two energies. Yin energy is dark, intuitive, compassionantly, and receptive. Yang energy is bright, strong, focused, and active. Yet each contains an element of its opposite. While all things feminine are predominantly yin, they contain an element of yang. And while all things masculine are predominately yang, they contain an element of yin.

I believe we all have latent inner energies—either masculine or feminine—awaiting development. Deep down, we are inherently *androgynous*.

The word *androgyny* may make you uneasy. The idea that you embody both masculine and feminine qualities may shock or upset you. If so, you're not alone. Most of us hold a single-sided view of ourselves. We've been acculturated to believe that a "real man" is all masculine. A "real woman" is all feminine. We don't even have a specific word for the balance of these human qualities. Androgyny, with all its baggage, is the only word that comes close.

When I was writing this section of the book, I asked quite a few friends and colleagues for feedback. I knew the topic was provocative and wanted to gauge people's reactions. Most women and quite a few men accepted the concept of androgyny and felt it reflected their experience. Yet some resisted it, to varying degrees—even those with well-balanced masculine and feminine traits. To their credit, they were willing to learn more. They were open to looking beyond the word to explore the idea. I hope you are, too.

# THE POTENTIAL OF ANDROGYNY

*If any human being is to reach full maturity both the masculine and femi-nine sides of the personality must be brought up into consciousness.*

—M. ESTHER HARDING, psychoanalyst

In our culture, most men are biologically, psychologically, and socially programmed to express their masculine sides. They're taught to dismiss or devalue their feminine sides. Most women experience a similar phenomenon. They're programmed to embrace their feminine sides and reject their masculine sides. Clearly there are exceptions, but, for most of us, this is true—at least during the early years of our lives.

How about you? If you're a man, were you dressed in blue as a child? Were you rewarded for assertive behavior while being made fun of for wanting to cook or clean? Were you told to tough it up? Reminded often that boys don't cry? Or pushed to play sports and become a winner?

If you're a woman, were you encouraged to wear dresses and not get dirty? Were you praised for being good and scolded for fighting with other kids? Were you expected to help around the house? Taught to cook and sew? Or asked to take care of others?

Wait a minute. Your childhood experience may have been entirely different. It was undoubtedly influenced by when you grew up, what kind of family you came from, and what your parents were comfortable with. Your ethnicity and culture also played a major role.

In his book *Cultures and Organizations,* Geert Hofstede sheds light on societal differences between men and women. Based on decades of rigorous research across the world and inside IBM, Hofstede states that the gap between the sexes varies by country. The most masculine countries are Japan, Austria, Venezuela, Italy, Switzerland, Mexico, and Germany. The most feminine countries are Sweden, Norway, Netherlands, Denmark, and Finland.

But whether you were encouraged to play with trucks and tanks or dolls and dishes, chances are you were socialized to play the traditional part of your gender to some degree. If you're lucky, you learned as you got older that it's important to accept and embrace all of who you are. You realized that masculine and feminine qualities do not have value per se, but are given value by society. Women growing up in male-dominated cultures probably figure this out sooner than their male counterparts. And whether or not we're aware of it, many of us naturally begin to take on our "opposite" traits as we mature.

Fortunately, the traditional boundaries between these polarities are really starting to blur. We are evolving. For example, the idea of purely masculine and feminine careers is rapidly disappearing. An increasing number of women are entering traditionally male jobs and conquering sports previously dominated by men. More women hold public office. More men are staying at home to care for the children. Today's children face fewer educational and professional limits dictated by gender. Gender-based expectations about whether or when to marry, and even what to wear, are melting away. This is all good. But there are more subtle, internal obstacles to overcome if we're to reach our full human potential.

We each have inherent tendencies toward masculine or feminine behavioral traits. Part of this is due to biology and hormones. The rest comes from how we were raised and our lifelong beliefs and expectations about what's appropriate, acceptable, or required in our culture. And these tendencies *may* or *may not* match our gender.

The more masculine among us are self-confident go-getters. We're committed to action and enjoy being in control. We're generally rational, direct, practical, and assertive. The world is ours for the taking. We keep a lid on our emotions and stay focused on what we want to accomplish. People sometimes see us as driven, cold, or distant. Our motto is "*I* can do it."

Those of us who are more feminine are compassionate givers. We're committed to helping others get what they want and need. Usually intuitive, nurturing, creative, and patient, we build great relationships. We're good advisers. Both reflective and emotionally expressive, we possess a real zest for life. Some people see us as overly emotional or pushovers. Our motto is "*We* can do it."

Your dominant tendencies and habits of mind influence who you are. They also impact your leadership style and the kind of organization you build. But remember: Not all men are masculine leaders and not all women are feminine leaders.

If your leadership style is primarily masculine, you tend to see it in terms of transactions. You exchange rewards for services rendered and punish people for poor performance. It's about winning and losing. You fight to preserve your independence and get ahead.

The dominant characteristic of a predominantly masculine organization is a firm hierarchy. Power comes from your position within the hierarchy, and the vertical structure encourages competition. End results are often more important than how you get there. In such an environment, information is power and communication usually flows only in one direction—from the top down.

If your leadership style is primarily feminine, you tend to seek solutions in which everyone wins. You encourage participation, share power and information, and enhance other people's self-worth. Your focus is on people. You work hard to create a sense of community, preserve intimacy, and avoid isolation.

| Masculine Leaders | Feminine Leaders |
|---|---|
| • Assign clear responsibility and accountability<br>• Focus on getting things done<br>• Respond rapidly and decisively<br>• Set strong boundaries<br>• Solve problems in practical ways<br>• Take risks to grow the business<br>• Weed out weak performers | • Align people around a shared vision<br>• Foster collaboration and teamwork<br>• Focus on human dynamics<br>• Intuitively know what's good for people<br>• Regularly share important information<br>• Respond to people's needs<br>• Spark creativity and innovation |

A predominantly feminine organization looks like a web, with the leader in the center. This structure fosters collaboration and open communication. Authority comes from your relationships. In a web culture, process is paramount and agreements rule.

A lopsided leadership style limits your options. Like shackles on a prisoner, it keeps you and your organization from moving forward. Without the full range of masculine and feminine strengths, you are more likely to delay, damage, or even destroy what you're trying to achieve.

One-sided masculine leadership can end up isolating employees and departments. This perpetuates rigid, impulsive, or "stovepipe" decisions. Most important, it deters collaboration and teamwork, which starves creativity and innovation. It creates *too much anxiety*. Without the feminine ability to nurture people, it's hard to get deep-seated commitment.

Fulfillment and inner satisfaction are elusive. People won't stay long in an environment where they don't feel valued.

One-sided feminine leadership can breed complacency. It can blur boundaries between people and functions, which weakens accountability. And its characteristic inclusiveness can lead to indecision or slow response times. It creates *too little anxiety*. Without the masculine ability to push people, it's hard to keep them focused on the task at hand. Objectives and goals are difficult to reach. People are constantly buffeted about by every wind of change.

No leader or organization is entirely one-sided, although business in general has been traditionally masculine-oriented for decades, even centuries. While this often worked well in a world with little change and complexity, today's business environment requires a broader, more balanced approach.

"Some people say that the feminine method of leadership is the wave of the future. That the masculine method of leadership is dead. I don't buy that," says REI CEO Sally Jewell, whom you'll read more about later in this chapter. "I think leaders have to create an environment where smart people choose to work. They have to play to the things that give people a sense of purpose." And that requires both masculine and feminine strengths.

It's time to embrace your dual nature. It's time to see that valuing one over the other is like thinking that your right foot is more important than your left foot. You need both feet to stand on. And you need both your masculine and feminine characteristics to live and lead in a world of change. It's essentially about power.

## REDEFINING POWER

*Nearly all men can stand adversity, but if you want to test a man's character, give him power.*

—ABRAHAM LINCOLN, sixteenth president of the United States

The word *power* comes from Spanish, Portuguese, and French root words meaning "to be able to." It has two definitions: (1) the ability to make unilateral, binding decisions for yourself or others; and (2) that which makes action possible, whether by constraining or enabling.

The first definition is steeped in traditional ways of thinking about masculinity. It puts the ultimate power in the hands of one individual whose decisions drive others' behavior. Leaders can express such power in various ways—through their expertise, charisma, or formal authority. This works fairly well when people will do what they're told. It's a viable prescription for leading in a predictable, unchanging world.

But what happens in a world marked by uncertainty and constant change? Where people have more to say about the course of their lives? Where loyalty to the organization has been usurped by mobility and volatility? Where the assets of the organization are sitting inside the minds of its people? Here the power resides in everyone. It is distributed throughout the organization.

Every person possesses some power. And power is usually reciprocal. As the leader, you have some control over salaries, working conditions, and hiring and firing. Your people have the power to work more or less diligently, support or sabotage your efforts, or leave. But you set the tone in your organization for how power is used or abused, and to what extent it is shared.

JEA leaders exemplify both types of power. They make things happen by using their own personal power and by unleashing other people's power—the human energy that turns the wheels of progress in their companies. This combination of making things happen (masculine trait) *and* empowering others (feminine trait) is the best way to succeed in a complex and ever-changing business environment. JEA leaders:

- Are courageous and caring.
- Direct and support people.
- Balance personal and shared power.
- Focus on process and results.
- Know when to charge ahead and when to wait.
- See present and future simultaneously.
- Push people to perform in constructive ways.
- Display confidence in themselves and others.

JEA leaders use both sets of qualities to get things done. But it's the power they share with others that creates the productive energy required for their organizations to succeed. Don't get me wrong. Leadership is still about command and control. It's also about cooperation and nurturing. JEA leadership combines both, to liberate, guide, and enable people to be the best they can be.

### Leadership Styles

| Masculine | JEA | Feminine |
|---|---|---|
| Command<br>Constrain<br>Control | Liberate<br>Guide<br>Enable | Cooperate<br>Nurture<br>Accommodate |

"It's important to have a broad leadership style," says Travelocity CEO Michelle Peluso. "Employees want vision. They want authority. They want clarity and direction. Yet people no longer come to work for a company for their lifetimes anymore. So loyalty has to be won. This requires softer skills, like team building, perceptiveness, graciousness, putting others first, and shining the spotlight on the team rather than yourself.

"Leaders need to cultivate all these skills. They need to have a generosity of spirit, a team orientation, and emotional intelligence. At the same time, they have to be firm and tough negotiators. They must be able to say, 'Okay, we're not going to debate this any further.'

"I'm a nonhierarchical person. I will always get back to anybody who e-mails me within twenty-four hours. I do brown-bag lunches a couple of times a month. I'm team-centered. But I'm also very direct. There have been times when I've slammed my hand on the table and said, 'This is the way it's going to be,' and then walked out of the room.

"We need to be good at blending these qualities. We need to set a clear direction and execute against a plan while being conscious of what it takes to build loyalty. We need to help people feel successful, like they're making a difference."

Four Seasons CEO Isadore (Issy) Sharp has his own unique way of balancing masculine and feminine leadership qualities. When he started the company in 1961, Issy was determined to run the business according to the Golden Rule. He told me it wasn't easy to get everyone on board.

"Some senior people in the company scoffed at it. They said, 'The soft stuff won't get us anywhere.' I said, 'Well, if you don't believe in it, then, for sure, it won't get us anywhere and we should part company.' Well, that was decades ago, and that theory has been proven over and over again.

There isn't a city or a village anywhere in the world that we couldn't go into and pull together a group of people to work by our values and standards. The Golden Rule is universally understood."

Here's a leader who is able to nurture the softer side of leadership, while firing top executives who can't lead the Four Seasons way. His balanced style has paid off. The Four Seasons is rated consistently as the top hotel chain in the world.

Far from washed-out, sexless abstractions, JEA leaders are full and robust human beings who express the best of both masculine and feminine qualities. This gives them a huge leadership toolbox from which to draw. Sometimes they walk into a room and tell people what to do. Other times they give advice or resolve conflicts. Most times they empower a group to manage themselves. They're able to use their feminine strengths in one situation and their masculine strengths in another. This integrated leadership style enables them to lead with just enough anxiety.

How can you become a more integrated leader? What do you need to do to blend your masculine and feminine traits?

If you're a predominately masculine leader, you need to increase your capacity for building healthy relationships. You need to come to terms with your emotions, vulnerabilities, and personal needs. And you need to show more patience, consideration, compassion, and tenderness. It's time to confront your fears of looking like a wimp.

If you're a predominately feminine leader, you need to become more action-oriented and claim your independence, courage, and power. You need to take more risks. And you need to demonstrate more assertiveness, control, strong opinions, and decisiveness. It's time to confront your fears of being seen as insensitive.

By learning to live with just enough anxiety, you can broaden your perspective and expand your repertoire of leadership skills, along with your leadership toolbox. Once you've begun to integrate your masculine and feminine sides, you will be better able to help others live with just enough anxiety. You will be better prepared to handle the roller-coaster ride called leadership.

You know that living in paradox is the key to living with just enough anxiety. You've read about the importance of realistic optimism and constructive impatience. Now it's time to tackle *confident humility*. This involves learning to lead with power and generosity—at the same time. Let's look closely at the two sides of this unusual paradox.

## LEADING WITH CONFIDENCE

| Too Little Anxiety | Just Enough Anxiety | Too Much Anxiety |
|:---:|:---:|:---:|
| Self-Doubting | Humble AND Confident | Arrogant |
| Ineffective Energy | Productive Energy | Chaotic Energy |

Confidence is an attitude. It's about believing in yourself and your ability to master your environment. It is also about believing in the people around you. It's being sure that your organization can meet challenges head-on, solve problems, and win in the marketplace. As Rosabeth Moss Kanter, the author of *Confidence*, says, "Confidence is the sweet spot between arrogance and despair—consisting of positive expectations for favorable outcomes." You can't build a winning team without it.

Some leaders have trouble feeling confident in a world of uncertainty. They may never have learned to be strong in the face of adversity. They may feel intimidated by the speed and complexity of change. Or they may truly believe, like the Victims and Fatalists I described earlier, that life controls them. These leaders are often flooded with doubts, swamped by anxiety, or washed away by events. A few may masquerade as confident in an attempt to hide their insecurity.

At the other end of the spectrum are arrogant leaders. Their unrealistically high opinion of themselves and low opinion of others makes them harsh and judgmental. They blame others for problems and refuse to accept responsibility for negative outcomes. Plus, they're often selfish, greedy, or overly competitive. Mesmerized by their own power and self-image, they use fear and manipulation to exploit others. Some may close themselves off from people; others may seek out attention. They all create too much anxiety for the people around them.

Most of us move in and out of confidence on a regular basis as we navigate life's uncharted waters. Change and uncertainty make us anxious. When this happens, it's not unusual to become temporarily hijacked by our emotional brains, to feel confused and unsure of ourselves.

Sometimes old memories trip us up. Other times our self-defeating beliefs get in the way—like expecting things to stay the same or always go our way.

JEA leaders know better. They exude confidence in themselves and express confidence in others, no matter what is going on around them. Yet they never lose sight of their humanity. Consider the two JEA leadership lessons about confidence that follow.

### Live Your Values Every Day

"Every six seconds somewhere in the world someone's life is improved by Medtronic's medical products or therapy," says chairman and former CEO Art Collins. A midwestern guy with midwestern values, Art leads Medtronic in touching the lives of more than 5 million patients each year. The Minneapolis-based company, which conducts business in more than 120 countries, has grown 20 percent a year for twenty years. It boasts a ten-year ROI of 23 percent, exceeding its four largest competitors by 110 percent.

"We are in business to use biomedical engineering to alleviate pain, restore health, and extend life. And our mission and values drive everything we do. They are embedded in the hearts and minds of every employee. They guide us and challenge us to achieve our highest performance.

"My job is to live and champion Medtronic's mission and values. I meet with groups of new employees all the time. I talk about the history of the company and how the mission came to be. And I use examples demonstrating how the mission is employed in the day-to-day conduct of people's jobs.

"But it can't simply be words. It has to be that we're walking the talk. One thing I learned very early in my career is that people are smart. They can sense when someone is all talk and really doesn't mean what he or she is saying. People watch their leaders very closely. It's not only what you say; it's what you do. If you want people to live the mission and values and act a certain way, start by acting that way yourself."

Art Collins knows what he values and is willing to live those values every day. It's what gives him his confidence and personal power. Then he models and teaches his values to others, creating alignment throughout the company.

JEA leaders like Art Collins stand for something. They know and share themselves, talk about their families, and are open about their fears and aspirations. They live their values personally and professionally. And they encourage others to do the same. This makes them predictable and trustworthy. It makes them real.

Their values define who JEA leaders are and how they run their businesses. They guide their decisions and relationships. They delineate acceptable and unacceptable behaviors. JEA leaders know when to stand firm, when to negotiate, when to be flexible, and when to let go. They lead with an inner confidence. And they impart their values—without proselytizing—by what they say and do.

Authentic values are not abstract ideals or hopes. They are deeply felt principles that provide a compass for action. They keep leaders and companies out of trouble, challenge everyone to reach for the highest and best, and provide people with a chart for navigating the murky waters of business.

Ogilvy & Mather chairman Shelly Lazarus has this to say about values: "Our founder, David Ogilvy, created this agency based on explicit beliefs and values about how a business should be run. He said, 'We encourage individuals, entrepreneurs, and inventive mavericks. We have no time for prima donnas or politicians. We value candor, curiosity, intellectual rigor, perseverance, and civility.'

"These values tell us what the Ogilvy brand is all about, whether we are operating in Brazil or China. If you don't have firm values to guide your decisions, you either have to be a dictator ruling from the center, which is impossible to do on a global scale, or be reduced to an amalgam of affiliated companies.

"Some people say I am maniacal about the way we treat clients. At the end of the day, it's all about the quality of the work we do. If we don't get excited by or judge ourselves by the quality of the product we deliver, we're not going to be a good agency. Like our founder, I must stand up for my principles. I have to be consistent in my management style because that will allow people to know and trust me."

Shelly sacrifices nothing to the fast-paced, glamorous world of brand advertising. "I'll never forget being in my boss's office one day when I first came to Ogilvy. One of our media planners was literally running around in circles because she was so distraught about an upcoming meeting. At least once a week, even now, I think about how my boss handled that situation. He got in front of her, stopped her from running, and said, 'What do you think they're going to do, take away your children?'

"Whenever people are feeling harried, I start by saying, 'Now, I just want to be clear on this, is anybody going to die because of this decision?' It lightens people up and lends perspective. This is just business, so let's be smart about it. Most decisions aren't about life and death. They don't have to do with whether you're going to keep your children or have them taken away.

"Being comfortable with yourself gives you confidence and perspective to determine what is and what is not important. It enables you to keep your perspective on life and work. Having a personal life reminds us about the nature of the decisions we are making. People don't like people who don't have life in perspective. They don't trust them."

By living her values, Shelly is creating an atmosphere that enables an unconventional, diverse, and creative workforce living in ninety-seven countries to feel valued and to truly excel. Her transparency about who she is helps people feel comfortable to be themselves. Her bold leadership style has landed the firm prestigious accounts such as IBM, American Express, Kodak, DuPont, and Unilever—and annual revenues of $800 million.

---

### How to Live Your Values Every Day

- Share your strengths and shortcomings.
- Bring your full self to work.
- Keep an open mind and open heart.
- Be consistent and predictable.
- Say what you mean and do what you say.
- Stand up for what you believe.
- Respect others' values.
- Communicate honestly and openly.

---

And then there is McKinney, a Durham, North Carolina–based advertising firm, which has a No Asshole policy. If you think you're becoming one, you're expected to stand up and scream. If you think someone else is acting like one, you can use the designated hand signal for Stop! McKinney is one of the top ten advertising firms in the United States. Its mission is "to make extraordinary things happen for our clients and their customers and our people." The company's values, including the No Asshole policy, help everyone do just that. Now that's what I call living your values.

## Share Your Power by Developing Leaders

Two minds are better than one. Many minds are best. Collective wisdom is simply greater than individual insight. In a complex, uncertain world you need as many good ideas as you can get. JEA leaders are masters at tapping into this collective wisdom. They know how to share power, manage egos, and develop leaders.

Take Alan Mulally, for example. When I first met Alan, he was vice president and general manager of Boeing's 777 business. He was overseeing 7,000 people in more than a dozen countries in a four-year, $4-billion effort to create a state-of-the-art airplane. The process involved 3 million parts from 1,500 suppliers in sixty-two countries. Managing this project was as tricky as assembling all the pieces, yet Alan said he deserved virtually no credit. "Our team did it," he says.

"I am not arrogant. I don't know whether humble is the right word, but I do know that I know relatively little. But when I talk to a lot of people, I get the feeling that they are trying to tell me how much they know. Well, we all know only what we know. So why don't we just work together and stop trying to tell each other what we know?

"Now if you really believe that's the way to go, like I do, then you know that your power is really outside of you. Your power is in everybody trying to figure out how to accomplish your plan, to accomplish your goal. Your job is enabling everybody to contribute, to feel appreciated for the great work with a 'Thank you.'"

To say that Alan is adept at sharing power is a gross understatement. He sees himself as a resource person, someone with great interpersonal skills who is supportive. This requires being secure with himself and his position. "The only way I can make the contribution I want to make is to get everybody involved in the work together and enable them to contribute," says Alan. "And I have to be self-confident to do this. If I worried that people were going to talk behind my back, I could never operate this way."

Not surprisingly, Working Together was the name given to the Boeing 777 project. The phrase was emblazoned on the first plane and was the central philosophy that governed the entire project.

Alan Mulally and other JEA leaders realize that everyone has access to their own personal power. It's the leader's job to unleash that power. It's the leader's job to focus people's discretionary power to achieve amazing results.

While others use their power over people to their advantage, JEA leaders share their power with others. This takes just enough anxiety—inside themselves, to let go and trust the process, and inside their people, to take responsibility and ownership.

Thousands of miles away from Everett, Washington, in Zurich, Switzerland, former UBS CEO Peter Wuffli harnessed people's power from the top of this global financial services firm. To be successful, Peter told me when we talked in July 2005, you must nurture the right kind of ego.

"There are two kinds of leaders. There is the larger-than-life kind with concentrated power whose ego will make it very difficult to tolerate somebody who comes close to their quality. When you talk to them, they tend to lecture rather than listen. When you meet them, you feel that their egos could fill a whole, empty cathedral.

"I find these leaders incredibly dangerous for their corporations and the economy, because there's just no human being so competent and skilled as to understand and drive the complexity of a large global firm. It just does not work. It would be a tremendous risk—you would get some good decisions, some brilliant, and then you would get some disasters. So I think, quite frankly, no large company with global impact can afford that kind of concentrated power in a single leader.

"Healthy leaders believe that they have a distinctive perception which may or may not be shared by others. They want the room to apply their talent and get credit for the outcome. That's the kind of leader we nurture at UBS. These leaders want to be visibly recognized for what they contribute. So to succeed, you need to reward people appropriately, tell them you appreciate what they do, and make their accomplishments visible internally and eventually to the public."

Peter was describing JEA leaders, including himself. When I met with him, this bright, forty-nine-year-old consultant-turned-banker was determined to turn UBS into "the best global-financial-services company" in the world. And he made great strides toward his goal during his five-year tenure. UBS stock performed well as the company attracted investments from the world's rich while executing a string of acquisitions that made it number five worldwide in terms of market value. But following three quarters of declining losses and an unsuccessful hedge-fund venture, Wuffli found himself out of a job in July 2007.

As I write this, it's unclear whether Wuffli's removal was the result of a power struggle or a change in UBS strategy. But his ousting does highlight the growing pressures facing chief execs of public companies as they grapple with the increasing scrutiny of their short-term performance. It also demonstrates the complexity involved in becoming a JEA leader.

Let's face it: Leaders do not operate in a vacuum. They lead in the context of their industry, the marketplace, and the global economy. They are helped or hindered by the people around them. Their success or failure is tied to the nature of their product or service and the times in which they find themselves. For these reasons, it's possible for a JEA leader to lose ground, to achieve only short-term success or no success at all. It's also possible for a non-JEA leader to build a winning organization, at least for a while.

At the time of our interview, Peter Wuffli came across as a solid JEA leader. It may be that his watch at UBS was cut short because of market volatility. It may be that the company needed a different leadership approach due to its more recent losses. Whatever the reason, I suspect that Peter will land on his feet. He is a confident guy with a healthy ego who knows where he's going and how to get there—even when the rules, or the game, change.

Developing leaders at PepsiCo has involved less drama. "PepsiCo's heritage is built on a long legacy of strong leaders," said the company's now retired CEO Steve Reinemund when I interviewed him in Purchase, New York, in the middle of his reign. "We spend a lot of time attracting, developing, and retaining world-class leaders. Leadership really matters to us.

"It matters with the innovation side of our business, because innovation is what fuels revenue generation. And it matters with our retail customers for the same reason. Our experience has been that leaders who can really understand the consumer can make a difference. We know it's a great competitive advantage."

"It's our responsibility as leaders to develop future leaders," says Steve. "Most importantly, that's what keeps people in a company, challenges them and helps them grow. If there isn't anybody in the company pushing you to develop as a leader, chances are you're not going to stay. It's not going to be attractive to you. You may be successful. You may stay for a while, but you probably won't stay for an entire career."

While PepsiCo has been focused on leadership development and succession planning, rival Coca-Cola has been experiencing a leadership crisis. In the past ten years, the company has had three chief executives, three general counsels, four chief operating officers, four heads of North America, and six chiefs of marketing. The president's post, Coca-Cola's number two spot, was vacant for nearly half a decade.

---

### How to Develop Powerful People

- See people bigger than they see themselves.
- Give people what they need to succeed.
- Celebrate others' successes.
- Reject showy signs of power.
- Be open to feedback.
- Let people run with good ideas.
- Encourage acts of civil disobedience.
- Model collaboration.

---

The numbers speak for themselves. Today, PepsiCo is the world's number one maker of snacks. Its revenues in 2006 totaled more than $35 billion. Company stock has risen 37 percent over the past five years, compared to Coca-Cola, which has fallen 9 percent. And PepsiCo now commands a 50 percent market share for noncarbonated drinks in the United States, with Coke a distant second at 23 percent.

Alan Mulally shares power. Peter Wuffli manages egos. Steve Reinemund develops leaders. This is the work of confident leaders. They think differently. They believe their influence is earned, not seized. Power increases as you give it away. Sharing power prevents stupid mistakes. And no matter how bright your reflection is today, your position of power will eventually fade away.

Ask yourself . . .

- How confident am I in myself? In the people around me?
- Am I my whole self at work? What values do I model?
- What more can I do to share power and develop leaders?

## LEADING WITH HUMILITY

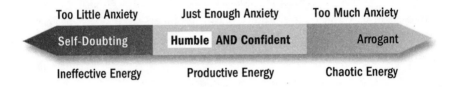

| Too Little Anxiety | Just Enough Anxiety | Too Much Anxiety |
|---|---|---|
| Self-Doubting | Humble AND Confident | Arrogant |
| Ineffective Energy | Productive Energy | Chaotic Energy |

Part of my job is public speaking. I speak to large audiences and facilitate dialogues with boards and executive teams. Early in my career, being smart was really important to me. If an audience walked away and said, "Now that guy is a real thought leader," I felt like I had accomplished my task. It was all about me, my ego needs, and my image to the public. Today, it feels different. I realize that I am just touching the surface when it comes to knowing about the world. I am listening more. And I am much more concerned about my audiences. Who are they? What are they interested in? How can I help them become better leaders?

Now don't misunderstand me. I still pride myself on being smarter than the average bear. I stumble over confidence from time to time. And I love applause. But now it's much more about you than it is about me. And that's a good thing.

Being humble involves admitting that you don't know everything and not feeling like you have to know. It entails listening deeply to others and being eager to learn something new. It also involves giving of yourself in service to others—being generous with your time and attention.

Generosity is the hallmark of humility. Humble leaders are generous in their compassionate and respectful attitudes toward others. And they are generous in their gentle and accepting attitudes toward themselves.

Humility is essential in today's complex world. Nobody can have all the answers. We need one another to thrive in a world of change. Humil-

ity enables us to build mutually rewarding relationships that are our cata-
lysts for success. This makes our lives more fulfilling and our organizations
more competitive.

Some leaders have trouble with humility. If they have grown up in
a culture that places a high value on confidence and expertise, they may
believe it's a sign of weakness to admit not knowing the answers or to rely
too heavily on others. They may have deluded themselves into believing
they are the most important person in their organization. Or they may be
lulled into a false sense of themselves by the collusion of silence that often
happens inside companies. People stop talking and the leader stops listening. It's no surprise that it is "lonely at the top."

Other leaders are too humble. Their low opinion of themselves makes
them uncomfortable with their power. They fear failure and get easily de-
railed. They're reluctant to take a stand. Indecisive and cautious, they're
often intimidated by strong people and afraid of change. They can also be
defensive or needy.

These self-doubting leaders delegate too much. They often misplace
their confidence in others and ignore their responsibility to develop the
people upon whom they've come to depend. Although they expect the
best from everyone, they willingly accept poor performance to avoid
confrontation. They give the same incentives and rewards to top performers and mediocre ones. Their leadership style usually creates too
little anxiety for the people around them. It can, however, create too
much anxiety for highly motivated self-starters who get frustrated by the
leader's passivity.

JEA leaders are comfortable not knowing, asking for help, and relying
on and learning from others. Let's look closely at two JEA leadership lessons on leading with humility.

## Listen Deeply and Build Great Relationships

Nothing shows your humility more than listening deeply. Everyone wants
to be heard. When you listen to people, you demonstrate your respect for
them and your willingness to learn. And you stay informed in a constantly
changing world.

When he isn't climbing mountains, earning a black belt in karate, or
preserving primeval forests, Toyota chairman Hiroshi Okuda is studying
global markets, monitoring competitors, and observing the needs of

customers. "The faster I make decisions, the faster Toyota can move forward. I have to anticipate what might happen in the future. To do that, I have to listen to people."

Toyota is the preeminent listener. This Japan-based company continuously gathers information about potential customers around the world. It videotapes them at work and play to understand their needs. It disassembles BMWs and Mercedes-Benz vehicles to determine how these mechanical mavens work. It collaborates with local dealers in each country and adapts its advertising to local tastes. The ad campaign featuring muscled bodies on the beaches of California, for example, spoke directly to Americans with its tag line, "We Build Hard Body Trucks." By paying attention to the changing preferences of its customers, Hiroshi and Toyota are able to stay ahead of the competition.

The Japanese are good at listening to their past (honoring their long heritage). They're good at listening to the present (understanding what they see around them). But Hiroshi Okuda has also mastered the art of *omoiyari* (listening for the future).

Japanese businessmen have always been good listeners and keen observers. In fact, much of what is said in Japan isn't said at all. The Japanese are highly attuned to the unspoken and intuitive elements of communication. Harmony and the preservation of relationships are central to Japanese business strategy. In a society where silence speaks loudly and context determines meaning, deep awareness in any given situation is vital.

Hiroshi is deeply invested in the younger generations. "I want Toyota to be a company full of youthful spirit and vitality," he told me, a company that can "pounce on consumer trends, drawing inspiration from human lifestyles. We have to operate globally, which requires new knowledge." And so he listens.

The keen ability to listen deeply gives Toyota true competitive advantage. With an exciting blend of new models such as the hybrid-powered Prius, bestsellers like the Camry, and its Lexus luxury-car line, the company is full of vigor and innovation. It is well on its way to achieving its goal of capturing 15 percent of the global automobile market by 2010. It's already captured a 41 percent market share in Japan and 34 percent in North America. And it is primed to become the number one carmaker in the world.

What does it take to listen deeply? First, you need to pay close attention to people—what they say and what they don't say. You also need to refrain from making quick judgments about people or their ideas. Give yourself time to obtain diverse views, explore new ideas, and weigh what you hear against your own perspective. And finally, you need to be open to surprises. Be ready to learn something new. Be willing to change your mind.

Deep listening is the foundation of great relationships. If you are in tune with the people around you, you will understand their wants and needs. You will know what motivates them and what scares them, what liberates them and what shuts them down. You'll be able to tell when and why they are feeling angry or anxious, complacent or bored, or enthusiastic and committed. This level of understanding is essential to unleashing human talent.

Just ask REI CEO Sally Jewell. Since taking the reins of REI, founded in 1939 as the company of outdoor enthusiasts, Sally has brought the company back from the brink of disaster by building solid relationships with employees, customers, and the world at large. Here's a former banker and Mobil engineer transforming a company full of tents, hiking boots, and granola bars.

"We were a company in crisis and we didn't know it. When you are a co-op (where the customers own the company and receive dividends on profits), you don't have the market hammering on you. And if you're providing members with good stuff, they aren't pounding on you either. Still, you need to prepare for what's coming. You need to think about the sustainability of the business.

"So we started town hall meetings, and I started sharing the fundamental building blocks of the financial side of our business. It was like a bucket of ice water on employees. They didn't realize that our performance had been declining on a number of key measures for several years. The company, on its present course, was not sustainable."

Fast-forward to today, and you'll find REI in a much different situation. It now operates more than eighty stores in twenty-seven states, with more than 8,000 employees—and also has the largest outdoor store on the Internet. Company sales in 2005 surpassed $1 billion, with a one-year sales growth of 15 percent. Consistently recognized as one of the "100 Best

Companies to Work For" in the United States by *Fortune* magazine, REI was ninth on the list in 2005.

"I'm not taking credit for all of this," says Sally, "but sharing information widely, helping employees understand what drives our business performance, and making difficult decisions really made the difference. It was an anxiety-raising exercise, but it also raised the confidence among our teammates that we were on top of things."

Today, every executive at REI meets regularly with employees. They do Let's Talk Sessions about what's happening and where the company is going. "It totally resonates with our employees," Sally told me. "They are so pleased that we are thinking long term and so thoughtful about how they can be part of the solution."

And here's the big secret behind Sally's success: She understands the importance of nurturing relationships—REI's relationship with employees, customers, local communities, and the environment. She's also discovered the burning platform inside each of her employees. "People at REI grasped the power of global climate change. And then they put gasoline on the fire to make it even brighter." By tapping into the hearts and minds of her employees, their higher purpose, Sally unleashed just enough anxiety lying dormant inside them.

"I'm a servant leader. And that makes it okay to volunteer and to be a part of your community. It brings people out of the closet who might have been volunteering for years, but doing it on their own time. I want to bring the idea of service to the forefront. To say, 'Not only do we value it, but we celebrate it. We want to support you and make you more successful.'

"Our competition is television, video games, and overscheduled people. We don't want our stores competing with the outdoor store down the street. We want you collaborating with them to go to your local community and schools to get people volunteering in the woods. To engage children in outdoor recreation. The more people, the bigger the market. So the outdoor store down the street wins, REI wins, and, most importantly, the community wins.

"We end up with healthier people who have a deeper connection to the planet and who will be more likely to recycle. They will use more fuel-efficient cars. They will understand what they have to lose if we don't solve some of the big environmental issues, even if they don't yet know what to do personally to effect change."

---

### Tips for Listening Deeply and Building Great Relationships

- Ask people what excites and motivates them.
- Show appreciation publicly.
- Give negative feedback privately.
- Give without expecting anything in return.
- Honor people with your full attention.
- View your company as a community.
- Respect and protect the environment.

---

At REI, people take their relationship to the planet very seriously. The company gives 3 percent of its operating profits—roughly 10 percent of its net income—to nonprofit organizations involved in conservation, recreation, and youth services.

"Last year, we did a supplemental grant as well. We crossed the $1 billion mark. Instead of a big party, we gave an extra million dollars to local parks around the country. So our grants last year were over $4 million, including a hundred parks chosen by our REI store employees. Every REI community had a park to give a $10,000 grant to—a park they could get out and work on themselves.

"We've always encouraged our employees to volunteer. It started in 1974, when stores would go out and work on a trail. But it was nothing like it has been in the last five years, where every single store is encouraged to do a service project every year. They clean up beaches and rivers, build trails, and remove invasive species from parks. It's been a way for our employees to be part of the solution."

Sally is helping her employees help REI customers help the planet. She knows that getting the employee piece of the business right is the key to getting the customer piece right. It's all about mobilizing human energy.

"We've got a very different notion of leadership here, because our employees are demanding it. They're looking for an environment they're proud to work in, where we are all committed to the same issues."

JEA leaders like Sally Jewell are leading the way. Their humility enables them to act on behalf of others, to benefit the greater good, and to make a profit. They assume positive intent and shed light on others. It's a leadership style that just might change the world.

## Be a Teacher and a Learner

Imagine lying in a hospital bed. It's 6:30 A.M. The door suddenly swings open. You're greeted by a group of white-coated people with friendly faces who have decided it's time to wake up. Welcome to morning rounds and your new best friends: the attending physician, resident, intern, medical student, and nurse. There's no place to go, so you sit up and observe confident humility in action.

Go to the best teaching hospitals and you will discover the value of teaching and learning. Places like Johns Hopkins Medical Center, the Mayo Clinic, and the Cleveland Clinic are built around action learning in real time. Doctors teach and learn with each patient. Residents supervise and mentor interns and medical students who learn at bedsides by testing their skills. Although there is a clear line of authority, the best teaching hospitals operate in a culture of collaboration. Everyone is responsible and accountable for each patient under his or her care. Problem-based group learning is the norm. Feedback is often immediate. Knowledge comes from failures as well as successes. People teach and learn on a daily basis. Their sense of community outweighs individual egos. They know what they don't know and are willing and eager to learn.

Clearly not all physicians work comfortably in this environment. But the best physicians are some of our best teachers. Mitch Rabkin, the former CEO of Beth Israel Hospital in Boston, is open to teaching and learning. Even when it comes as a surprise.

"I remember vividly one man who used to sweep floors. He and I had never said much more than good morning. One day I sat down at lunch with him in the cafeteria and we were chatting, and I asked him how long he had been working here, and he said, 'Seventeen years.' I said, 'That is quite a long time.' And he said, ''Well, I have been working at Children's for nineteen years.'

"It turned out that he had been working eight hours a day at Children's and then coming over here for another full shift. We went on talking, and I asked him how many kids he had, and he said nine. I thought to myself, Okay, a typical family with no possibility of social advancement. I asked, 'Where are they and what do they do?' And he said, 'Well, my oldest is a professor of microbiology at Stanford, and the next one teaches law at Yale.'

"The man had put every single kid through graduate school, but what you saw walking down the corridor was this guy pushing a broom. What I came to realize in talking to him was here was a man of extraordinary strength and determination, and very few people knew it. And you wonder how many other people working here are like that."

Mitch Rabkin learned that every interaction is a learning opportunity. His genuine interest in the janitor enabled him to see new possibilities inside the hospital. He had just met a guy with more personal power and leadership qualities than he could have imagined. Later Mitch became one of the national leaders in strengthening the collaborative relationships between physicians and nurses.

---

### How to Be a Teacher and a Learner

- Understand the different ways people learn.
- Tailor your teaching to people's needs.
- Be a mentor.
- Help people learn on the job in real time.
- Ask questions more often than you give answers.
- Be willing to not know.
- Cultivate curiosity.
- Learn something new every day.
- Work with an executive coach.
- Let yourself by challenged, work through discomfort, and be open to new ways of doing things.

---

JEA leaders like Mitch Rabkin are active learners. Their eyes and ears are always open to new ideas, knowledge, and feedback. They continually question themselves and the impact they are having on the people around them. Many even have their own coaches.

JEA leaders are also great teachers. They're constantly on the lookout for teachable moments—those windows of opportunity when they can share what they know with others. Or help someone solve a problem. Or communicate their vision or values. Or give feedback, convey a new strategy, or talk about how the business works. They enjoy teaching people how to learn and how to look beyond their industries for new perspectives and solutions.

Steve Reinemund teaches throughout PepsiCo's senior high-potential program. Michelle Peluso teaches at Travelocity, Eric Schaeffer teaches at Signature Theater, and Todd Stitzer teaches at Cadbury Schweppes. Each one teaches the leadership skills required to address tomorrow's challenges. They talk about their vision and values, tell their own leadership stories, and discuss what's working and not working inside their organizations.

You, too, can be a great teacher and learner. If you acknowledge that you don't know everything. If you're willing to learn in real time with others. If you're comfortable living in the gap between where you are and where you want to be. If you ask the hard questions, take risks, and share what you are learning with others. By asking, What am I teaching? and What am I learning? you are showing confident humility at its best.

Ask yourself . . .

∘ How comfortable am I not knowing? Asking for help?
∘ What more can I do to listen deeply and build great relationships?
∘ Am I more of a teacher or a learner? How can I better balance the two?

## CONFIDENT HUMILITY IN ACTION

*Never let your ego get so close to your position that when your position goes, your ego goes with it.*

—GENERAL COLIN POWELL, American four-star general and statesman

Early in my career, I was fortunate to receive a multiyear grant from the MacArthur Foundation to study leadership and healthy organizations. I talked with leading academic researchers, corporate executives, consultants, and union leaders. I wanted to know how healthy leaders create healthy organizations where everyone gets what he or she needs and wants from each other. What sets these leaders apart? What do their organizations look like? The single quality that stood out was *confident humility.*

Let me introduce you to Mike Petters. At Northrop Grumman Newport News (NGNN) it takes eight years and 18,000 people to create just one of the company's products—nuclear-powered aircraft carriers and submarines. That kind of life cycle requires a special kind of leader and extraordinary commitment and sustained top-level performance from everyone. Mike Petters, the president, is the right man for the job.

"People are at the heart of everything we do," says Mike. "We have the world's best shipbuilders. They come to work each day looking to do well, to be part of something bigger than they are. We have a responsibility to create an environment where they can be successful. That starts with me but includes every leader in the shipyard."

Mike's leadership philosophy and style revolve around people. "The single most important process in the shipyard is the relationship that you have with your people," he says. "I get a lot of energy from spending time with our shipbuilders, seeing what they do and watching the success they achieve. It makes for great days. I also get a lot of energy from talking about them. I have so much confidence in what our people do, and I enjoy spreading the word."

Over the past four years, Mike's people-centered approach has been instrumental in reinvigorating the workforce, improving productivity, and satisfying NGNN's primary customer, the U.S. Navy. It has been a total team effort of which Mike is extremely proud. "When one of our ships goes down the river, everybody in the shipyard can say, 'I had a piece of that.'"

A graduate of the U.S. Naval Academy and a consummate lifelong learner, Mike Petters balances the power of his position with his commitment to build a culture of leaders. "I spend more time developing leaders than anything else," he told me. "By raising everyone's leadership skill level, the entire community performs better. I have a fundamental belief that the team is a lot stronger than any individual's ability or interest. If the team doesn't win, nobody wins."

Mike is also deeply aware of his own strengths and vulnerabilities. He knows when to take charge, when to involve others, and when to turn things over to his colleagues. "I have a gut feel for when a decision has to be made and the impact of not making the decision." Yet he admits, "When I'm dealing in an area where I'm weak, I will be more nervous and will call in for more help. If you lose sight of the things that you do well and the things you need help on, you can lose perspective and open yourself up to arrogance or self-doubt. My approach is to be as collaborative as I can be. The people that work around me are a lot smarter than I am."

Mike is a champion of leadership. He talks about it, models it, and invests in leadership development at every level of the shipyard. But don't underestimate Mike. He's unabashed about asking people to deliver consistently on their commitments.

"There's a part of everybody's job where they get to choose to put in something over and above going through the motions. It's not about working harder. It's about people being more engaged and acting like they own the business.

"Ownership starts with your job. Let's say someone is doing a pipe job on an aircraft carrier. He's meticulous about getting insulation put in and positioned right. It's down to a millimeter, and perfectly installed so it can handle fifty years of life. And he smokes a cigarette when he's done and throws the butt on the floor. He assumes somebody else has the responsibility for cleaning it up. Ownership is when he says, 'I'm not going to do that,' and instead throws the butt in the trash. He takes responsibility for himself, his job, and the shipyard."

Mike Petters personifies confident humility. He models and shares his leadership philosophy and deep-seated values. He is authentic. He listens deeply and develops productive relationships throughout the shipyard. He understands that developing people is essential to closing the gap between NGNN's current and desired realities. By making good use of learning opportunities, stretch assignments, and incentives and rewards, Mike differentiates good from poor performers. He's a great teacher and a lifelong learner. He creates just enough anxiety for people to achieve their highest potential, which enables NGNN to optimize its human talent and be the premier shipbuilder in the world.

## WHAT'S YOUR CONFIDENT HUMILITY POTENTIAL?

Confident humility may be the most challenging of the three paradoxes to master. It certainly has been for me. And lessons can come from the most unexpected places.

Ten years ago I got a hair transplant—one thousand new follicles on the top of my head. We won't get into why I did it. That's for another book. Needless to say, however, I was a little self-conscious about going back to work. My first appearance was facilitating an executive team meeting in a Midwest company. I figured that, coming from the heartland, people would be nice and accommodating. So I walked up to the front of the room, feeling both timid and courageous, with my little brown Scottish cap on my head. I thought I'd introduce myself by referring to the transplant.

"Now you might be wondering why I'm wearing this cap today," I said. "Well, to be honest, it's because I'm phallically challenged." Everyone in the room broke into hysterical laughter. My follicle humor had worked. And then I realized what I actually had said. So much for confident humility.

We each come from a family or culture that tends to promote one side of the confident humility continuum. If you were taught to be strong in the face of adversity, and to solve problems on your own, you probably developed a high degree of self-confidence. You are comfortable with your personal power. However, you may have difficulty asking others for help. You may think you have to do everything yourself.

If you were taught to ask for help, or that two heads are better than one, you probably developed a deep sense of humility. You are open to learning from others. However, you may find it hard to tackle tough problems by yourself. You may doubt your abilities.

JEA leaders are able to hold on to their self-assurance and accept their shortcomings—at the same time. They are comfortable with who they are. They know clearly what they can and cannot do. These leaders are adept at taking bold actions without becoming arrogant, and maintaining healthy egos without feeling self-important. They feel at ease with their own power. They also readily share power, and, as developers of talent, they're adept at empowering others.

A leader with confident humility can walk into an intense, politically charged boardroom, hold his own with confidence and grace, and then walk into a factory or a cafeteria, sit down with an average worker, and have an honest, open conversation—one human being to another. He feels comfortable in both situations. And so do the people around him.

Confident humility is born from a positive self-image and compassionate respect for others. It grows with the development of personal power and generosity of spirit. And it blossoms with lifelong learning, strong values, and a desire to share power and serve others.

Use the quiz and table on the next pages to figure out where you sit on the continuum of confident humility. Once you know where you are, you will be able to move toward the center. As you learn to master both sides of this paradox, you will be better equipped to balance your power with the power distributed throughout your organization.

---

### How Confident and Humble Are You?

*Instructions:* Place an "X" next to the *one characteristic in each pair* that best describes you. Consider asking your colleagues or direct reports to complete the checklist to learn how other people see you.

I AM . . .
1. ___strong-willed.
2. ___generous.

3. ___someone who is aware of my strengths.
4. ___someone who is aware of my vulnerabilities.

5. ___able to hold my own with strong personalities.
6. ___able to talk openly with people at all organization levels.

7. ___concerned primarily with leading teams.
8. ___concerned primarily with building teams.

9. ___comfortable with power.
10. ___uncomfortable with power.

11. ___likely to trust myself more than others.
12. ___likely to trust others as much as myself.

13. ___unusually open to taking risks.
14. ___unusually open to others' ideas.

15. ___prone to act decisively.
16. ___prone to serve others.

17. ___good at taking charge.
18. ___good at working collaboratively.

19. ___inclined to teach.
20. ___inclined to learn.

*Results:* Count how many "X"s you have for odd-numbered items and how many "X"s you have for even-numbered items. Having more odd-numbered "X"s means you are more confident. Having more even-numbered "X"s means you are more humble. If your answers are equally distributed, you are able to balance being both confident and humble. You are a JEA leader.

Learning to be both confident and humble will enable you to tap into the best—in yourself and others. It will ensure that you and your organization are lifelong learners and teachers. This, in turn, will strengthen your ability to stay ahead of the competition through creativity and innovation.

JEA leaders who demonstrate confident humility have mastered the human side of leadership. Like Michelle Peluso, they recognize what people need and tailor their leadership style accordingly. Like Art Collins and Shelly Lazarus, they live and champion their values. Like Alan Mulally, they know that the lion's share of power resides outside of them. Like Steve Reinemund, they strive to unleash that power and develop leaders. They listen deeply, like Hiroshi Okuda, and build powerful relationships, like Sally Jewell. And, like Mitch Rabkin, they are great teachers and lifelong learners.

If you find yourself leaning too far to the left or right of confident humility, you need to bring yourself back to the center. To move from arrogant to confident:

- Take time to find out what others think and feel before you act.
- Practice sharing leadership and key responsibilities.
- Ask someone you trust to help you understand your vulnerabilities.

To move from self-doubting to humble:

- Take on additional responsibilities one step at a time.
- Enroll in an assertiveness class.
- Work with a coach or mentor to deepen your skills and increase your confidence.

|  | Too Little Anxiety | Just Enough Anxiety | | Too Much Anxiety |
| --- | --- | --- | --- | --- |
| If you are . . . | Self-Doubting | Humble | Confident | Arrogant |
| On the inside you . . . | question your abilities<br><br>are insecure about your power<br><br>fear failure | accept your vulnerabilities and shortcomings<br><br>listen and learn from others<br><br>have respect for what other people know | possess positive self-esteem<br><br>have clear values<br><br>are courageous | are self-serving<br><br>feel entitled to special treatment<br><br>think you are better than others |
| On the outside you . . . | rely heavily on others and delegate too much<br><br>accept poor performance to avoid confrontation<br><br>hesitate to take strong course of action | seek to learn from others<br><br>empower people to succeed<br><br>recognize and reward others' contributions | develop and celebrate people's strengths<br><br>share power with ease<br><br>delegate responsibility and authority | motivate through fear, intimidation, and manipulation<br><br>rarely delegate and keep people out of the loop<br><br>exaggerate your contributions |
|  | Ineffective Energy | Productive Energy | | Chaotic Energy |

The JEA leaders I've talked about in the last three chapters are masters at each of the three leadership paradoxes. They balance realism and optimism. They're both constructive and impatient. And they exude confident humility.

Now it's time to see how everything comes together. How do JEA leaders use the three paradoxes, along with an open heart and open mind, to create just enough anxiety in their organizations? How can you put just enough anxiety to work?

# 8

# PUTTING JEA TO WORK

| CHANGE & UNCERTAINTY | → | LEADER'S WORK | → | JUST ENOUGH ANXIETY | → | THE THREE PARADOXES | → | WINNING PERFORMANCE |
|---|---|---|---|---|---|---|---|---|
| | | Open Mind | | Too Much Anxiety | | Realistic Optimism | | Productive Energy |
| | | Open Heart | | Too Little Anxiety | | Constructive Impatience | | Profitable Growth |
| | | Performance Gap | | | | Confident Humility | | |

*The way to get started is to quit talking and begin doing.*
—WALT DISNEY, business innovator and founder of Disney entertainment

Kumar Mangalam Birla was only twenty-eight when he took the reins of the Aditya Birla Group in Mumbai, India, due to the untimely death of his father. Nobody expected him to lead the company into the ranks of the Global 500. But that's exactly what he did.

The young Birla infused the Birla Group with a passion for winning. He embraced Western management methods, placed young MBAs in senior positions, and abandoned his family's preference for hiring fellow members of their *marwari* business subcaste. In a culture committed to saving face, Kumar bucked social mores and began eliminating unprofitable businesses and balancing tough decisions with respectful benevolence. He shifted the company's focus from fiber-based to ferrous metals and consolidated each business. He institutionalized systems and processes that enabled high-potential managers to be entrepreneurs, and changed management systems to emphasize merit rather than seniority. He hired people he thought were brighter than he was. And through it all, Kumar balanced persistence with patience, self-assurance with the willingness to learn, and today's reality with tomorrow's vision.

Through his JEA leadership, Kumar has created a results-driven, decentralized, and networked group of independent companies, run by leaders he both trusts and holds accountable for results. The Birla Group employs 100,000 people worldwide and attracts the best talent from all over the globe. More than 50 percent of its revenues come from operations around the world.

His transformation of the family company into a $24 billion conglomerate demonstrates Kumar's understanding of how to generate just enough anxiety to propel people forward. "Organizational longevity requires that there be some level of ferment and internal challenge, some level of constant boil," he says. Yet "the process is full of anxiety, uncertainty, and silent suffering," and "leaders need to be sensitized to these issues, to create conditions that are conducive to continuous learning."

Kumar also knows that generating too much anxiety can be disastrous. You have to make a "conscious decision to pace the change," he advises. "Initially, there was the fear that if I rocked the boat too hard the outcome would be worse than what it is now." Today, however, adaptability is an inherent part of the Birla culture. "Change is in the organizational psyche, and it doesn't create any disruptions anymore."

Despite his wealth, education, and power Kumar remains a humble executive with great respect for others. He's a mature, modern, modest person with a sense of confidence and an unassuming nature, a man with extraordinary aspirations and self-awareness. He believes that when employees underperform, a part of the fault lies with their boss. "My leadership style differs from my father's, but if he were here today, I think he'd agree with everything I'm doing," he says.

It was with his father in mind that the young leader designed the Birla Group's first corporate logo: a rising sun. The image was both a literal translation of Aditya, his father's name, and a unifying symbol for the rapidly growing global organization. According to Kumar, "The sun embodies the values we stand for: its journey is never ending, and we never stop in our own search for excellence."

Here's a leader who thrives in uncertainty. He lives comfortably in the present and the future. He stretches his organization while creating an environment that is healthy and collaborative. And he develops and mentors others while continually learning himself. He is a JEA leader.

Kumar Birla's leadership challenges are universal. You may live in a different time zone, work in a different industry or sector, have responsibility for a larger or smaller organization, or lead a different kind of team. But the issue is the same.

Your challenge is to build a winning JEA organization. To do this, you need to get rid of the shackles forged by old mental models and outdated leadership methods. You need to understand how anxiety affects you and your organization and develop new ways of thinking about uncertainty and change. You need to chart and navigate the gaps between where you are and where you want to be. To develop an open mind and open heart. To balance between too much and too little anxiety. To live in paradox. These actions will enable you to create just enough anxiety and unleash the productive energy inside your organization.

---

### The JEA Leader's Lens: The New Way of Looking at Leadership

- It's time to embrace change, uncertainty, and anxiety as facts of life.
- We can use our healthy anxiety as a positive force for growth.
- Just enough anxiety is the key to living and leading in our complex world.

---

The ability to live and lead with just enough anxiety is the great differentiator. You see the world through a fresh lens. This enables you to travel into the unknown (*leadership*) and manage change and uncertainty (*strategy*). It helps you inspire and challenge people to stretch into their discomfort zone and perform beyond their expectations (*engagement*). Just enough anxiety enables you to imagine possibilities and discover opportunities (*innovation*) to expand your business (*growth*). This translates to increased profitability and sustainable value creation. It is the proven formula for building a winning JEA organization.

## BECOMING A JEA LEADER

*If your actions inspire others to dream more, learn more, do more and become more, you are a leader.*

—JOHN QUINCY ADAMS, sixth president of the United States

## WHAT MAKES A JEA LEADER

You sit at the center of your organization. Your success depends on your ability to develop an open mind and heart, and to master realistic optimism, constructive impatience, and confident humility. These essential qualities of a JEA leader enable you to live and lead with just enough anxiety.

You are a JEA leader if you *think* with an open mind. You are self-aware, a lifelong learner, and not attached to a single point of view. In fact, you're able to hold seemingly contradictory thoughts in your mind at the same time. You blend the best of Eastern and Western perspectives, like Ping An Insurance's Peter Ma. You balance your inherent drive for protection with your desire to grow and develop. And like the U.S. Air Force general John Jumper, you embrace both your personal power and the certainty of uncertainty.

You believe change and uncertainty are opportunities. By admitting what you can and can't control, you are able to take charge of your life while remaining open to the unexpected.

You have reframed the idea of power. Like Alan Mulally at Ford, you know that your real power comes from harnessing the power inside others. And like Travelocity's Michelle Peluso, you know there is power in being your full self at work, in integrating your masculine and feminine qualities.

You understand what makes you anxious—your genetics, personal development, life experiences, and beliefs and expectations. You know your strengths. Yet you also know what trips you up, where you're vulnerable. You understand how your perceptions can help or hinder you. Like Linda Rabbitt at Rand Construction Corporation, you monitor your thoughts and expectations to keep them positive and in sync with your highest goals.

You are a JEA leader if you *feel* with an open heart. You exhibit emotional honesty, empathy and compassion, and emotional resilience. Like Isadore Sharp at Four Seasons Hotels, you follow the Golden Rule. You experience the full range of human emotions—from pain and fear to love and gratitude—and express each emotion in healthy ways. Because you're familiar with what too much, too little, and just enough anxiety feel like, you're able to keep your anxiety at a healthy level. And like Jimmy DePriest conducting the Oregon Symphony, you help others do the same.

You feel at home in uncharted territory and, like NSBA executive director Anne Bryant, are willing to take risks to lead people through change. You're at ease with healthy conflict. You accept your vulnerabilities and are willing to poke fun at yourself. You're comfortable with discomfort, in yourself and others. By making friends with ambiguity, you are able to thrive in a permanent state of transformation.

You are a JEA leader if you *act* with realistic optimism, constructive impatience, and confident humility. Like Alan Lafley at Procter & Gamble and Dave O'Reilly at Chevron, you continually assess where you are while crafting a bold vision of the future. Like Arlington County's Ron Carlee, you push people to do their best while creating an environment in which it's safe to stretch and grow. You trust yourself and others to get the job done while being committed to learning along the way. And you dare to dream and deliver, like Stonyfield Farm's Gary Hirschberg.

You tackle problems head-on in creative ways, like Muhammad Yunus at Grameen Bank, to close the gap between where you are and where you want to be. Whether that means raising the bar, like Ken Samet at MedStar Health, or helping people face their anxieties, like Eric Schaeffer at the Signature Theater, you strive for and achieve continuous improvement.

These beliefs and behaviors reflect the healthy, dynamic interplay of your emotional and executive brains. They demonstrate your ability to consciously control your anxiety, and to develop new habits of mind and action. Here are five principles to help you develop just enough anxiety in your life.

- *Know yourself.* Reflect on the kinds of situations that have made you anxious. Learn to recognize the signs of too much, too little, and just enough anxiety within yourself. Understand your strengths and shortcomings. Practice stepping outside yourself and observe how you perceive, interpret, and evaluate situations. You may be creating your own anxiety in the way you see the world.
- *Get comfortable with uncertainty.* Develop an acceptance of change as a natural part of life. Cultivate an open mind to positive and negative experiences as opportunities to learn and grow. The more you recognize what you can and cannot control in your life, the more able you will be to handle uncertainty and change.
- *Befriend your anxiety.* Acknowledge your fears. Get comfortable with competing emotions inside yourself. Allow yourself to see your feelings as indicators that it's time to pay attention to a key aspect of your life. Remember: Your conversations with yourself influence how you experience and interpret your anxiety. Practice deep breathing and listen to what your anxiety is "saying" to you.
- *Practice nonattachment.* Avoid unnecessary attachments to success, objects, fame, people, and money. Watch for repetitive thoughts that intensify or exaggerate your anxiety (e.g., generalizing, magnifying, and beating up on yourself). You can refuse to entertain thoughts that cause you too much anxiety.
- *Be real.* Life is full of pleasure and pain. Allow yourself the freedom to experience both and enjoy the full range of human emotions. Develop a self-monitoring capacity to see and react to the world. Make sure you're not shutting yourself off from your feelings or drowning in negatives.

    Ask yourself . . .

    ○ In what ways am I a JEA leader?
    ○ What JEA attitudes do I need to develop?
    ○ How can I act more like a JEA leader?

## CREATING A JEA TEAM

*The leaders who work most effectively never say "I." They think "we"; they think "team."*

—WARREN BENNIS, author of *On Becoming a Leader* and founder of the Leadership Institute at USC

As a leader, you are most likely responsible for one or more teams. You may be a top executive, middle manager, entrepreneur, factory manager, or office head. You may work in a large corporation, a not-for-profit organization, a government agency, or a small mom-and-pop business. You may have responsibility for 2 or 20,000 people. Whatever your position, you will inspire or inhibit the people you lead with the kind of environment you create around you. Let's take a look at how this works.

*An open heart invites passion.*

Everyone harbors a deep desire to succeed, to win. It's an emotional longing tied to our inherently human desires to feel good about ourselves, be productive, and live meaningful lives. We want to make a difference in the world.

## WHAT MAKES A JEA TEAM

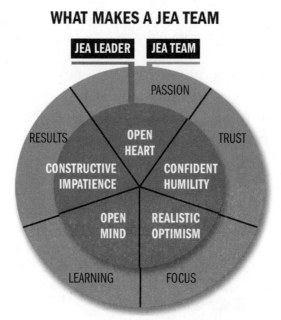

As a leader, it's your job to tap into these desires. It's how you motivate people to perform in service to the organization and to themselves. Just watch great coaches, teachers, ministers, and bosses. There's something magical in what they do that touches people's hearts and cultivates passion.

Passion ignites the energy within your business. It's what turns people on, fires them up. People with passion care deeply about what they're doing. They put in extra effort and extra hours to get the job done. In a world of uncertainty, passion helps you scale mountainous problems and navigate the murky waters of change. And passion is contagious.

Having an open heart is the key to invoking passion in your team. By being emotionally honest, you connect with people on a deeply human level. By being empathic and compassionate, you honor who people truly are. By being emotionally resilient, you show people how to handle life's inevitable ups and downs.

*Confident humility nurtures trust.*

We all have an inherent need to trust ourselves and each other. This is especially true in today's ever-changing world. Everything happens at lightning speed. Misunderstandings and missed deadlines lurk around every corner. Without trust, we are doomed.

Trust has two parts: believing in others (*trusting*) and being worthy of others' belief in you (*trustworthy*). It is your job to make sure both elements are present in your team. When you are trusting, people feel valued. They are more open and honest. They do their best. And they want to trust you. When you are trustworthy, you confirm their trust, and the cycle continues.

Trust is the glue that holds your relationships together. Your relationships, in turn, hold your team together. Without trust, your team's productivity, commitment, and quality all decline. The ground around you seems to give way. People turn on each other. Anxiety increases. Chaos reigns.

Building trust depends on your ability to demonstrate confident humility. Your confidence in yourself enables you to model your values and be authentic. Your confidence in others enables you to share power and develop leaders. Your humility enables you to listen deeply, be generous with your time and attention, and remain open to learning. These are the building blocks of great relationships.

Remember: Trust takes a long time to earn, yet it can be lost in a moment's thoughtlessness. We all know in our hearts if we do or don't trust ourselves or the people around us. And they know it, too.

*Realistic optimism focuses energy.*

Most of us are not inspired by the prospect of a higher net margin. We're not inspired to increase market share. And we're not inspired—at least not for very long—by a bigger paycheck. None of these things drives us to achieve extraordinary results.

We need something to believe in. It might be a vision, a personal goal, or a lifelong dream of success. We're eager to get from *here* to *there* only when *there* is someplace we want to go.

Your work as a leader takes place in the gap between where your team is and where you want it to be. It's up to you to help people focus on current problems and opportunities, burning platforms, and day-to-day business objectives. It's also up to you to help them keep their eyes on the desired outcome, the reason for all their hard work.

It's all about energy. Every gap contains human energy waiting to be unleashed and harnessed. What will you do with this energy? Will you allow it to become too much or too little anxiety? Or will you turn it into productive and focused JEA energy?

Focus is the guiding light that keeps your team on the right path. It's what they need to close the gap. Without focus, your team will flounder like a group of people lost in the woods without a compass or sunlight.

Realistic optimism is the secret to providing focus. When you tell people the truth about where things stand, you give them a clear starting point for their journey across the gap. When you articulate a compelling vision, you let them know where they're going. You give them something to focus on that inspires, stretches, and unites them—a North Star. When your vision is grounded in reality and hopeful about the future, you instill a sense of common purpose and a clear mental image of success.

*An open mind fosters learning.*

Most of us want to grow and improve. But we're also wary of change. We crave stability. But nothing stays the same. Not us. Not our organizations. Not even the air we breathe. The only way we can thrive in a world of constant change is to be willing and able to change ourselves.

To be a leader in today's world, you must expand your knowledge and skills continually. You must reinvent your leadership every day. And you must help your people learn and grow. It's your job to balance between your team's needs for protection and growth. To help people get comfortable with discomfort. And to learn from their mistakes.

Continual learning is what's going on behind the curtain of successful change. It's how people handle uncertainty. It's how you leverage your organization's human assets. Learning keeps people engaged in their jobs. Without new knowledge, insights, skills, and ways of doing things, you and your team will fall farther and farther behind.

Having an open mind is the way to foster learning in your team. By being self-aware, you encourage others to learn more about themselves. By being eager to learn yourself, you set an example for your team. You turn every interaction into a learning opportunity. By not getting attached to the way things are, you create space for people to stretch into the future.

*Constructive impatience produces results.*

Most of us are willing to work hard. But we're willing to go the extra mile only for a worthwhile goal. And we want to be appreciated for our efforts. It's your job to focus people on execution and results. You need to harness your team's creativity and drive. To develop outcome thinking. To cultivate a sense of ownership.

Without ownership, your people put in their hours and then go home. They feel indifferent, perhaps even hostile or destructive. Your team has no galvanizing identity. But when your people own their jobs—and are truly engaged with the team—their commitment soars. Everything matters. They act as mature business partners. They take initiative, accept responsibility, and care about results. Any anxiety they feel is directed toward growth and performance. It becomes a constant source of energy.

Constructive impatience is the fuel you need to ignite top performance. When you create a safe environment, you make it possible to challenge people into their discomfort zones. You create passion for winning and get the results you want. You mobilize people and give them the tools they need to succeed. And you lead your team through the ups and downs of the business.

How does all of this come together to create JEA teams? Let's check in with Arbitron chief administrative officer Kathie Ross to find out.

"Our core competency at Arbitron is measuring audiences in the radio industry," says Kathie. "Like most businesses, our world is changing so fast that if you're not constantly looking for new knowledge and products, then you're behind the game. We now have out-of-home technology for measuring different kinds of media. So we're moving from a legacy company to 'Arbitron on the Edge.'

"We're trying to introduce that same edge on our executive team. We want to create an environment that is comfortable enough for people to function in, but edgy enough that if people don't deliver, or don't keep their commitments to the team, they get called out. So it's a very exciting time, but it's very nerve-racking."

Kathie's job is to harness that anxiety. As the adviser and steward of the executive team, she coaches and aligns executive staff and links directly to the board.

"It's critical that we have people who have the capacity to thrive in success and navigate in uncertainty. Some of the executives are retiring after many years at Arbitron, and a new generation of people is coming on board. It's great having new executive team members from different arenas, people with different experiences. They are relying on those of us who have been around for a long time to help them learn, not only about the business but about the culture at Arbitron. And we're learning enormous amounts from them about how we might look at our business differently.

"We're also becoming more comfortable with conflict. We see it not as something to avoid but something to harness, albeit in a civilized way. But you need to get the big issues on the table. So as leaders, we need to hold and modulate the anxiety of the team. We need to be in touch with our team, to read people, to know where they are, both individually and collectively. Then we need to ask the provocative questions that bring someone out of too little anxiety to just enough. Or open our hearts to someone with too much anxiety to bring them into just enough. Mining these opportunities in real time is what creates a high-performing team."

Kathie knows what makes a great team tick. We've all been on a team that was broken down or impaired—where people didn't bring their full selves to the table, where there was constant conflict, or where one or two

| How to Put JEA into Practical Action | |
| --- | --- |
| When setting goals and priorities . . . | • Be crystal clear about your expectations.<br>• Create stretch targets that tap into people's potential.<br>• Make sure everyone understands and agrees with the goals. |
| When leading change . . . | • Imagine together what success could look like.<br>• Give people time to think through and comment on proposed changes.<br>• Encourage people to take informed risks while defining their boundaries. |
| In meetings . . . | • Share your thoughts, feelings, intentions, and concerns.<br>• Pay attention to spoken and unspoken communication.<br>• Give people opportunities to vent their anxiety. |
| When managing performance . . . | • Build on people's strengths and manage around their shortcomings.<br>• Involve people in defining their own performance goals.<br>• Manage your anxiety about giving and receiving feedback. |
| When solving problems and making decisions . . . | • Stay attuned to your anxiety in the gap.<br>• Explore your options and the impact on people's level of anxiety.<br>• Define current reality and desired outcomes in clear, straightforward language. |
| When communicating on key issues . . . | • Be open and direct about your views and goals.<br>• Listen more than you talk and speak the truth.<br>• Ask for feedback and manage your anxiety when you receive it. |
| When measuring success . . . | • Define desired results for individuals and teams.<br>• Consider "soft" signs of success such as engagement, collaboration, and loyalty.<br>• Measure the attitudes, behaviors, and outcomes you want to see. |

voices dominated. Inevitably, these poorly functioning teams lead to poor business decisions. They get mired in too much anxiety or undermined by too little.

Great teams are built by JEA leaders. By inviting passion, nurturing trust, focusing energy, fostering learning, and producing results, JEA leaders use just enough anxiety to achieve winning team performance.

Ask yourself . . .

○ Is my team a JEA team?
○ How does my team demonstrate passion? Trust? Focus? Learning? Results?
○ What are our strengths? Where can we improve?

## BUILDING A JEA ORGANIZATION

*Good is the enemy of great.*

—JIM COLLINS, *Good to Great*

Jack Welch was obsessed with the financial side of the business in his early years as CEO of General Electric (GE). "Neutron Jack," as he came to be known, was all about cutting costs, creating efficiencies, selling off underperforming businesses, pushing top performance, and, most important, raising profits. While he made many key business moves during this time, he later admitted he had undervalued the human side of the business. Clearly, many of his decisions set the stage for GE's twenty-year success. But by that point, Jack had realized it was the people who mattered most. Developing leaders, he concluded, was a leader's most important job. And the numbers don't lie. According to *BusinessWeek*, thirty-four of the top executives at Fortune 500 companies in the early years of the twenty-first century had come up through the ranks of GE.

Some leaders never discover that people are the most influential factor in business success. Others find out late in the game, perhaps through a personal or business crisis. Or they grow into the idea. Whether they come to it early, late, or just know it in their bones, JEA leaders understand that people are the real engine for growth.

Your organization is human at its core. It is a collection of people brought together to create value. Only by embracing its human nature can you become intimately attuned to your business and guide it to consistent success. You must interact with your organization as a great conductor interacts with his orchestra. You must lead the players, not the instruments.

The players, of course, are infinitely more complex than any instrument. Their complexity is what makes people so problematic—and so powerful. You can never know anyone completely. You cannot fully control someone's actions or reactions. Each of us is a mystery, laden with infinite layers of potential. The potential of your organization, therefore, lies in your capacity to understand, inspire, focus, and empower your people. This is every leader's greatest challenge.

If you're a JEA leader, you know that *people drive business success.* I know this from talking with hundreds of CEOs from successful companies around the world. These are men and women across all industries, sectors, and national cultures who deliver superior numbers year after year in constantly changing conditions. What they share is their penetrating insight into what makes their organizations thrive. By understanding people, as well as business, and by focusing on the human drivers of business success, these JEA leaders gain powerful and sustainable competitive advantages.

In the mind of a JEA leader, the soft stuff is the hard stuff. Medtronic chairman and former CEO Art Collins describes it this way: "The people drive everything. The income statement, the balance sheet, and the cash-flow statement are the results of what the organization and the people do. It's not the other way around. If you focus only on the financials, you lose the spirit or soul of the company. That leads to stagnation and a decline in performance. Now, I'm not saying the financials are not important. If you don't earn a fair profit, and if you're not financially solid, you don't have a future."

Not every leader thinks this way. Many believe that their financial strategy (e.g., investments, cash flow, debt, and stock price) drives the business, followed by their market strategy (e.g., customers, suppliers, sales, brand, and reputation) and their operational strategy (e.g., R&D, manufacturing, planning, and product development). To them, their human strategy (e.g., leadership, culture, learning, and execution) is no

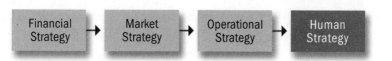

more than a tool to support higher-priority agendas, as depicted in the graphic above. As a result, people become second-class citizens instead of being truly managed or "owned" by the CEO or business unit leader.

At Healthy Companies International, our research has shown that JEA leaders upend these four traditional strategies. They elevate human capital from a secondary tool to a primary driver. They understand that people drive the operational strategy of the business, which in turn drives the market strategy. And the finances of the business are simply the score-card, as depicted in the graphic below.

This turnaround in business priorities is taking hold. CEO surveys report that top leaders are paying increasing attention to their human agendas. More and more "Most Admired Companies" are championing the human aspect of business. And companies that prioritize people are rapidly becoming the biggest winners in the marketplace.

Yes, finance, marketplace, and operations agendas are critical for your business. But they are the price of entry. It's the human agenda that gives your company its real competitive edge.

If you're a JEA leader, you put people at the front of the value chain. You hire the best and brightest people and make sure they're in the right jobs. You engage their hearts and minds. You inspire and challenge them to do their best work. You give them the authority and tools they need to exceed expectations. And you acknowledge, reward, and celebrate their accomplishments.

Ten years ago I met an amazing leader known as the "transformation man" at Allstate Insurance Company. His name is Jack Callahan. Jack would go into struggling divisions within the company and bring them back to life. He was the ultimate JEA leader. He told me, "I've learned that

the hard stuff—top-down command and control—is the easy way. It's the soft stuff that's hard to do, but what really makes the difference.

"If you provide the right tools and environment, if you focus on individual employees and give them a framework for success, and allow them to focus on the customer, you are bound to win. Instead of workers coming to the job and, at best, feeling satisfied with pay, benefits, and working conditions, you get people who feel good about what's happening and are willing to perform above and beyond what's expected. If you focus on the people side of the business, you can create extraordinary results. That's when a company takes off."

## FIVE LEADING INDICATORS OF BUSINESS SUCCESS

*If you don't know where you're going, you'll end up somewhere else.*
—YOGI BERRA, former Major League
Baseball catcher and manager

When you put financials first, you end up focusing on revenues, production, profits, budget compliance, and ROI. These are *lagging* indicators. They tell you what your company (or one of its component parts) has already done. They are backward-looking measures of performance.

When you put people first, you focus on *leading* indicators. These are the measures that help you foresee how your company will likely perform in the future, based on its present strengths and weaknesses. They are forward-looking.

Leading indicators are the DNA of your business. They determine your company's ability to sustain dynamic growth. They let you know when something isn't working or is about to fail. They help you recover from short-term problems or rebuild after a crisis. Most important, they enable you to keep your company healthy and responsive to change.

The concept of leading indicators comes from economics. The Federal Reserve, for example, uses leading economic indicators (e.g., the consumer price index, unemployment claims, housing starts) to gain insight into the emerging economic climate (e.g., inflation, recession, growth).

Armed with such knowledge, the Fed adjusts the variables it can control (e.g., interest rates and money supply) to influence the economy in desired directions.

In much the same way, you can use leading indicators to determine where your organization is headed. Then you can decide where to invest your time, attention, and energy *now* to optimize your results *later.* You can determine where you will get the biggest return on your investment. It's how you get ahead and stay ahead in business.

At HCI, we have identified five leading indicators for business success based on hundreds of CEO interviews over two decades. They are:

- Purpose and Values
- Productive Relationships
- Shared Direction
- Creativity and Innovation
- Performance Excellence

Each indicator specifies a crucial strength your organization needs to produce superior business results. And each one offers you clear opportunities to do something today that will improve your results over time.

Together these leading indicators take the mystery out of building a JEA organization. Let's look at how JEA leaders and teams generate high marks on all five of them.

*A JEA organization stays on purpose and lives its values.*

When you have an open heart and invite passion around the values of your organization, you construct a foundation that can withstand any storm. You define what your company stands for. This gives people purpose and inspires them to do their best. When these values live inside the hearts and minds of every employee, they guide business decisions and drive every system and process inside your organization. Your people become ambassadors of your business.

"Medtronic saves lives." Chairman and former CEO Art Collins creates the working environment that brings this core value to life. He hires and fires people, recognizes and celebrates accomplishments, and rewards and penalizes performance based on this value. He says what he means and does what he says. He leads by example. Art's open heart,

## WHAT MAKES A JEA ORGANIZATION

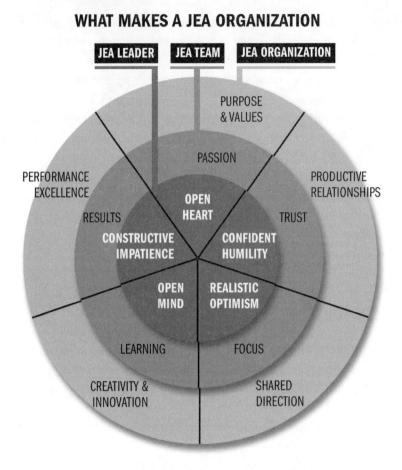

combined with people's passion for saving lives, has molded this success-ful, values-driven business.

Your organization is living its values when people act courageously to maintain high ethical standards. Communication is open and decisions are transparent. Every person's contribution is respected. Doing the right thing is as important as doing things right. And emotional honesty, em-pathy and compassion, and emotional resilience are the name of the game.

*A JEA organization mobilizes productive relationships.*

If you're a JEA leader, your confident humility creates two-way trust with your employees. You are authentic, dependable, and consistent. You build solid relationships and teams. You encourage honest dialogue and healthy debate. You emphasize teaching and learning, and develop strong leaders. And you let everyone know that it's their responsibility to shed light on the people around them.

Sally Jewell at REI understands the power of productive relationships. A servant leader with a strong commitment to collaboration, she blends the best of masculine and feminine leadership to mobilize REI employees. She regularly conducts "town meetings" and shares the financials of her business to get her people on board. Then she leverages people's concern for the environment—both inside and outside the company—to get all of us to care more about this planet we call home.

You know your organization is mobilizing people and building productive relationships when people are both trusting and trustworthy. Collaboration is the norm. Leaders at all levels share power, authority, and decision making. People value one another and embrace diversity. They effectively convert conflicts into creative opportunities because they believe "we are all in this together."

*A JEA organization creates shared direction.*

As a JEA leader, you use realism and optimism to create focus for people. You know that shared direction is the glue that holds your organization together. So you tell the truth about the present and paint a vivid picture of the future. You make sure your vision is shared at every level. You create a strategy that is winning and actionable. You set goals that are focused and aligned. This enables your organization to move forward like a well-coordinated armada of ships sailing the Mediterranean during the height of the Greek empire.

Dennis Nally of PricewaterhouseCoopers is a master at creating shared direction. He continually holds two pictures in his mind: the company's current reality and its desired future—to become *the* distinctive professional-services firm. Then he lives and leads in the gap between the two. Dennis tells the truth about today while remaining hopeful about tomorrow. He talks about change as opportunity. By focusing PwC's 2,200 partners on *both* challenges *and* possibilities, he gets everyone on board the same boat, headed in the same direction, and energized to reach the same goal.

You have created shared direction when everyone in your organization understands where you are and where you're going. And they know why and how. Their individual and team goals are in sync with your company's strategic ones. Their performance standards and plans also match. People at all levels know how their jobs fit into the bigger picture.

*A JEA organization unleashes and harnesses creativity and innovation.*

When you have an open mind, you embrace learning, for yourself and others. This opens the door to the creativity and innovation you need to keep up with a changing business environment. There are many ways to grow. You might change the way you make money, add value to your products and services, or redesign your offerings. You might invest in research, create new experiences for your customers, or rebrand your business. Or you might join forces with others through new networks, alliances, and distribution channels. However you do it, you are adept at unleashing the creative energies of your people to build and sustain a winning company.

We can learn a lot about creativity and innovation from J. P. Garnier at GlaxoSmithKline. His ability to step outside the box to imagine the best R&D organization in the world set the stage for a remarkable transformation. His ability to remain unconstrained by how things had always been done enabled GSK to step out of the box as well. J.P. defined a clear course of action that people could understand and endorse. He encouraged learning and experimentation throughout the company. And he realigned systems and structures and redeployed resources to support the new model.

You know you have a culture of creativity and innovation when learning is everyone's top priority. People seek to understand themselves and how the business works. They routinely question assumptions. In fact, they question everything. Learning from one another, and from mistakes, is how your organization improves performance. By not clinging to old ways of doing things, people at all levels freely create the future.

*A JEA organization achieves performance excellence.*

Your constructive impatience as a JEA leader is what produces results. It's all about finding the right level of anxiety to maximize performance. You are driven by your abiding passion for winning. Your aspirations are bold, your expectations clear. You manage costs to maximize value. You push decisions down to the right people at the right level. You let people know where they stand through ongoing feedback. And you make it safe for everyone to be their best selves.

Cadbury Schweppes's Todd Stitzer has always challenged himself to do better—in school, sports, and business. So his vision to take Cadbury to greatness was not that surprising. With his bold, courageous leadership, he challenged people to be the best. He set bold targets and transmitted his sense of urgency and passion throughout the company. But Todd never forgot that people drive the business. They create the strategy, understand the markets, interpret the numbers, motivate teams, and execute the business. His ability to be both constructive and impatient was a winning combination.

You have achieved performance excellence when accountability is clear and metrics mean something. Results consistently exceed expectations. People feel safe and protected as well as motivated to outperform. They channel their anxiety into productive energy. Your organization is fast, flexible, and responsive to change.

JEA organizations get high marks in all five leading indicators. Their people live the values, build productive relationships, share direction, are creative, and achieve performance excellence. People are the engine that drives business. And just enough anxiety is the fuel that fires up that engine and creates speed and success.

Being a JEA leader is about making the most of the energy inside your organization. Just as you might rev your car engine to keep it from stalling, or downshift to negotiate a sharp curve, you need to modulate the engine inside your organization. You need to monitor and manage people's energy—creating just enough for peak performance. It's your job, as the steward of your organization.

Yet building a JEA organization is everybody's job. In fact, we must all be the JEA leaders in our own lives—whether we are CEOs or factory workers, division heads or team leaders, stay-at-home parents or global leaders. As we develop the five qualities of a JEA leader, we are more able to embrace change, bounce back from adversity, tackle problems, seize opportunities, and feel positive about who we are and where we're going.

Change happens one person at a time. By becoming a JEA leader, you will set the standard for your life and your leadership. You will help others become JEA leaders and build JEA teams. And, together, you will create a JEA organization.

Ask yourself . . .

- What drives my business—finances or people?
- For which leading indicators does my organization have high marks?
- Which leading indicators require more time, attention, and energy?

# THE ROAD TO WINNING

*What man actually needs is not a tensionless state but rather the striving and struggling for some goal worthy of him.*

—VIKTOR FRANKL, *Man's Search for Meaning*

Organizations, like humans, grow in stages. And whether you're an athlete, a musician, or a business, the best way to get to the next stage is to know what stage you're in. You can then set your sights—and your goal—on your desired level of performance. You can identify milestones to mark your progress as you close the gap. This allows you to engage in a *sustained* process of continuous improvement.

Your ultimate goal as a leader is to create winning performance—a JEA organization. Hopefully, by now you believe that just enough anxiety can help you do this. Let's look at the stages of performance your organization may travel through on its journey.

At HCI, we've identified four stages: high-risk, mediocre, solid, and winning. Diagnosing where you are is the first step toward winning.

| High-Risk Performance | Mediocre Performance | Solid Performance | Winning Performance |
|---|---|---|---|
| • Frequently staggered by change | • Threatened by change | • Adaptive to change | • Proactive change agent |
| • Easily bested by competitors | • Under constant competitive pressures | • Able to secure its marketplace position | • Able to excel in marketplace |
| • Stagnant financial and operational performer | • Erratic financial and operational performer | • Consistent financial and operational performer | • Superior financial and operational performer |

*High-risk* organizations live in chaos or lethargy and have difficulty surviving competitive threats. *Mediocre* organizations are all over the map, up one day and down the next; their change strategy consists of guessing and gambling. *Solid* organizations enjoy relative stability even in the midst of change and are financially and competitively viable. *Winning* JEA organi-

## THE STEPS TO WINNING

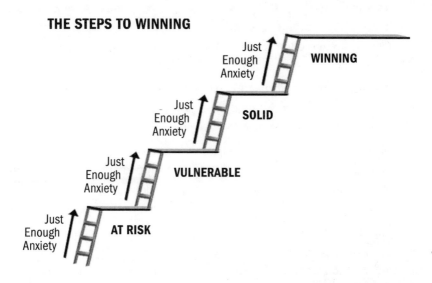

zations anticipate or even create change, lead their markets, and excel in their measures of success.

Every leader wakes up Monday morning wanting to win. Those who actually achieve this do so by moving their organizations from where they currently sit on the performance continuum toward the ideal winning stage—day in and day out, one step at a time.

Imagine walking into your office one morning to discover that you have lost one of your key customers to the competition. You're upset. Your organization has consistently performed in the solid range. Your products and services are well received and you have a great reputation with your customers, or so you thought. You have a reasonably good track record of performance. And you have competent leaders and smart people who work hard and care about the business. What's the problem?

You call your executive team together. Most have already heard the news. You ask, "What's going on? Why have we lost this customer?"

You watch and listen as individual team members react differently to the problem. One tries to downplay the situation and shows little concern. Several start pointing fingers at one another, becoming defensive and argumentative when possible problems in their units come up. Some of the discussion is quite heated. Fortunately, over time, most show their willingness to uncover the truth of the matter and explore the real reasons behind the incident. After considering all you've heard, you come to three conclusions:

- *Execution is getting sloppy.* Some people are complaining that they don't understand the strategy. Others are ignoring customer feedback. Targets are too often missed. There's a growing lack of passion for results.

- *Communication is starting to erode.* Information sharing is inconsistent, people are working at cross-purposes, and there's a declining sense of trust and teamwork.

- *Teams are showing signs of complacency.* Some people are not keeping their commitments. Productivity has dropped. Loyalty is waning. And a couple of key people recently left to join the competition.

You realize that these are all people problems. Relationships in general are becoming less productive. You're not moving fast enough or responding well to the marketplace. You're starting to backslide into mediocre performance.

| | High-Risk Performance | Mediocre Performance | Solid Performance | Winning Performance |
|---|---|---|---|---|
| **Execution** | Poor and unpredictable | Focused on activities rather than results | Sufficient to meet performance goals | Performance-driven, results-focused, with passion for winning |
| **Communication** | Closed and unreliable | Selective and rarely reliable | Generally open and reliable | Open, honest, and reliable in all situations |
| **Teamwork** | Aimless and unproductive | Undirected and rarely productive | Effectively utilized and productive | Widely utilized, diverse, and high-performing at all levels |

You've diagnosed the problems. You know where you are and where you want to be. So what do you do? Here are the three things you can do to respond like a JEA leader.

*Live and lead in the gap.*

You were dragged into the gap by a specific problem. You widened the gap by exploring the issue with your executive team. Now it's time to lead them through the gap. So shine a light on the challenge at hand. Make sure you fully understand existing strengths, weaknesses, opportunities, and threats—and help others do the same. Imagine your desired outcome. Define the gap in detail and determine your ability to close it. Then take action.

Chances are that you are both part of the problem and part of the solution. So become a participant observer. Use the time to learn more about yourself. Experiment with new behaviors. Apply what you learn in real time. As you lead people through the gap, be prepared for excitement and disappointment, boredom and surprise, and being stuck and moving ahead. It's all part of the process.

*Turn anxiety into productive energy.*

Rather than seek to eliminate anxiety, strive to utilize and direct it. Start by gauging people's level of anxiety. Who in the meeting was showing too much or too little anxiety? Then watch for signs that your organization is moving ahead or back on the performance continuum. Acknowledge people who are comfortable with uncertainty and change. Reward those who face the tough issues head-on. And celebrate those who are willing to stretch into their discomfort zones and reach for fresh solutions These are the next JEA leaders in your organization.

Remember that how you deal with your own anxiety has a huge impact on how others deal with theirs. Manage your emotions and express yourself honestly. Trust yourself and express trust in others. Model hope and optimism. And use healthy conflict to get at the truth.

*Travel the middle way.*

Learn to recognize when your organization is sliding into too much or too little anxiety. Create a plan for coming back to just enough, and follow it. Then continually monitor and manage that anxiety. Keeping people in the healthy range of just enough anxiety is the key to your success.

Do the same for yourself. Take note if you begin to take on too much anxiety to become egotistical, perfectionistic, volatile, or suspicious. Watch for signs that you are lapsing into too little anxiety to become idealistic, detached, overpleasing, or cautious. Allowing yourself to gravitate to either extreme puts your organization at risk. Keep your balance. Take the middle way. Remember: All anxiety is contagious.

If you follow these three steps, you can create just enough anxiety for positive change in any scenario. By leading with an open mind and heart and demonstrating realistic optimism, constructive impatience, and confident humility, you will lead people up the performance continuum. It will take work, lots of work. Be patient. Creating just enough anxiety inside your organization is one of the most important—and powerful—things you can do.

### Dos and Don'ts of Living and Leading with Just Enough Anxiety

| DO | DON'T |
|---|---|
| • Accept and learn from life's experiences. | • Try to avoid negative life experiences. |
| • Acknowledge your hopes and concerns. | • Ignore or deny your feelings. |
| • Mediate your anxiety through meditation, nature walks, exercise, etc. | • Try to hide from your anxiety. |
| • Get comfortable with competing emotions. | • Attempt to think and feel the same way all the time. |
| • Give yourself credit for handling anxiety. | • Convince yourself you can't live with anxiety. |
| • Honestly assess your strengths and shortcomings. | • Be too hard or too easy on yourself. |
| • Know what you value in your life. | • Get too attached to success, fame, or money. |
| • Learn to ask and live with tough questions. | • Fight change and uncertainty. |
| • Approach anxiety as your friend. | • Approach anxiety as the enemy. |
| • Recognize what you can and cannot control. | • Fool yourself by thinking you're in control of everything. |

## RAISING THE BAR

*Make the most of yourself by fanning the tiny, inner sparks of possibility into flames of achievement.*

—GOLDA MEIR, co-founder and fourth prime minister of Israel

ING, which helped finance the Louisiana Purchase in 1803, is full of history and culture. Yet when Michel Tilmant took over as CEO in 2004, the Amsterdam-based company's steady performance seemed to have hit a wall as thick as the dikes protecting Holland from the North Sea. Stock was stagnant, morale was only average, and the bank was not reaping the expected synergies from its global brand. Analysts were not impressed. Neither was the new CEO.

Michel quickly changed ING's structure and strategy, refocusing its more than 118,000 employees in fifty countries on three markets: banking, insurance, and asset management. He introduced new programs to improve value creation and make the company easier to deal with. But his biggest gamble was the reshaping of ING's strong culture—a move that would radically change how employees thought about their roles and measured their performance in the race to rebuild ING's brand and sustain profitable growth.

Three years later, the results of ING's culture change are everywhere. The company raised total shareholder return by 109 percent over that period—the second best performance in its peer group of global financial institutions. Its life insurance sales are up 30 percent in Central Europe and 20 percent in its Asia Pacific territories. The company reported $98 billion in sales and a net income of $9 billion in 2006. ING Direct is now a global leader in electronic banking and is adding Japan to its turf. And to promote its global brand, the company is now the official sponsor of the Renault Formula One team.

Michel raised the bar at ING. He built a winning performance culture on what I see as four foundational leadership principles: organize for change, communicate honestly, focus on execution, and track and reward progress. Let's see how he did it.

## Organize for Change

"When I took over as CEO, we were a very content company. We had good people but only managed to achieve average performance in all our operations. We needed to improve our leadership, management, communication, and direction. We had to remove the feeling of complacency that had built up over the years.

"The first challenge was to create clear direction and structure. The driving goal was to reach excellence in each of our businesses. We began by reorganizing. We knew that people had to focus on their own business first, before we could change the whole company.

"Our framework for building a winning performance culture grew out of these initial changes. It was difficult to explain at first, but I knew we had to design a new approach to lead the business. We had to radically move our performance bar and stretch ourselves in different ways."

Michel knew that to preserve the existing culture would strangle the drive and urgency that ING needed to compete in the global arena. He organized the culture change in staged efforts, rather than create a revolution. By changing the structure and focusing first on managing value, he laid a solid foundation for ING's transformation.

### Communicate Honestly

"As the CEO, I think you have to be very straight with people. You can't be afraid to confront the tough issues. I told people that if we didn't change our culture, we'd lose our competitiveness. By making this transition, we'd be preparing ING for the future and avoiding drastic measures.

"Honesty sometimes creates anxiety, but it's necessary, and you owe it to your people. The best way to handle resistance to change is to convince the skeptics. After a while you know who they are. If people can't get on board, we just accept that they'll leave. It's always a fear. But you have to accept that a small percentage will never be convinced. If you're patient for too long, you're not the leader.

"Now when I meet with management or employees, I talk about creating a winning performance culture. You've got to communicate relentlessly about what a winning performance culture is so managers can translate it in their daily work. This has to cascade down to all levels of the organization. You can't repeat the message enough."

Like most European CEOs, Michel has a deep historical and social sensitivity. But he's also direct and honest. This combination of sincere and candid communication enabled him to overcome the initial resistance to change at ING. His courage and resilience allowed him to win employees' hearts and minds. But his real success came from his passion for execution.

### Focus on Execution

"Over the long term, you distinguish yourself by execution. It requires hard work, attention, and challenging people. It requires the personal discipline to get things done. It's not necessarily exciting, but you just have to do it.

"Good execution starts with your mind-set. If you accept poor execution, you get sloppy performance. When we started our focus on a winning performance culture, we challenged ourselves to reach a higher level of execution.

"As leaders, we have to be role models for the culture we're trying to build. We have to make sure people behave properly as we manage execution. I don't think you can use good performance to justify poor behavior. Nor can you use performance challenges to push people around and create a climate of fear or high anxiety. It's not sustainable.

"I believe strong leaders reduce the anxiety level of the people working for them. They give them peace of mind by supporting them and coaching them. You need to recognize success as much as you point out performance challenges."

Leaders in every company have the twin challenges of balancing behavior and performance. It's about striking the right balance between setting goals and holding people accountable. It's about recognizing the positive leadership behaviors that fuel employee engagement and doing right by your customers. By addressing *how* people achieve their goals, leaders like Michel Tilmant are sending the message that they are not just in the game for the short term, but truly want to build lasting value.

## Track and Reward Progress

"Every year, we do a performance culture scan throughout the company to find out how we're doing. The results are shared with management, who can decide on actions to close the gaps within their business.

"We know that we're still far from reaching the winning state, but we're improving on the scan. Even in the business units that were very complacent and difficult to get on board, the scan tells us we're making striking improvements.

"We're also embedding the winning performance culture into the performance appraisals of our top 200 leaders across the company. For the first time ever, their performance evaluations will be based not only on *what* they achieved during the year but *how* they achieved it.

"The way we're tracking progress on the winning performance culture has created the right amount of anxiety for us to sustain change across the company. Our top 200 leaders know that we are putting our money where our mouth is. They can't say anymore that behavior is a soft issue."

Building a winning performance culture does not happen overnight. By creating a benchmark and allowing each business to track its performance over time, Michel achieved two important goals: He let everyone know where they stood. And he created healthy tension inside the organization, as leaders took stock and aimed to improve their performance. By asking everyone to put skin into the game, he made sure that the entire company would play by the new rules.

I've had the privilege of observing ING's transformation firsthand. HCI has worked closely with Michel Tilmant and the top ING leaders throughout the process. It's clear that this is a company committed to transformation. ING is a good example of just enough anxiety in action.

## THE BOTTOM LINE

*In the end, it is important to remember that we cannot become what we need to be by remaining what we are.*

—MAX DEPREE, former CEO of Herman Miller

No organization is ever static. It is either growing or declining, every minute of every day.

Your organization may be growing with changes in top leadership, global opportunities, or new products or customers. It may be expanding because of a reorganization, merger, or acquisition. Or it may be experiencing a growth spurt due to a new strategy, a new strategic alliance partner, or a repositioning of your business. If your organization is growing, your job as a JEA leader is to unleash human energy, increase capability, foster innovation, and execute for results.

If your organization is declining, it may be suffering from a lack of unified direction, poor execution of strategy, financial losses, or a drop in market share. It may be experiencing flat growth or waning productivity. Or it may be losing employees due to a weakened reputation, disgruntled workforce, or extraordinarily high levels of stress. In these instances, your job as a JEA leader is to diagnose the problem, provide direction, and guide your organization through the change.

Whether your business is growing or declining, you can use just enough anxiety to move in the direction of your goals. You can use JEA as the catalyst to achieve winning performance.

Without just enough anxiety, your organization will sooner or later teeter on the brink of decline. On the *human* side, you will see increasingly ineffective leadership, the loss of good people, underperformance in critical arenas, slowed innovation, and an inability to change. In *operations,* you will notice excessive costs, poor product quality, inefficient processes, slower and slower speed to market, and low service delivery. In the *marketplace,* you will discover lagging growth, declining market share, growing competitive pressure, withering brand value, and poor customer feedback. And on the *financial* side, you will witness declining stock price, falling return on capital, low analyst ratings, and lower margins.

When you lead with just enough anxiety, however, you will experience an entirely different outcome. You will have a capable and committed workforce, a well-executed vision and strategy, operational excellence, a world-class reputation, and a strong capacity for change and reinvention. You will enjoy profitable growth and long-term value creation.

Just enough anxiety is what you need to drive positive change. It is the fuel that stimulates growth. It is the productive energy that solves problems and averts crises. Just enough anxiety is the hidden driver of business success—inside you and your organization.

# 9

# CHANGE BEGINS WITH YOU

Kun-Hee Lee, chairman and CEO of Samsung Electronics, walked onto the stage. The room was still, the people curious and anxious about what he would say. The company had been going through a very difficult period, and major change was absolutely essential. This was his leadership moment.

"Change begins with me," said Lee. "Each of us must initiate change, not passively wait for others to act. Once you have made the decision to change, you are strong. Once you have recognized your limitations, you can transcend them. Once you understand what you know and don't yet know, you begin to realize wisdom. Change begins with me."

Kun-Hee Lee was the architect of Samsung's global success in the twenty-first century, taking personal responsibility and shining a light on himself. At some deep level he knew the power of living and leading with just enough anxiety.

Just enough anxiety can be a powerful force in your life. It can bring out your best performance, help you build great teams, and inspire and challenge your organization to ever greater heights. It truly is your catalyst for change. But to tap its full potential you must make a commitment to yourself: to know yourself, to be yourself, to challenge yourself, and to love yourself.

*Knowing yourself* is the foundation for living and leading with just enough anxiety. It's about being real with yourself—your strengths and shortcomings, your aspirations and fears. It's also about learning every day of your life. By performing on stage and being in the audience at the same time, you will always have an honest sense of who you really are.

*Being yourself* grows out of knowing yourself. It takes just enough anxiety to be who you truly are. Here you learn to embrace what you find with open arms. You learn to express your full self, to find your real voice, to discover your full power. You become the architect of your own future.

*Challenging yourself* is how you create just enough anxiety in your life. It involves traveling into uncertainty, asking the tough questions, and getting comfortable with discomfort. This takes you into the gap between your current reality and your desired future, where anxiety lies. By stretching yourself you unleash the human energy lying dormant inside you.

*Loving yourself* makes it safe for you to live and lead with just enough anxiety. Grounded in deep personal values, you allow yourself to experience the full range of human emotions. Healthy anxiety becomes a positive force in your life.

Every morning, before I start my day, I take time to meditate, to travel inside myself. It's my gift to myself to reflect on each day and to renew myself. It's my special time alone in my open mind and open heart. Some days my mind is active and anxious; other days it is quiet and serene. Sometimes I review what happened yesterday. Other times I prepare for the new day. Often I simply stay quiet and do nothing. Or I use the time to remind myself what's important in my life: Being real and telling the truth. Loving with my heart's abandon. Being committed and staying detached. Making a contribution every day. And living in the moment.

On one of my quiet mornings, for some unknown reason, Nelson Mandela came across the ticker tape in my mind. As one of the world's most admired statesmen, Mandela is a real hero of mine. His native country of South Africa is such a special place, a land of gorgeous scenery, fantastic animals, wonderful people, and a real social laboratory for change.

While working in South Africa in 2006, I decided to take some R&R in Capetown. One sunny afternoon I visited Nelson Mandela's former "home" on the cape. But Robben Island is not your typical residence. It is the isolated camp in which Mandela was incarcerated with his friends for most of his twenty-seven years in prison. Getting off the boat, I was immediately struck by an overwhelming sense of sadness that such a great man would have to waste so much of his adult life living in such a barren, life-denying place.

As we approached the barracks where Mandela had lived, we were greeted by one of his old prison mates who today spends his time as a tour guide. Down a long gray hallway was Mandela's cell. It had a small bed, tiny window, and miniature sink. Each day, this great man would get up and perform hard labor in a lime quarry. I couldn't imagine what it would be like to live in such squalor from age twenty-four to age forty-eight.

In 1990, Mandela was released from prison. On the day of his release, he made a speech to the nation, declaring his commitment to peace and reconciliation. After years of oppression and persecution, Nelson Mandela emerged a hopeful, courageous, and loving man. He eventually became the president of South Africa and led the transformation of his country to become the multiracial democracy that it is today. In 1993, Nelson Mandela received the Nobel Peace Prize.

Nelson Mandela is a man who found peace with just enough anxiety. For his adult life, he lived in the gap between his current reality and his desired future. He lived with an open mind and an open heart. He mastered all three paradoxes, being both realistic and optimistic, constructive and impatient, and confident and humble simultaneously. And he lived and led with just enough anxiety his entire life.

After living fifty years of my own life and observing people like Nelson Mandela, I've come to realize that, despite all the change, challenge, and complexity in the world today, life is really quite simple. For me it comes down to two things: fear and love. Fear shuts us down and holds us back. Love opens us up and propels us forward. In life and in business, people are motivated best by a little fear and a lot of love.

Finally, let me leave you with an old Native American folk tale. It's a story about a Cherokee elder who one evening told his grandson about the battle that goes on inside people. He said, "My son, the battle is between two wolves inside us all.

"One is Evil. It is anger, envy, sorrow, regret, greed, arrogance, cynicism, self-pity, guilt, resentment, inferiority, lies, false pride, superiority, and ego.

"The other is Good. It is joy, peace, love, hope, curiosity, confidence, humility, kindness, benevolence, empathy, generosity, truth, compassion, and faith."

The grandson thought about it for a minute and then asked his grandfather, "Which wolf wins?"

The old Cherokee simply replied, "The one you feed."

Yes, indeed, it is all about the one you feed. And the choice is yours.

## HEALTHY COMPANIES INTERNATIONAL

Healthy Companies International is a change consulting and new media firm founded in 1988. Our mission is to help CEOs and executive teams build winning organizations. HCI brings the "CEO perspective" into focus on issues of human strategy and business performance. We work as strategic partners focused on delivering great, measurable results.

*Research:* HCI has studied the world's most successful companies and interviewed more than 250 world-class CEOs from more than thirty countries. Our ongoing proprietary research in CEO leadership, leading change, growth leadership, and human strategy provides deep insights into how leaders create competitive advantage. HCI works with top executives to translate these insights into practical solutions to achieve outstanding results.

*Consulting:* HCI provides customized change management solutions to executives around the world by identifying and strengthening the human drivers that matter most to business success. As experts in the human side of execution, HCI senior consultants provide a variety of services, including CEO and executive coaching, organization diagnostic tools, facilitation of strategic change initiatives, executive team facilitation, and the formation of human capital strategy.

*Performance tools:* HCI offers an array of online leadership and performance tools to help leaders at all levels identify and solve problems, make decisions, boost creativity, and effectively manage performance. The e-tools are available anytime, anywhere, via the Internet, and are designed to be used by managers in a variety of situations. They include assessments, surveys, interactive exercises, and best practices.

For more information on HCI, see www.healthycompanies.com.

For more information on Just Enough Anxiety speeches, educational programs, and tools, visit our Web site at www.justenoughanxiety.com.

# ACKNOWLEDGMENTS

*Just Enough Anxiety* is my life's work. It didn't take a lifetime to write. It just took a lifetime to experience.

So many people are hidden in the pages of this book. It reflects a rich life filled with loving family and friends and memories that will last a lifetime.

To Jay Fisette for our deep partnership. You are an extraordinary person who has brought out the best in me.

To my parents, Barbara and Dick, for giving me the courage to walk the diving board.

To my sister Randi and to Rich, Dan, Chris, Ryan, Devon, Margot, Jerry, Lynne, Mark, Erin, Amanda, Michael, Paul, Nancy, Kyle, and Melanie for bringing joy to my life every day.

To my dear friend Jeff Akman, whose wisdom and humanity shines a light on so many people.

To my business partner and great friend Jim Mathews, who has been by my side the entire ride.

To Suzanne Goldberg, who saw the path before I did and brought love and liberation into my life.

And to my great friends who challenge and support me all the time.

Special thanks to our writing team. Rae Thompson, you are an absolute gift. A woman with an amazing mind and a huge heart. I am forever grateful to you and for our partnership. And to Aaron Wunder, whose global mind and deep compassion are all over this book.

To my colleagues at Healthy Companies International, who inspire and challenge me every day: Eric Sass, Leigh Shields, David Rippey, Nancy Medford, Dierck Casselman, Stephanie Lokmer, Marsha Johnson, Monique Farmer, and JuKrisha Kingwood.

To my friends and colleagues who were kind enough to read this manuscript and give me their advice and counsel: Judy Rosenblum, Eric Beaudan, Kathy Ross, Sam Paschall, Berard Tierney, and David Mills.

To my colleagues at Duke Corporate Education, the Darden School of Business, and the Barbados Group, who stretch my thinking and expand the reach of our ideas around the world.

To my good friend and agent, Gail Ross, and to Howard Yoon, for believing in me and my voice over many years.

And to my friends at Portfolio: Adrian Zackheim, Adrienne Schultz, Will Weisser, and publicist Mark Fortier, for seeing the power of *Just Enough Anxiety*.

Finally, to the hundreds of leaders I have met over the years. You have been my teachers.

# NOTES

## Chapter 1: It's Time to Evolve

1 **Just ask Alan Mulally:** Mulally story adapted from Healthy Companies International, "Channeling Anxiety into Productive Energy: An Interview with Alan Mulally," *What CEOs Do*, December 2007.

3 **Ford won five top-quality awards:** "Press Release," J. D. Power & Associates (June 6, 2007).

5 **"We have data overload":** Judith M. Bardwick, *Seeking the Calm in the Storm: Managing Chaos in Your Business Life* (London: Financial Times Prentice Hall, 2002).

8 **The human brain has been programmed:** Discussion of the historical understanding of the brain compiled from Joseph LeDoux, *The Emotional Brain: The Mysterious Underpinnings of Emotional Life* (New York: Simon & Schuster, 1996); Elkhonon Goldberg, *The Executive Brain: Frontal Lobes and the Civilized Mind* (New York: Oxford University Press, 2001); and Sharon Begley, "The Evolution Revolution," *Newsweek*, March 19, 2007.

11 **"When you make a choice":** Robert Fritz, *The Path of Least Resistance* (New York: Fawcett Columbine, 1984).

13 **As Lars Ramqvist, chairman and CEO:** Taken from Robert Rosen, Patricia Digh, Marshall Singer, and Carl Phillips, *Global Literacies: Lessons on Business Leadership and National Cultures* (New York: Simon & Schuster, 2000).

18 **Jean-Pierre (JP) Garnier at GlaxoSmithKline:** Garnier story adapted from Healthy Companies International, "Building a High Performance Culture: An Interview with Dr. Jean-Pierre Garnier," *What CEOs Do*, March 2007.

## Chapter 2: A New Understanding of Anxiety

24  **Manuel (Manny) Pangilinan:** Pangilinan story taken from Robert Rosen, Patricia Digh, Marshall Singer, and Carl Phillips, *Global Literacies: Lessons on Business Leadership and National Cultures* (New York: Simon & Schuster, 2000).

25  **Do we run because we're afraid:** Information on James, Cannon, and Freud compiled from Joseph LeDoux, *The Emotional Brain: The Mysterious Underpinnings of Emotional Life* (New York: Simon & Schuster, 1996); Elkhonon Goldberg, *The Executive Brain: Frontal Lobes and the Civilized Mind* (New York: Oxford University Press, 2001); and "Freud Is Not Dead," *Newsweek,* March 27, 2006.

26  **Around the 1930s, Anna Freud:** Historical information and list of ego defense mechanisms compiled from "Personality Theories: Anna Freud," http://webspace .ship.edu/cgboer/annafreud.html; and "Defence Mechanism," http://en.wikipedia. org/wiki/Defense_mechanisms.

27  **Psychiatrists who served in World War II:** Historical perspective based on G. N. Grob, "Origins of DSM-I: A Study in Appearance and Reality," *American Journal of Psychiatry,* 148 (1991): 421–31.

27  **seven types of anxiety disorders:** Compiled from Anxiety Disorders Association of America, http://www.adaa.org/aboutadaa/Introduction.asp; *Diagnostic and Statistical Manual of Mental Disorders,* http://en.wikipedia.org/wiki/; "Anxiety Disorders Research at the National Institute of Mental Health," http://www.nimh.nih .gov/publicat/anxresfact.cfm; and "Psychiatric Disorders," http://www.allpsych .com/disorders/anxiety/index.html.

27  **Meanwhile, back in the laboratory:** Information on MacLean and Selye compiled from LeDoux, *The Emotional Brain*; and Raymond Lloyd Richmond, "The Psychology of Stress" in *A Guide to Psychology and Its Practice,* http://www.guidetopsychology.com.

28  **The rise of psychopharmacology:** Text and list of medications compiled from "Medication Options for the Treatment of Anxiety," http://www.cncplan.com/anxi etymed.htm; and "History of Psychology" in *Discovering Psychology,* http://www .learner.org/discoveringpsychology/history/history_nonflash.html.

29  **Cognitive behavioral therapy (CBT) erupted:** Robert Langreth, "Patient, Fix Thyself," *Forbes,* April 9, 2007.

29  **Fast-forward to today:** See bibliography for full citations of books mentioned here.

29  **Anxiety in the United States Today:** Compiled from Anxiety Disorders Association of America, http://www.adaa.org/aboutadaa/Introduction.asp; and "Anxiety Disorders Statistics and Facts," http://www.healthyplace.com/Communities/Anxiety/ statistics.asp.

31  **Fortunately, a new group of leaders:** Compiled from various interviews cited throughout the book.

32  **The brain has been described:** Discussion of the parts and workings of the brain compiled from "A User's Guide to the Brain," *Time,* January 29, 2007; "Who Do You Think You Are: A Survey of the Brain," *The Economist,* December 23, 2006; LeDoux, *The Emotional Brain*; Goldberg, *The Executive Brain*; Esther M. Sternberg, M.D., "Can Stress Make You Sick," in *The Balance Within* (New York: W. H. Freeman, 2000);

and Jeffrey Kluger, "Why We Worry About the Things We Shouldn't and Ignore the Things We Should," *Time,* December, 4, 2006.

37  **Although genetic research:** Compiled from Edmund J. Bourne, *The Anxiety & Phobia Workbook,* 4th edition (Oakland: New Harbinger Publications, 2005); T. J. Hendricks, D. V. Fyodorov, L. J. Wegman, N. B. Lelutiu, E. A. Pehek, B. Yamamoto, J. Silver, E. J. Weeber, J. D. Sweatt, and E. S. Deneris, "Pet-1 ETS Gene Plays a Critical Role in 5-HT Neuron Development and Is Required for Normal Anxiety-Like and Aggressive Behavior," *Neuron* 37, no. 2 (January 23, 2003): 233–47; Steven Taylor, Dana Thordarson, Kerry L. Jang, and Gordon J.G. Asmundson, "Genetic and Environmental Origins of Healthy Anxiety: A Twin Study," *World Psychiatry* 5, no. 1 (February 2006): 47–50; and Murray B. Stein, M.D., Kerry L. Jang, and W. John Livesley, M.D., "Heritability of Anxiety Sensitivity: A Twin Study," *American Journal of Psychiatry* 156 (February 1999): 2.

38  **Psychologists talk about this:** John Bowlby, *Attachment* (New York: Basic Books, 1969).

41  **Scholars of the Kabbalah:** "Anxiety Relief: The Kabbalah Approach to Mental Health: Positive Anxiety," http://www.inner.org/mental/mental32.htm.

41  **This kind of anxiety:** From Bob Rosen interview with Jeffrey Akman, January 2007.

43  **Symptoms of anxiety disorders:** "Brief Overview of Anxiety Disorders" from Anxiety Disorders Association of America, http://www.adaa.org/GettingHelp/BriefOverview.asp.

44  **"Good leaders make friends with anxiety":** Peluso story adapted from Healthy Companies International, "Embracing and Using Anxiety: An Interview with Michelle Peluso," *What CEOs Do,* November 2007.

46  **"Even when the brain suffers":** Sharon Begley, "How the Brain Rewires Itself," *Time,* January 29, 2007.

46  **Recent research, however, has revealed:** Compiled from ibid.; and "Brain Plasticity: What Is It," http://faculty.washington.edu/chudler/plast.html.

48  **Evidence of our adaptive brain:** Compiled from Sharon Begley, "How the Brain Rewires Itself"; and Mariko Yashumoto, "Aging Japanese Keep Their Minds Moving," *Washington Post,* March 21, 2007.

48  **"If we literally put enough energy":** David Rock, *Quiet Leadership* (New York: HarperCollins Publishers, 2006).

49  **Walk into the headquarters:** Ma story adapted from Healthy Companies International, "Blending Eastern and Western Business Thinking: An Interview with Peter Ma" *What CEOs Do,* November 2005.

50  **The Western perspective gives us logic:** Compiled from Rosen et al., *Global Literacies;* and Lama Surya Das, *Awakening the Buddha Within: Tibetan Wisdom for the Western World* (New York: Broadway Books, 1997).

52  **"I first became aware":** Bruce Lipton, "Growth and Protection," in *The Biology of Belief: Unleashing the Power of Consciousness, Matter, and Miracles* (Santa Rosa, CA: Mountain of Love/Elite Books, 2005).

53  **The turnaround success:** GlaxoSmithKline story adapted from Healthy Companies International, "Building a High Performance Culture: An Interview with Dr. Jean-Pierre Garnier," *What CEOs Do,* March 2007.

56  **Nobody understands how to use:** Jumper story adapted from Healthy Companies International, "Leading Transformation: An Interview with General John P. Jumper," *What CEOs Do,* April 2007.

## Chapter 3: Living in the Gap

64  **After decades of self-regulation:** Nally story adapted from Healthy Companies International, "Turning Challenge into Opportunity: An Interview with Dennis Nally," *What CEOs Do,* October 2007.

64  **Like Ken Samet, the CEO:** All references to Samet in this chapter come from a Healthy Companies International interview with Samet in February 2007.

67  **In the words of Daniel Vasella:** All references to Vasella in this chapter come from Robert Rosen, Patricia Digh, Marshall Singer, and Carl Phillips, *Global Literacies: Lessons on Business Leadership and National Cultures* (New York: Simon & Schuster, 2000).

72  **Dave O'Reilly at Chevron Corporation knows a lot:** O'Reilly story adapted from Healthy Companies International, "Mobilizing Human Energy: An Interview with Dave O'Reilly," *What CEOs Do,* October 2006.

74  **"Good enough isn't good enough":** All references to Rabbitt in this chapter come from Healthy Companies International, "Become an Authentic Leader: An Interview with Linda Rabbitt," *What CEOs Do,* April 2005.

75  **When Eli Lilly's Prozac patent:** Taurel story adapted from Healthy Companies International, "Strong Values Drive Renewal and Inspire Change: An Interview with Sidney Taurel," *What CEOs Do*, August 2005.

75  **Lilly has since clinched:** "America's Most Admired Companies 2007," in *Fortune*, http://money.cnn.com/magazines/fortune/mostadmired/2007/industries/industry _47.html.

76  **Our prefrontal cortex creates:** Elkhonon Goldberg, *The Executive Brain* (New York: Oxford University Press, 2001).

76  **This thinking about thinking:** "Metacognition," http://en.wikipedia.org/wiki/ Metacognition.

80  **At PepsiCo, CEO Steve Reinemund:** Reinemund story compiled from Healthy Companies International, "Great Leaders Are Great Teachers: An Interview with Steven Reinemund," *What CEOs Do,* July 2005; and "PepsiCo's Steve Reinemund to Retire as Chairman in May 2007," PepsiCo press release, October 1, 2006.

82  **"a condition of the heart":** All references to DePree in this chapter come from Robert Rosen, *Leading People: Transforming Business from the Inside Out* (New York: Viking Penguin, 1996).

83  **Italian, Jewish, and Latin cultures:** Robert Rosen et al., *Global Literacies*.

84  **One leader stands out:** Bodson story taken from ibid.

84  **Not at Four Seasons:** Sharp story adapted from Healthy Companies International, "Turn Your Values into Action: An Interview with Isadore Sharp," *What CEOs Do,* March 2005.

85  **"control the uncontrollable":** Pema Chödrön, *Comfortable with Uncertainty: 108*

*Teachings on Cultivating Fearlessness and Compassion* (Boston: Shambhala Publications, 2003).

86  **Such renewal, according to:** Richard Boyatzis and Annie McKee, *Resonant Leadership* (Boston: Harvard Business School Press, 2005).

87  **"When these partners interact":** Daniel Goleman, *Emotional Intelligence: Why It Can Matter More Than IQ* (New York: Bantam Books, 1995).

87  **"As we perceive and react":** Doc Childre and Deborah Rozman, *Transforming Anxiety: The HeartMath® Solution for Overcoming Fear and Worry and Creating Serenity* (Oakland: New Harbinger Publications, 2006).

88  **Eric Schaeffer lives in the gap:** Story compiled from a Healthy Companies International Interview with Schaeffer in March 2007.

## Chapter 4: The Three Faces of Anxiety

92  **Milo of Croton dreamed:** The story of Milo and other remarks by Carlos Berio taken from Bob Rosen's interview with Berio in January 2007.

93  **Cognitive research reveals:** Information on research results and Yerkes-Dodson law compiled from Miguel Humara, "The Relationship Between Anxiety and Performance: A Cognitive-Behavioral Perspective," *Athletic Insight: The Online Journal of Sport Psychology*; Graham Jones, "Pre-Competitive Feeling States and Directional Anxiety Interpretations," *Journal of Sports Sciences*, June 1, 2001; and "Finding Your Optimum Stress Level," http://www.mindtools.com/stressrt.html.

94  **How champion athletes enter the *Zone*:** Compiled from Luis Valdes, "Peak Performance Pulse," http://www.squidoo.com/valdes/; Anne Fricker, "Lance Armstrong," http://www.tuftsdaily.com; Netliberty, http://www.netliberty.com/sports.html; "Hank Aaron Biography," http://www.biography.com/search/article.do?id=9173497; "Venus Williams," http://en.wikipedia.org/wiki/Venus_Williams and http://thinkexist.com/quotes/venus_williams/.

95  **"The happiest among us":** Gilbert Brim, *Ambition: How We Manage Success and Failure Throughout Our Lives* (New York: Basic Books, 1992).

97  **Several years ago I spent the day:** DePriest story adapted from Robert Rosen, *Leading People: Transforming Business from the Inside Out* (New York: Viking Penguin, 1996).

98  **"inexorably drawn into an intimate":** Daniel Goleman, *Social Intelligence: The New Science of Human Relationships* (New York: Bantam Books, 2006).

98  **We are hardwired:** Compiled from Ulf Dimberg and Maria Petterson, "Facial Reactions to Happy and Angry Facial Expressions: Evidence for Right Hemisphere Dominance," *Cambridge Journals*, October 2000; "Hard to Keep a Straight Face" in *Innovations Report: Forum for Science, Industry and Business*, http://www.innovations-report.com/html/reports/social_sciences/report-13848.html; and N. Wager, G. Fieldman, and T. Hussey, "The Effect on Ambulatory Blood Pressure of Working Under Favourably and Unfavourably Perceived Supervisors," in *Occupational and Environmental Medicine* 60 (2003): 468–74, http://oem.bmj.com/cgi/content/full/60/7/468.

99 **Cadbury Schweppes CEO:** Stitzer story adapted from Healthy Companies International, "Inspiring a Passion for Winning: An Interview with Todd Stitzer," *What CEOs Do,* May 2007.

99 **Good organizations make good leaders:** Dirk J. Louw, "Ubuntu and the Challenges of Multiculturalism in Post-Apartheid South Africa," in *An African Journal of Philosophy*, http://www.quest-journal.net.

102 **I interviewed Vivendi CEO:** Compiled from Michael E. Raynor, "Making Choices Versus Creating Options," in *The Strategy Paradox: Why Committing to Success Leads to Failure (and What to Do About It)* (New York: Doubleday, 2007); and Robert Rosen, Patricia Digh, Marshall Singer, and Carl Phillips, *Global Literacies: Lessons on Business Leadership and National Cultures* (New York: Simon & Schuster, 2000).

105 **Over the years:** Descriptions of TLA leaders come from HCI research and my personal observations, as well as from David L. Dotlich and Peter C. Cairo, *Why CEOs Fail: The 11 Behaviors That Can Derail Your Climb to the Top and How to Manage Them* (San Francisco: Jossey-Bass, 2003); Michael Maccoby, *Narcissistic Leaders: Who Succeeds and Who Fails* (Boston: Harvard Business School Press, 2007); Manfred F. R. Kets de Vries and Danny Miller, *The Neurotic Organization* (San Francisco: Jossey-Bass, 1984); and Robert Lawrence Kuhn, "12 'CEO Diseases' and How to Treat Them," *Chief Executive*, October/November 2006.

109 **Expectations were high:** Compiled from "A Brief History of Lucent Technologies," http://www.bell-labs.com/history/lucent.html; Dawn Kawamoto, "Lucent CEO Walks Tightrope as Stock Tumbles," *News.Com*, October 13, 2000; and Steve Rosenbush, "Can Rich McGinn Revive Lucent," *BusinessWeek Online,* June 26, 2000.

110 **Joe Nacchio's cowboy mentality:** Compiled from Carrie Johnson, "Nacchio Guilty of Insider Trading," *Washington Post,* April 20, 2007; Stephanie N. Mehta, "Qwest Joe Nacchio's Dream Has Unraveled," *Fortune,* April 14, 2002; and Steve Raabe, "Regulators' Lawsuit Cites Qwest CEO's 'Culture of Fear' in Fraud Allegations," *Denver Post,* March 17, 2005.

114 **Let's look at four different ways:** Descriptions of TMA leaders come from HCI research and my personal observations, as well as from David L. Dotlich and Peter C. Cairo, *Why CEOs Fail;* Michael Maccoby, *Narcissistic Leaders*; Manfred F. R. Kets de Vries and Danny Miller, *The Neurotic Organization*; and Robert Lawrence Kuhn, "12 'CEO Diseases.'"

119 **They called him "Chainsaw Al":** John A. Byrne, *Chainsaw: The Notorious Career of Al Dunlap in the Era of Profit-at-Any-Price* (New York: HarperCollins Publishers, 2003).

121 **"A loving person lives":** Ken Keyes Jr., *Handbook to Higher Consciousness* (Berkeley, CA: Living Love Center, 1986).

121 **Rand Construction Corporation founder:** Rabbitt story adapted from Healthy Companies International, "Become an Authentic Leader: An Interview with Linda Rabbitt," *What CEOs Do*, April 2005.

## Chapter 5: Realistic Optimism

124 **When Jimmy DePriest:** DePriest story adapted from Robert Rosen, *Leading People: Transforming Business from the Inside Out* (New York: Viking Penguin, 1996).

125 **Ancient Chinese philosophy:** "Yin and Yang," in *Chinese Philosophy,* http://www .wsu.edu.

127 **In psychology, we call this:** "Cognitive dissonance," http://en.wikipedia.org/wiki/ Cognitive_dissonance.

128 **"Most companies don't face":** Larry Bossidy and Ram Charan, *Execution: The Discipline of Getting Things Done* (New York: Crown Books, 2002).

130 **Two billion times a day:** Story compiled from a Healthy Companies International interview with Lafley in May 2006.

133 **Who is making this possible?:** Yunus story adapted from Robert Rosen, Patricia Digh, Marshall Singer, and Carl Phillips, *Global Literacies: Lessons on Business Leadership and National Cultures* (New York: Simon & Schuster, 2000); "Grameen Bank at a Glance," http://www.grameen-info.org/bank/GBGlance.htm; and "Muhammad Yunus," http://en.wikipedia.org/wiki/Muhammad_Yunus.

135 **"The foremost challenge for leaders":** Rosamund Stone Zander and Benjamin Zander, *The Art of Possibility: Transforming Professional and Personal Life* (New York: Penguin Group, 2000).

135 **"In order to survive":** O'Reilly story adapted from Healthy Companies International, "Mobilizing Human Energy: An Interview with Dave O'Reilly," *What CEOs Do,* October 2006.

136 **Tips for being realistic and optimistic:** H. B. Gelatt, "Positive Uncertainty: A Paradoxical Philosophy of Counseling Whose Time Has Come," http://www.ericdigests .org.

136 **"Don't let folks tell you":** Story compiled from a Healthy Companies International interview with Hirschberg in August 2006.

137 **Just ask Dennis Nally:** Nally story adapted from Healthy Companies International, "Turning Challenge into Opportunity: An Interview with Dennis Nally," *What CEOs Do,* October 2007.

## Chapter 6: Constructive Impatience

143 **"Chaos is actually":** William Bridges, *The Way of Transition: Embracing Life's Most Difficult Moments* (Cambridge, MA: Perseus Publishing, 2001).

143 **"I'm an accomplishment junkie":** All mention of Stitzer in this chapter comes from Healthy Companies International, "Inspiring a Passion for Winning: An Interview with Todd Stitzer," *What CEOs Do,* May 2007.

145 **Arbitron chief administrative officer:** All mention of Ross in this chapter comes from a Healthy Companies International interview with Ross in March 2007.

155 **"Leaders probe and push":** Jack Welch, *Winning* (New York: HarperCollins Publishers, 2005).

156 **"I love change":** Story compiled from a Healthy Companies International interview with Bryant in March 2007.

158 **You might be surprised:** Story compiled from a Healthy Companies International interview with Carlee in January 2007; and "2004 Citizen Survey," Arlington County, VA, http://www.arlingtonva.us/web/survey/Survey.aspx.

## Chapter 7: Confident Humility

165 **He referred to the feminine:** Eric Neumann, "Anima/Animus," from *The Origins and History of Consciousness*, reprinted by Barbara McManus in "The Feminine Archetype in Myth and Art," http://www.cnr.edu/home/bmcmanus/anima.html.

166 **The yin-yang symbol:** "About Yin and Yang," http://www.thetao.info/tao/yinyang .htm; and "Yin and Yang," http://en.wikipedia.org/wiki/Yin_and_yang.

167 **In our culture:** Discussion on masculine and feminine traits compiled from Robert Rosen, *Leading People: Transforming Business from the Inside Out* (New York: Viking Penguin, 1996); John and Micki Baumann, "Understanding the Masculine & Feminine Side," in *Women's Issues,* http://www.selfgrowth.com/articles/baumann.html; Geert Hofstede, *Cultures and Organizations: Software of the Mind* (New York, McGraw-Hill, 1997); Ayal Hurst, "Balancing Masculine & Feminine," http://www .trans4mind.com/counterpoint/shamanic5.shtml; Eric Neumann, "Anima/Animus"; Michael D. Pollock, "Balance Your Masculine and Feminine Energies," http:// psychology.articlesarchive.net/balance-your-masculine-and-feminine-energies .html; and Jeanie Marshall, "Masculine and Feminine Energies," http://www.mhmail .com/articles/masculine-feminine-energy.html.

170 **"Some people say that":** All references to Jewell in this chapter come from a Healthy Companies International interview with Jewell in April 2007.

170 **The word *power* comes from:** "Power," http://en.wikipedia.org/wiki/Power_ %28sociology%29.

172 **"It's important to have":** Peluso story adapted from Healthy Companies International, "Embracing and Using Anxiety: An Interview with Michelle Peluso," *What CEOs Do,* November 2007.

172 **Four Seasons CEO:** Sharp story adapted from Healthy Companies International, "Turn Your Values into Action: An Interview with Isadore Sharp," *What CEOs Do,* March 2005.

174 **"Confidence is the sweet spot":** Rosabeth Moss Kanter, *Confidence: How Winning Streaks and Losing Streaks Begin and End* (New York: Crown Business, 2004).

175 **"Every six seconds":** Collins story adapted from Healthy Companies International, "Champion Your Mission and Values: An Interview with Art Collins," *What CEOs Do,* January 2005.

176 **Ogilvy & Mather chairman:** Lazarus story taken from Robert H. Rosen, Patricia Digh, Marshall Singer, and Carl Phillips, *Global Literacies: Lessons on Business Leadership and National Cultures* (New York: Simon & Schuster, 2000).

177 **Closer to home:** Drawn from Robert Rosen's experience facilitating a panel with McKinney leaders at a May 2007 conference.

178 **Take Alan Mulally:** Mulally story adapted from Healthy Companies International, "Channeling Anxiety into Productive Energy: An Interview with Alan Mulally," *What CEOs Do,* December 2007.

179 **Thousands of miles away:** Wuffli story compiled from Healthy Companies International, "It's All About Relationships: An Interview with Peter Wuffli," *What CEOs Do,* February 2005; and Peter Thal Larsen and Haig Simonian, "Unease About Day-to-Day Management Cost Wuffli His Job," *Financial Times,* July 7, 2007.

180 **Developing leaders at PepsiCo:** Reinemund story compiled from Healthy Companies International, "Great Leaders Are Great Teachers: An Interview with Steven Reinemund," *What CEOs Do,* July 2005; and Andrew Martin, "Does Coke Need a Refill?," *New York Times,* May 27, 2007.

183 **When he isn't climbing mountains:** Okuda story adapted from Rosen et al., *Global Literacies.*

188 **Mitch Rabkin, the former CEO:** Rabkin story adapted from Robert Rosen, *Leading People.*

189 **How to be a teacher and a learner:** Developed from conference on learning sponsored by Duke Corp. Education, Fuqua Business School, at Duke University, May 2007.

190 **Steve Reinemund teaches:** Compiled from various interviews cited throughout the book.

190 **At Northrop Grumman Newport News:** Story compiled from a Healthy Companies International interview with Petters in April 2007.

196 **JEA leaders who demonstrate:** Compiled from various interviews cited throughout the book.

## Chapter 8: Putting JEA to Work

Brief mentions of JEA leaders in this chapter come from interviews cited throughout the book.

197 **Kumar Mangalam Birla:** Birla story adapted from Healthy Companies International, "Leading India into the 21st Century: An Interview with Kumar Mangalam Birla," *What CEOs Do,* January 2006.

207 **"Our core competency at Arbitron":** Story compiled from a Healthy Companies International interview with Ross in March 2007.

209 **"Good is the enemy":** Jim Collins, *Good to Great: Why Some Companies Make the Leap and Others Don't* (New York: HarperCollins Publishers, 2001).

209 **Jack Welch was obsessed:** From "Jack Welch: Management Evangelist," *BusinessWeek,* October 25, 2004.

210 **"The people drive everything":** All references to Collins in this chapter come from Healthy Companies International, "Champion Your Mission and Values: An Interview with Art Collins," *What CEOs Do,* January 2005.

211 **At Healthy Companies International:** Conclusions drawn from HCI research and white paper on the four leadership agendas (Healthy Companies International, 2003).

212 **Ten years ago I met:** Callahan story adapted from Robert Rosen, *Leading People: Transforming Business from the Inside Out* (New York: Viking Penguin, 1996).

212 **These are *lagging* indicators:** Information on lagging and leading indicators drawn from "Leading Indicators" (Healthy Companies International background paper, 2005); "Global Business Cycle Indicators" on the Conference Board, http://www.conference-board.org/economics/bci/pressRelease_output.cfm?cid=1; and "Economic Indicators" on GPO Access, http://www.gpoaccess.gov/indicators/07janbro.html.

218 **"What man actually needs"**: Victor Frankl, *Man's Search for Meaning*, rev. ed. (New York: Pocket Books, 1997).

222 **Yet when Michel Tilmant**: Tilmant story adapted from Healthy Companies International, "Building a Winning Performance Culture: An Interview with Michel Tilmant," *What CEOs Do*, September 2007.

## Chapter 9: Change Begins with You

228 **Kun-Hee Lee**: Story taken from Robert Rosen, Patricia Digh, Marshall Singer, and Carl Phillips, *Global Literacies: Lessons on Business Leadership and National Cultures* (New York: Simon & Schuster, 2000).

# SELECTED BIBLIOGRAPHY

Aron, Elaine N. *The Highly Sensitive Person: How to Thrive When the World Overwhelms You.* New York: Broadway Books, 2000. First published in 1996 by Carol Publishing Group.

Bardwick, Judith M. *Seeking the Calm in the Storm: Managing Chaos in Your Business Life.* London: Financial Times Prentice Hall, 2002.

Berkow, Robert, M.D., Mark H. Beers, M.D., Robert M. Bogin, M.D., and Andrew J. Fletcher, eds. *Merck Manual of Medical Information: Home Edition.* New York: Pocket Books, 1997.

Bossidy, Larry, and Ram Charan. *Confronting Reality: Doing What Matters to Get Things Right.* New York: Crown Publishing Group, 2004.

———. *Execution: The Discipline of Getting Things Done.* New York: Crown Business, 2002.

Boyatzis, Richard, and Annie McKee. *Resonant Leadership.* Boston: Harvard Business School Press, 2005.

Bridges, William. *The Way of Transition: Embracing Life's Most Difficult Moments.* Cambridge, MA: Perseus Publishing, 2001.

Brim, Gilbert. *Ambition: How We Manage Success and Failure Throughout Our Lives.* New York: Basic Books, 1992.

Burns, David. *When Panic Attacks: The New Drug-Free Anxiety Therapy That Can Change Your Life.* New York: Morgan Road Books, 2006.

Calarco, Alan, and Joan Gurvis. *Adaptability: Responding Effectively to Change.* Greensboro, NC: CCL Press, 2006.

Carroll, Michael. *Awake at Work: Discovering Clarity and Balance in the Midst of Work's Chaos.* Boston: Shambhala Publications, 2004.

Childre, Doc, and Deborah Rozman. *Transforming Anxiety: The HeartMath® Solution for Overcoming Fear and Worry and Creating Serenity*. Oakland: New Harbinger Publications, 2006.

Chödrön, Pema. *Comfortable with Uncertainty: 108 Teachings on Cultivating Fearlessness and Compassion*. Boston: Shambhala Publications, 2003.

Collins, Jim. *Good to Great: Why Some Companies Make the Leap and Others Don't*. New York: HarperCollins Publishers, 2001.

Conner, Daryl R. *Leading at the Edge of Chaos: How to Create the Nimble Organization*. New York: John Wiley & Sons, 1998.

Csikszentmihalyi, Mihaly. *Finding Flow: The Psychology of Engagement with Everyday Life*. New York: Basic Books, 1997.

Das, Lama Surya. *Awakening the Buddha Within: Tibetan Wisdom for the Western World*. New York: Broadway Books, 1997.

Dodd, Dominic, and Ken Favaro. *The Three Tensions: Winning the Struggle to Perform Without Compromise*. San Francisco: Jossey-Bass, 2007.

Dotlich, David L., and Peter C. Cairo. *Why CEOs Fail: The 11 Behaviors That Can Derail Your Climb to the Top and How to Manage Them*. San-Francisco: Jossey-Bass, 2003.

Fink, Steven. *Crisis Management: Planning for the Inevitable*. Lincoln, NE: iUniverse, 2002.

Fritz, Robert. *The Path of Least Resistance: Learning to Become the Creative Force in Your Own Life*. New York: Fawcett Columbine, 1984.

Goldberg, Elkhonon. *The Executive Brain: Frontal Lobes and the Civilized Mind*. New York: Oxford University Press, 2001.

Goleman, Daniel. *Emotional Intelligence: Why It Can Matter More Than IQ*. New York: Bantam Books, 1995.

Goleman, Daniel. *Social Intelligence: The New Science of Human Relationships*. New York: Bantam Books, 2006.

Healthy Companies International. *Leading People*. Arlington, VA: HCI, 2004–2008.

———. *What CEOs Do*. Arlington, VA: HCI, 2004–2008.

———. "Winning Performance Scan®." Arlington, VA: HCI, 2005.

Hofstede, Geert. *Cultures and Organizations: Software of the Mind*. New York: McGraw-Hill, 1997.

Hodgson, Philip, and Randall P. White. *Relax: It's Only Uncertainty*. London: Prentice Hall Financial Times, 2001.

Kets de Vries, Manfred F. R., and Danny Miller. *The Neurotic Organization*. San Francisco: Jossey-Bass, 1984.

———. *Unstable at the Top: Inside the Troubled Organization*. New York: Penguin Group, 1988.

Kuhn, Robert Lawrence. "12 'CEO Diseases' and How to Treat Them." *Chief Executive* magazine, October/November, 2006.

LeDoux, Joseph. *The Emotional Brain: The Mysterious Underpinnings of Emotional Life*. New York: Simon & Schuster, 1996.

Loehr, Jim, and Tony Schwartz. *The Power of Full Engagement: Managing Energy, Not Time, Is the Key to High Performance and Personal Renewal*. New York: Free Press, 2003.

Maccoby, Michael. *Narcissistic Leaders: Who Succeeds and Who Fails.* Boston: Harvard Business School Press, 2007.

"Managing Uncertainty," in *Harvard Business Review.* Boston: Harvard Business School Press, 1999.

Manktelow, James. "Introduction to Sports Psychology." (http://mindtools.com/sprintro.html).

Prince, C. J. "When Bad Things Happen to Good CEOs." *Chief Executive* magazine, October/November, 2006.

Raynor, Michael E. *The Strategy Paradox: Why Committing to Success Leads to Failure (and What to Do About It).* New York: Doubleday Currency, 2007.

Rock, David. *Quiet Leadership.* New York: HarperCollins Publishers, 2006.

Rosen, Robert H., Patricia Digh, Marshall Singer, and Carl Phillips. *Global Literacies: Lessons on Business Leadership and National Cultures.* New York: Simon & Schuster, 2000.

Rosen, Robert. *Leading People: Transforming Business from the Inside Out.* New York: Viking Penguin, 1996.

Rosen, Robert. *The Healthy Company: Eight Strategies to Develop People, Productivity, and Profits.* Los Angeles: Jeremy P. Tarcher, 1991.

Ulrich, Dave, Jack Zenger, and Norm Smallwood. *Results-Based Leadership.* Boston: Harvard Business School Press, 1999.

Valdes, Luis. "Peak Performance Pulse." (http://www.squidoo.com/valdes/).

Welch, Jack. *Winning.* New York: HarperCollins Publishers, 2005.

White, Randall P., Philip Hodgson, and Stuart Crainer. *The Future of Leadership.* Lanham, MD: Pitman Publishing, 1996.

Zander, Rosamund Stone, and Benjamin Zander. *The Art of Possibility: Transforming Professional and Personal Life.* New York: Penguin Group, 2000.

# INDEX

Aaron, Hank, 94
accountability, 16, 170, 188, 198, 217, 225
adaptation, 2, 6–7, 8, 14, 28, 55, 68, 81, 198
adrenaline, 34
Afghanistan, Enduring Freedom in, 57
African tribal communities, 100
Air Expeditionary Force (AEF), 57, 58, 60
Akman, Jeffrey, 41–42
Allstate Insurance Company, 211–12
American Psychiatric Association, 27
amygdala, 27–28, 29, 33, 34, 37, 40, 72
androgyny, 165–66, 167–70, 172–73, 200, 215
anxiety: as abnormal, 28; affects of, 21– 22; avoidance of, 27, 28; as bad, 4; benefits of, 1–3, 25, 41–42; brain origins of, 8, 26; confronting, 45–46, 59–60, 201; as constant, 4–5; as contagious, 98–99, 221; coping with, 26– 27; denial of/resistance to, 104; embracing, 31, 58, 202; evaluating your own, 41, 228–31; exaggeration of, 202; as fact of life, 4, 45; fear of, 78; listening to, 202; managing, 3, 31, 36– 46, 47, 67, 71, 77, 79, 83, 97, 100, 123, 149, 202, 221; as mental health problem, 4; modulating, 31, 58, 59, 81, 207; new understanding of, 4, 11–14, 19, 21, 23, 24–60, 199; options for response to, 35– 36; physical training compared

with, 92– 93; prevalence in U.S. of, 30; recognizing, 67; reluctance to use word, 30–31; statistics about, 30; tips for living with, 13; treatment for, 30, 44; triggers for, 2, 34–35, 36–44, 137, 159, 160, 200, 224; as weakness, 31. *See also* just enough anxiety; too little anxiety; too much anxiety; *specific topic*
anxiety disorders, 27, 43
Arbitron, 145, 150, 206–7
Arlington County, Virginia, 158–61, 201
Armstrong, Lance, 95
athletes, 94–95
attachment, 38. *See also* nonattachment
authenticity, 148, 149, 176, 192, 214

balance: importance of, 123. *See also* paradox
Bangladesh, 133–34
Beck, Aaron, 29
beliefs and expectations: and becoming a JEA leader, 201; and building a JEA organization, 211, 212; and confident humility, 174, 175, 176; conflicting, 68, 69; and constructive impatience, 153, 155; core, 2; and creating a JEA team, 205; and gaps, 68, 69, 74, 75, 77, 85; gender-based, 168; and just enough anxiety, 122–23, 199; and leading indicators of success, 216, 217;